THE RECORD OF

TRANSMITTING
THE LIGHT

THE RECORD OF

TRANSMITTING THE LIGHT

ZEN MASTER KEIZAN'S DENKOROKU

Translated by Francis Dojun Cook

Foreword by John Daido Loori

Wisdom Publications • Boston

Wisdom Publications
199 Elm Street
Somerville MA 02144 USA
www.wisdompubs.org

Library of Congress Cataloging-in-Publication Data

Keizan, 1268-1325.
   [Denkōroku. English]
   The record of transmitting the light : Zen master Keizan's denkoroku / translated by
Francis Dojun Cook ; foreword by John Daido Loori. — 1st Wisdom ed.
    p. cm.
   Includes bibliographical references.
   ISBN 0-86171-330-3
   1. Sōtōshū—Early works to 1800. 2. Priests, Zen—Biography—Early works to 1800.
I. Cook, Francis Harold, 1930– II. Title
   BQ9415.K4513 2003
   294.3'927—dc21

                         2002155428

First Wisdom Edition
07 06 05 04 03
5   4   3   2   1

Interior designed by Stephanie Doyle
Cover designed by Rick Snizik

Wisdom Publications makes grateful acknowledgment to Andy Ferguson for assistance
with this new edition.

Wisdom Publications' books are printed on acid-free paper and meet the guidelines for the
permanence and durability of the Production Guidelines for Book Longevity set by the Council
on Library Resources.

Printed in the United States of America

Dedicated to my wife, Elizabeth B. Cook,
with thanks for so many good things

TABLE OF CONTENTS

FOREWORD

The Record of Transmitting the Light is a work that many that rank alongside Zen Master Dogen's *Shobogenzo* as a major classic of Japanese Soto Zen. It documents the enlightenment experience and transmission of the Dharma through successive generations beginning with Shakyamuni Buddha down through Zen Master Koun Ejo, Dogen's successor. The collected cases and accompanying commentary and poems by Zen Master Keizan are used in several modern lineages as part of koan study.

Keizan Jokin was born in 1268, fifteen years after the death of the great Master Dogen in 1253. He studied Zen under Dogen's first successor Ejo, and then continued with Zen Master Tettsu Gikai, Ejo's successor at Eihei-ji. He played a pivotal role in the development and expansion of Japanese Soto Zen, which earned him the title of Great Ancestor. Master Keizan is held in as high regard as Master Dogen, and has in fact been referred to as the mother of Japanese Soto Zen, while Dogen is considered the father.

After the death of Dogen in 1253, while Gikai was the third abbot of Eihei-ji, factional splits began to develop at Eihei-ji among monks of various other schools of Buddhism, such as the Tendai and Daruma lines. Master Gikai, then in his seventies, found himself at the center of the conflict and was ultimately banished from Eihei-ji. He took up residency at the gatehouse of the monastery, and although he had Ejo's full trust—had in fact received transmission from him—he was forced to leave Eihei-ji and went on to establish Daijo-ji in Kaga (Ishikawa Prefecture).

The internal disputes and disorder became quite serious and began to threaten the very existence and continuance of the Japanese Soto lineage that was established by Dogen. Disciples left Eihei-ji. Supporters decreased in number. The vital and vigorous atmosphere that was originally established at the Eihei-ji monastic community began to disintegrate.

By this time, Master Keizan, having now succeeded Gikai as the second abbot of Daijo-ji, began a series of talks tracing the lineage of the rightly transmitted Buddhadharma from India to China, and from China to Japan, in an attempt to confirm that the teaching of the essence of the treasury of the true Dharma eye rests in zazen and realization—a point that had became lost as a result of the ongoing disputes at Eihei-ji. These talks were later collected as *The Record of Transmitting the Light*.

The word *light* in the title refers to the enlightenment experience that was transmitted, mind to mind, generation to generation, from Shakyamuni Buddha through twenty-eight ancestors in India and twenty-three ancestors in China, and finally carried from China to Japan by Dogen and transmitted to Ejo. The *Record* was Keizan's attempt to heal the rift that had developed at Eihei-ji and to assert the legitimacy of the lineage that master Dogen carried from China. He thus attempted to fend off much of the criticism of Gikai, as well as to assert his own legitimacy and the legitimacy of his successors. Dogen himself had begun to establish the legitimacy of the lineage, but had not completed this work before his death.

Slowly, the sangha of Eihei-ji began to heal and the vitality of the practice returned. Keizan then established Soji-ji, and along with Eihei-ji, these two became the head monasteries of the Japanese Soto Zen tradition, and remain so to this day.

After establishing Soji-ji, Keizan traveled around Japan creating thousands of temples within his lineage. At its peak, the Japanese Soto School had about twenty-five thousand temples with over thirty thousand priests and some ten million followers. It became—and remains—the largest Buddhist denomination in Japan. The propagation philosophy of Keizan is embodied today in the Soto School of Japan where it promotes the international development of Soto Zen. In the early part of the twentieth century, Japanese Soto Zen Buddhism began to spread to Europe, America, and southeast Asia. Today it is one of the largest Buddhist schools in the West.

In collecting the stories that make up *The Record of Transmitting the Light*, Keizan traced his own lineage back through history to Shakyamuni Buddha. The fifty-three accounts he recorded present historical information on the bloodline of Keizan's Dharma ancestors as documented in the Ancestral Lineage of Succession, a document every Soto priest receives at the time of

Dharma transmission. But more important, each anecdote is also a koan Keizan's students had to unravel, and in time the *Record* became established as a koan collection for future generations of Zen students to contemplate.

Koans appear in a number of different ways in the traditional records of Zen Buddhism. In *The Record of Transmitting the Light* each koan is presented as the biography of one of the Zen masters. Koans also appear as individual cases collected in the various records of the masters, usually by a later-generation disciple. These koans or "public cases" usually contain factual information regarding the teacher's training, teaching career, birth, and death, as well as a dialogue or dialogues between master and disciples, contemporaries, or visitors. During the Song Dynasty in China, several masters collected koans they regarded as being particularly valuable for the training of their own students. The masters then usually added to the koan their own commentary or verse, as both a challenge and a helpful pointer for their students.

At the time Keizan delivered the discourses in the *Record*, three of the major koan collections were already in existence. *The Blue Cliff Record,* the oldest of the three, was introduced to Japan by Dogen in 1227. Dogen had just completed five years of study in China with his teacher, Master Tiantong Rujing, and had received the Soto transmission. Shortly before leaving for Japan, he discovered a copy of *The Blue Cliff Record* and spent his entire last night in China hand-copying it. This text is known within the Soto School as the "One-night Blue Cliff Record."

The second koan collection, *The Book of Serenity,* essentially follows the same form as its predecessor, *The Blue Cliff Record.* The third collection was *The Gateless Gate.* Its form is less poetic and literary than that of its predecessors, but rather more direct and straightforward in its exposition of and commentary on the recorded dialogues.

These three collections no doubt provided a model for Keizan's work. Each of the chapters in the *Record* consists of four basic sections. The first is the main case, which includes the essential elements that sparked the realization and transmission of the disciple, mind to mind, from the master. Next is a section with biographical and historical information to set the context in which the encounter is taking place. The third is Keizan's discourse or *teisho* on the case. Here Keizan guides the student to realize the koan by directly pointing. Teisho are said to be "dark to the mind but radiant to the heart," so they must be received with the whole body and mind, rather than through linear, discursive thought. They challenge students to make a quantum leap of consciousness and see directly *into* the koan, thereby turning the ancestor's realization into an intimate part of their own being. The fourth and last section is Keizan's verse, a few lines that capture the essential point of the koan, following the Zen tradition in which students or teachers present in poetic form their understanding of a particular point in the teachings.

Koan introspection is significantly different than koan study. In koan study, the student tries to develop an intellectual understanding of the koan and the teachings it contains. Koan introspection, on the other hand, is a process in which the student sits with the koan for long periods of time and presents his or her understanding to the master. When there is a clear identity between the insight of the master and that of the student, the student passes on to the next koan in a series. Therefore, the traditional use of koans in Zen represents the transmission of the Dharma mind to mind from teacher to disciple, generation to generation. As part of systematic koan introspection, Keizan's *Record of Transmitting the Light* is found in several lineages, its study preceding the formal transmission of the Dharma.

More than seven hundred years have passed since Keizan began the series of talks that became the *Record,* yet this invaluable collection still contains the heart of the teachings of the inexhaustible light of the Dharma.

Francis Cook's translation was first published in 1991, and in the years that followed, it has played an important role in illuminating the Way for thousands of first-generation Western students. Cook's skill and insight as a translator come from his well-earned scholarly authority in the field of Buddhism, as well as by experiential authority obtained through many years of study as a Zen practitioner—and specifically, as a student of koans. May this edition of *The Record of Transmitting the Light* continue to illuminate the Way for the next generation of Zen practitioners.

John Daido Loori, Abbot
Zen Mountain Monastery
Winter 2003

ACKNOWLEDGMENTS

Translating a text such as the *Denkoroku* is never an easy task even under the most favorable conditions, but my work was made much easier because of invaluable help from several sources.

First, my thanks and gratitude to Taizan Maezumi Roshi. He loaned me books from his own private library and otherwise made sure I had any materials I needed for the translation. Most of all, however, he met with me many times during the time I worked on the translation to answer questions and to offer invaluable advice on many difficult problems in the text. His knowledge of the language and world of the *Denkoroku* has made the translation much better than it would have been had I not conferred with him. I should note, however, that I made the final decision as to whether to accept his advice, and any deficiencies in the work remain my own. I am grateful for the many happy hours we spent together discussing the text at Yoko-ji, the Zen Center monastery in the San Jacinto Mountains.

I wish also to give my special thanks to Chief Abbot Umeda Shinryu and Chief Administrator Saito Shingi of Soji-ji, and to Chief Abbot Suigan Yogo of Saijo-ji, for generous financial contributions to help in the initial publication of the *Denkoroku* through Center Publications of the Zen Center of Los Angeles.

I cannot thank Michael Shodo Rotter enough for transferring my typescript onto the computer and revising and correcting the manuscript as I sent changes to him. This spared me a huge amount of retyping, made the project move much faster, and ensured a splendid final draft. He played a big part in getting the *Denkoroku* into print, and I am really grateful.

My heartfelt thanks to friends and fellow members of the Riverside *zazenkai* Kelly Stevens and Stan MacGregor for their interest and moral support during the two years of translation.

Finally, in this new addition I'd like also to gratefully acknowledge the assistance of Sensei Wendy Egyoku Nakao, Burt Wetanson, and Professor Edward Slingerland.

Francis Dojun Cook

Notes on Translation

1. All personal names, place names, and the like have been restored to their original form, regardless of how Keizan pronounced them. A case could be made that they should all be pronounced as Keizan pronounced them, but I believe that one function of translation is to make these restorations. Thus, Indian names have been restored to a Sanskrit original, although some Indian names were probably originally in Pali. All Chinese names are given in Chinese (in Pinyin transliteration) rather than in Japanese as Keizan would have pronounced them. A chart of alternative transliterations and pronunciations appears on page 275 at the back of this book.

2. Japanese and Chinese personal names are given in the Japanese and Chinese manner; that is, family name first, followed by given name. Thus, Fujiwara Moroie is Mr. Fujiwara, whose parents named him Moroie.

3. I have capitalized such words as *Buddha*, *Tathagata*, and *Master*, the latter when it is part of a title, such as "Master Touzi." *Dharma* is capitalized when it is a synonym for "Buddhism" or "Truth," but is not capitalized when it means "experiential datum," or "phenomenal object." I have capitalized *Self* and *Mind* when they are synonyms for "Buddha nature," but not for other senses.

4. All material enclosed within square brackets is my own addition to the original text. I have depended on this device often throughout the translation in order to avoid an unreasonable number of endnotes. In almost every case, the interpolation is a small expansion of the original text, made to clarify the text. For example, I often interpolate a better-known name beside a lesser-known name, as when I write, "Eihei [Dogen]." Sometimes, I specify a speaker or grammatical subject where the text typically does not. In other cases, I add material which eliminates the

need for an explanatory note, such as when I write, "the three times [of past, future, and present]" or "the four forms of birth [which are birth from a womb, birth from an egg, birth from moisture, and spontaneous birth]." In all cases, my intention has been to spare the reader a needless trip to the notes at the end of the translation.

5. Manuscript copies of the *Denkoroku* do not divide each chapter into four sections as I have done. Each chapter runs unbroken from start to finish without break or section titles. The custom of pointing out these four sections with headings began soon after the text was published. The two-volume publication by Yoshida Gizan (Kyoto, 1886), for instance, indicates the four sections with interlinear notes *(bokun)*. The four sections are *hon soku,* the "main koan case that begins each chapter; the *kien,* or "story" surrounding the enlightenment experience of the subject; Keizan's *nentei* commentary on the main case or story; and finally, the *juko* verse, which concludes the chapter. Professor Kochi followed this practice in the text I used for my translation, and I have also divided each chapter into four parts. My one deviation from the precedent of Yoshida and others has been to use the more familiar term *teisho* in place of *nentei,* since some dictionaries appear to consider the two terms to be synonyms, and I believe the more familiar term serves equally well.

6. In the Far East, a person is considered a year old at birth. Thus, a year after his birth, he or she is considered two years old. Throughout the introduction and translation, I have "translated" ages into their Western equivalents. Thus, if the Japanese text says that a person was seven years old when he did a certain thing, I have changed this to his Western-reckoned age, which is six.

A Note on This Book's Design

The section heading device that appears in this volume at the beginning of each section of the *Record* is a *kao*—a unique design adopted by Zen priests and other cultured Japanese which functioned like a signature and was related only loosely to orthography. The *kao* opening each section is Master Keizan's.

INTRODUCTION

I. The Text

The *Record of Transmitting the Light* (*Denkoroku* in Japanese) is a type of literature that can be called "spiritual genealogy." Like ordinary genealogies, it traces the history of a family, locating its origins in some ancestor long ago and tracing that ancestor's descendants down through the successive generations to the present. This accomplishes several goals that are important for the family: It provides a panoramic view of the continuity of a line rooted in distant antiquity; it records the exploits and special distinctions of each generation; it provides a basis for family pride and style; and, perhaps most important, it provides a strong sense of family identity. Together, these things create a sense of rootedness, as well as continuity and identity through, history.

But unlike traditional family genealogies tracing a genetic bloodline, the *Record* traces a spiritual bloodline. Thus, the fifty-three generations recorded in Keizan's work are not related by blood but rather by spiritual kinship in which the inheritance of each generation is one of spiritual endowment and authority.

Keizan took it as his task to trace the genealogy of the Soto line of Zen Buddhism, which was his "family." The founding ancestor to which Keizan's line is heir was the Buddha Shakyamuni, who passed on his spiritual endowment and authority to his own spiritual son, Mahakashyapa, who, in turn, passed it on to his own spiritual son, Ananda, and so on, through twenty-eight generations in India, twenty-two generations in China, and two generations in Japan, ending with Zen Master Koun Ejo, the fifty-second patriarch of the family. In the process of recording these generations, Keizan discusses the spiritual struggles and victories of such well-known figures in

Buddhist history as Mahakashyapa, Ananda, Ashvaghosa, Vasubandhu, Bodhidharma, Huike, Qingyuan, Dongshan, and Dogen, along with a number of
others in the Indian line who are unknown outside Buddhist genealogies of
this kind. Thus, the *Record* shows a straight and unbroken line of descent
starting from the Buddha and continuing through India, China, and Japan,
ending with Ejo, who was Keizan's own spiritual grandfather. Keizan omits
any mention of himself out of modesty, although he was the fifty-fourth
patriarch of the family, and he also does not include his predecessor and spiritual father, Tettsu Gikai, who was still living and whose inclusion Keizan
apparently felt was inappropriate. Gikai is only mentioned briefly in the
account of Ejo as having established the family at Daijo Monastery.

At the heart of the *Record* lie such genealogical matters as transmission,
succession, and inheritance—words that are encountered frequently in the
text. There are also the related matters of continuity, legitimacy, and authenticity. The structure of each chapter is fairly uniform. The current patriarch
of the family is wandering about teaching, or is an abbot of a monastery, and
he is searching for a suitable individual to inherit his authority. He encoun-
ters a young man of unusual commitment and talent who has forsaken secular life and seeks enlightenment. After some passage of time, during which
the young man struggles valiantly and single-mindedly, he achieves enlightenment, often during an encounter with the patriarchal master. The master
confirms the awakening and recognizes the younger man as a fit successor.
Thus, the younger man succeeds the older in a process that has continued
unbroken over many generations. The point of such a narrative is that at
any point in the chain of successors, an individual can demonstrate his legitimacy and his claim to the family name by proving that his predecessor was
so-and-so, whose own claims derive from his own predecessor, and so on
back to the founding ancestor. Ultimately, Shakyamuni himself, as the
founder of the family, is the ultimate legitimator of all subsequent successors.

There are other Zen genealogies besides Keizan's *Record*, each with its
own structure and purpose, and there are also genealogies in traditions outside Zen, such as Pure Land and Huayan. However, Keizan's *Record* is
unique within this genre of literature. Each of the fifty-three chapters begins
with a koan case *(hon soku)*, which records the master's awakening in a dialogue with his master, upon hearing some remark made by his master, or

upon pondering some spiritual problem. The short introductory case is then followed by a story *(kien)* about the master, including his birthplace and parentage, religious yearnings as a youth, home departure and tonsure, spiritual struggle, awakening, and succession to the title of patriarch. The main purpose of this section is that of providing the circumstances surrounding the awakening experience announced in the preceding koan case. This latter section is often the occasion of stressing the master's special virtues and abilities, his unique fitness to become a patriarchal successor, and his later success as a Zen teacher. Occasionally, especially in the accounts of the Indian patriarchs, the master is shown exhibiting marvelous supernatural powers in an atmosphere charged with the miraculous and fabulous. This section can be lengthy in the case of particularly important pivotal figures such as Bodhidharma, or it can be perfunctorily brief in cases where the background information on an individual is practically nonexistent. At any rate, the material for this section of a chapter is not Keizan's own invention but rather was drawn from other genealogies such as the Chinese *Jing De Chuan Deng Lu (Keitoku Dentoroku)* and *Wu Deng Hui Yuan (Goto Egen)*, which were Keizan's two main sources. Hence, these stories were well known in the Zen tradition and could be found elsewhere. However, a comparison of Keizan's telling of these stories and their presentation in other sources shows the author editing, abbreviating, expanding, shifting emphasis, and otherwise exercising a critical choice in what to include or exclude.

The third section of each chapter consists of Keizan's commentary on either the main case or, rarely, on the second section. This section, named *nentei* in many modern editions, is very similar to the traditional *teisho* given by the master to his monks. Neither the *teisho* nor the *nentei* is a simple explanation or discussion *about* the koan case, but rather functions as an occasion for the master to speak "from the heart," to explore the case from an enlightened perspective. Such an occasion may stimulate the monk's own spiritual search and provide pointers for the individual who is prepared to understand as a result of considerable practice and his own inquiring spirit. Keizan's talks, like the classical *teisho*, provide him with the opportunity to guide practice, exhort, correct, and encourage, as he clarifies the import of the koan case. I have given this section of a chapter the more familiar heading of *teisho* in order to alert the reader to the nature of the section.

Most readers will probably find this section of a chapter the most reward-
ing and interesting. The main case that introduces each chapter will not be
significant to anyone who has not had a considerable amount of experience
with Zen koans, although these cases can often be striking and thought-
provoking. The story section offers its own difficulties for the reader. Sometimes the material is flatly factual and perfunctory, limited to a bare
description of the master's family and the circumstances surrounding his
later enlightenment and patriarchal succession, and these are not particularly interesting, colorful, or edifying. Sometimes, particularly in the stories
of the Indian patriarchs, the stories are rather colorful in their accounts of
supernatural beings, dragons and demons, magic, and paranormal powers,
but modern readers are likely to find all this incredible and thus perhaps
meaningless, albeit colorful, in a way not thought so by earlier generations
of readers.

The observant reader will notice an interesting difference between the
biographical and historical accounts of the earlier Indian patriarchs and
the later Chinese masters. The Indian stories contain a large amount of the
miraculous and supernatural mentioned above. However, once the patriarchal transmission reaches China, this kind of material almost disappears.
Whereas a large percentage of the twenty-nine Indian biographies contain
material of this sort—physical transformations, demons and celestial beings,
strange accounts of rebirth, apparitions, and omens—there are only about
three or four of these stories in the accounts of the twenty-four Chinese and
Japanese patriarchs. Of these, the most remarkable is the story of a Chinese
monk who, through an act of will, incarnates himself in the womb of a virgin
and subsequently is born of a virgin. But what is striking is the almost complete absence of this kind of material in the Chinese and Japanese stories. In
these latter accounts, Keizan concentrates almost totally on the encounter
between master and disciple, spiritual struggle, and ultimate succession. A
close comparison of stories in the *Record* and Keizan's Chinese sources will
often reveal that such supernatural material was present but that Keizan
made conscious and deliberate omission of it. Why the omission? The reason
may only be conjectured about, but the impression is that Keizan, writing
in about 1300 in a land far away from India, considered the Indian patriarchs to be practically mythological beings living a very long time ago in a

mysterious and sacred land where such events could and did happen with amazing regularity. Men such as Mahakashyapa, Ashvaghosa, and Kapimala may have been thought of as spiritual giants not known outside the Holy Land or in more recent "degenerate" times. Time, distance, and the special aura surrounding the Indian Holy Land and the giants of yesteryear might very well make conceivable what would be considered incredible in one's own everyday time and place.

If the main case and biographical and historical sections are problematic for modern readers, Keizan's commentary on the koan cases is another matter. These commentaries provide him with the opportunity to display his own understanding of the nature of Zen and the special "family style" of his own Soto line of Zen. Consequently, from these commentaries the reader has an opportunity to gain a better understanding not only of what Zen teaches generally but also of what Zen meant to one seminally important figure in the development of Japanese Buddhism. As a result, this section, perhaps along with the concluding appreciatory verse (juko), gives us an insight into what may be called Keizan's Zen. In many ways, Keizan's Zen is a continuation of the Zen of the founder of Japanese Soto Zen, Dogen— and this should not be particularly surprising. Yet, the two men were different individuals with different teaching methods and different emphases in their writings.

In the course of documenting the patriarchal succession over the generations, Keizan centers his talks primarily on two topics. One is the necessity of being totally committed to achieving awakening, of taking the Zen life most seriously, and of making a supreme effort in Zen practice. This is also a focal point in Dogen's writing, and both men, as Zen patriarchs, are equally concerned with the training of monks and the selection of successors. The second emphasis, and, indeed, the overwhelmingly central focal point of all these chapters, is the *Light* of the title of the work. It is this light that is transmitted from master to disciple as the disciple discovers this light within himself. In fact, once the light is discovered, this itself is the transmission. The light is one's Buddha nature or True Self. Keizan uses a number of striking and provocative epithets and titles for this True Self, including "That One," "That Person," "The Old Fellow," and "The Lord of the House." Such language is uncommon in Dogen's writings, as is any focus on discussing the existence and nature of this Old Fellow—that is part of what constitutes Keizan's Zen as distinct from Dogen's Zen.

The fourth and final section of each chapter is a short verse, usually made up of two lines of seven ideographic characters each or, occasionally, of four lines of five characters each. These verses are the occasion for Keizan to present the gist of the introductory koan, to summarize his remarks in the commentary section, and to express his appreciation and praise for the koan case. These verses are excellent examples of the highly literary nature of Zen and the literary tastes of Zen masters, and, at the same time, they serve the reader by providing a handy reference for the interpretation of the main case and Keizan's commentary. In a word, the verse is the case and its commentary in a poetic nutshell.

Earlier it was said that the *Record* has another function beside those mentioned as being part of all genealogical work—namely to demonstrate the legitimacy of the Japanese Soto Zen tradition founded by Dogen three generations before Keizan. There were several reasons why Keizan believed that he had to give this demonstration. First, there was the oft-repeated claim by Dogen and his successors, including Keizan, that their Buddhism was the only true Dharma in Japan. It was the only true Dharma because the other traditions were corrupt and worldly, they did not teach Zen meditation, which is the primary Buddhist practice, and they did not base their own legitimacy on the transmission of the enlightened mind. On the other hand, the Soto Zen line was a newcomer to the Japanese religious scene (as was the Rinzai line), dating only from the early thirteenth century. The older, established traditions, such as Tendai, were persistently antagonistic to Dogen's line of Zen and sought to turn secular authorities against it. Zen also had to compete with other newly established forms of Buddhism that had risen at the same time, namely, Pure Land and Nichiren Buddhism. A further consideration may have been the need to deal satisfactorily with the internal dispute that is said to have occurred at Eihei-ji (the temple founded by Dogen), which is believed to have centered around Keizan's own predecessor, Gikai.

Gikai is said to have been finally forced to step down as abbot of Eihei-ji and to have established a new center at Daijo-ji, resulting in a split in the patriarchal line, with the Eihei-ji line continuing on with a new abbot, and Gikai starting a new, separate transmission line at Daijo-ji. Keizan was the second abbot of Daijo-ji and later became the founder of a new headquarters at Soji-ji, in Noto. Thus, the line that had existed presumably unbroken from the time of Shakyamuni down to Gikai had become divided in Japan in the third generation. For all these reasons, as well as Keizan's determination to popularize and propagate his teaching, there was a need to argue in a convincing way that the form of Buddhism he represented was not merely legitimate, but was in fact the Treasury of the Eye of the True Dharma (Shobogenzo), bequeathed by the Buddha to Mahakashyapa and, through him, down through over fifty generations.

What better way to do this than through a genealogy? An individual whose pedigree is in doubt can demonstrate through the family tree that he or she is truly a legitimate heir to the family name and inheritance. It is the unbroken succession of generations, with the clearly established link between each, that proves authenticity. It is interesting in this regard to compare Keizan's Record with another genealogy, the Chinese Chuan Deng Lu (Dentoroku). Like Keizan's work, the Chuan Deng Lu traces the transmission of spiritual authority and authenticity from Shakyamuni through a single line of successors through India into China. There is also a single line stretching from Bodhidharma, the "Blue-eyed Brahmin," down to the sixth Chinese patriarch, Huineng. However, unlike the Record, the line of succession branches out at this point, so that as all genealogies show, Huineng had five successors, two of whom, Qingyuan Xingsi and Nanyue Huairang, became founders of their own important lines of transmission. One of Nanyue's successors was the important Zen master, Mazu Daoyi, who in turn had a number of successors, including Baizhang Huaihai and Nanquan Puyuan. The same branching out of the family tree continues over the generations, branches proliferating and producing more proliferations. Consequently, the Chuan Deng Lu is much more like a real family tree in showing all the "children" of a parent, the children of each of those children, and so on into the present. This can be seen in any Zen genealogical table.

Keizan's Record takes a much different form, showing a single line of descent from a spiritual father to a spiritual son, as if there were no other children, or as if, if others existed, only one son got rights to the family name and inheritance. This is because the two genealogies have different purposes. The primary purpose of the Chuan Deng Lu is not to show that a single individual is the sole repository for authority, but rather, to show how the light of the Buddha is inherited by many in each succeeding generation. Thus, in the Chinese work, we find the records of lay people, for instance, who were confirmed as enlightened by their masters but who had no successors and thus were themselves the end of their "line." They were not links in an unbroken line of succession but their accomplishments were nevertheless recorded as significant, and this seems to be the purpose of the text.

Sometimes, a successor was a monk who left no successors of his own but, again, his accomplishment is recorded in the *Chuan Deng Lu* because it celebrates the proliferation of the light. It does not seem to be concerned with the question of genuineness or legitimacy in the way the *Record* seems to be. The *Record* ignores the fact that a master may have had a number of enlightened disciples who established their own lines. Thus, Keizan's work does not have the biographies of Mazu, Zhaozhou, Deshan, Baizhang, or a host of other Zen luminaries, as does the *Chuan Deng Lu*. Keizan's genealogy is more of a sectarian document than is the Chinese work. Keizan's work says, in effect, that the spiritual bloodline runs from the father to an only son, who becomes the new family patriarch, and so on. The effect of this is to argue that at any given time, the present patriarch can demonstrate his authority and power by simply proving who his father was and that he, himself, is his father's descendent. The model for the *Chuan Deng Lu* is the true family tree that shows all the sons and daughters of a family, and the sons and daughters of each of them, as the "branches" grow and multiply. The model for Keizan's *record* is that of patrilineal descent, in which the family inheritance is passed on from father to eldest son in each generation. It is still a genealogy, but one that ignores all members of the family except the chosen son.

The importance of this model is so evident in Keizan's *Record* that one is left with the clear perception that nothing is more important for a Zen master than to have a spiritual son who is worthy of being a vessel for the Dharma succession. Nowhere is this clearer than in the account of the forty-fourth patriarch, Touzi Yiqing. The previous patriarch Dayang Jingxuan had the misfortune of reaching the end of his life without finding a suitable successor. However, a Linji (Rinzai) monk named Yuanjian (Fushan Fayuan), who was already a successor to the Linji Zen Master Shexian, visited Dayang, who found him in complete accord with his own understanding. He wished to make Yuanjian his successor, but the latter declined because he was already a successor to another master in the Linji lineage. However, overcome with sadness and regret that Caodong line (as Soto was known in China) would become extinct, he volunteered to become a temporary holder of Dayang's Dharma and the Caodong patriarchy and later transmit it to a worthy vessel in the Caodong line when he found him. This turned out to be Touzi. Yuanjian convinced Touzi that he was a temporary stand-in for Dayang and truly possessed the master's Dharma. Touzi trusted him and became, indirectly, Dayang's Dharma heir. Consequently, although Dayang is listed in the *Record* as the forty-third patriarch and Touzi is listed as the forty-fourth, there was a break in the Caodong line with Yuanjian, a Linji master, serving as the temporary bridge between the two.

This must have been a terrible situation for Dayang, but it must also have been a difficult problem for Keizan, who was so concerned with the question of legitimacy. His need to deal with the problem seems evident from the fact that his *teisho* on this chapter is one of the longest in the *Denkoroku* and concerns not the main koan case but the story of the break in the lineage. Given the nature and tone of the *Record*, it would seem incredible that this is all a fiction. It must have been an indubitable fact widely known in Buddhist circles and one that could not be passed over. So, he faced the problem head on, dealing with it in a manner the reader can discern for himself or herself in that chapter of the translation.

The success of the Japanese Soto tradition from the fourteenth century on was, as historians agree, due in no small part to Keizan's efforts to make it widely known and practiced. His historical importance in Japanese Buddhism consists of his success in making Soto Zen a popular religion. Some of this success was due to the incorporation of elements of liturgy and practice from outside of Zen, and there is little doubt that had Soto retained the austere, noncompromising, eremitical style associated with Dogen, it would not have become the school with the large following and numerous temples and priests that it has become in recent centuries. Keizan's important place in this development is enshrined in his title, Taiso, the "Great Patriarch," which places him almost as high as the founder, Dogen, the Koso, or "Eminent Patriarch." It is often said that if Dogen were the father of Japanese Soto, Keizan was the mother.

Perhaps the *Denkoroku* did play some part in this great expansion and the eventual success of Soto Zen in becoming an accepted part of the Japanese religious establishment. By demonstrating that Soto held a legitimacy and authority based on a Dharma succession that could be traced all the way back to the Buddha in India, Keizan could counter any claims that his tradition was a mere upstart and interloper; he could achieve a standing of legitimacy and acceptability in the eyes of secular authorities who were often closely allied politically with the older, established traditions; and he could win acceptance among a population already increasingly proselytized by the growing Pure Land and Nichiren traditions. In so doing, the *Record* served as a certificate of respectability in the same way any genealogy does.

However, this should not be construed as implying that the *Record* was composed merely as an expedient tool designed to win acceptance for Keizan's tradition among a hostile or indifferent audience. While its structure and content indicate that it also had that purpose, its primary function seems to have been to celebrate the "light" of its title. Two facts support this conclusion. First, the fifty-three chapters of the text were delivered orally on formal occasions to a community of monks. It was not presented to the court or to the military powers as a document supporting a claim. In fact, no evidence indicates that it was ever presented to authorities as a kind of petition or memorial. The place of presentation (Daijo Monastery), the audience (Zen monks), and the contents of the text support a conclusion that the primary purpose of the text was to instruct and encourage monks. A second point is that the *Denkoroku* does not appear to have been widely known outside Soto monasteries until the mid–nineteenth century, when it was first printed and circulated widely. Thus, from the first, its audience seems to have been the Soto priesthood. It provided them with an authoritative review of the essentials of Soto Zen teachings; reminded them of the seriousness of their vocation and the need to practice hard; and, at the same time, in documenting their genealogical heritage, provided them with a sense of confidence, pride, and legitimacy.

All these functions of the text are based on the evidence of the existence of the "light" of the title. It is likened to a pearl that is bright and lustrous without need for carving and polishing, a vermilion boat so beautiful that no artist could capture its beauty in a painting, the wind that circulates everywhere and shakes the world but cannot be seen or touched, and an icy spring so deep that no traveler can make out its bottom. The occurrence of such epithets and figures of speech throughout the text shows the author not only recording a transmission from master to disciple, in which the disciple realized finally the existence of the "Undying Lord of the Hermitage," but also expressing his profound reverence for this light in the heightened emotional language of poetry.

It is this "Old Fellow" whom we all truly and essentially are, says Keizan. "This True Self has been our constant companion in life after life and has never left us" (Furong Daokai).† It is beyond all predication such as pure and impure, annihilation or eternity, and is identical in fools and sages (Shitou Xiqian). It never divides itself into self and other, or subject and object, but merely wears the faces of self and other (Daman Hongren). Mind, the objective world, delusion, and awakening are all nothing but "names for one's True Self" (Dayi Daoxin). All that we are and do is the result of its presence. It gives us life and makes us die (Yaoshan Weiyan), and we see and hear through the presence of this "Faceless Fellow" (Xuedou Zhijian). It is the source of our minds and bodies (Xuedou Zhijian), and even the use of ordinary discriminative thinking is the doing of the True Self (Tongan Daopi). It itself is speechless and mindless, has no form or sense faculties, but it is not mere nothingness or emptiness (Xuedou Zhijian). It is, on the contrary, a reality possessed by all beings and the true place to which we all return (Danxia Zichun). Although we are born here and die there, constantly arriving and departing in the cycle of rebirth, the True Self does not die, nor is it reborn but remains eternally the Undying Lord of the House who merely wears the different faces of ordinary beings, Buddhas, demons, and donkeys. When the world is periodically destroyed by fire, water, and wind, it is not destroyed (Xuedou Zhijian). In humans, it is "nothing but bright light" (Xuedou Zhijian), a "clear, distinct knowing" (Dongshan Liangjie).

Again, it is this light that is mentioned in the title of Keizan's Record as being transmitted from Shakyamuni through fifty-two generations to Ejo and, by implication, to Tettsu Gikai and Keizan himself. Whatever else may be said about one's essential nature, it is the self as the brilliant light of clear and alert knowing of events that most clearly concerned Keizan. He emphasizes this aspect of the self in chapter after chapter, saying that it is "a thor-

† Parenthetical names in the next two paragraphs indicate the patriarch in whose section of the Record this phrase occurs.

oughly clear knowing" (Daman Hongren), an "alert knowing" (Qingyuan Xingsi), "a clear and distinct, constant knowing" and "a perfectly clear knowing" (Dongshan Liangjie), "boundless clarity and brightness" and "just alertness" (Xuedou Zhijian), to mention just a few instances from the text.

We learn from the *Record* that this True Self or essential nature is the origin of all things and remains their imperishable essential nature, and among humans it takes the form of a capacity for knowing events clearly, without delusion. This clear knowing always lurks just beneath the surface, so to speak, whether the individual is wise or foolish, learned or ignorant, a genius or a simpleton. However, among all these, it remains obscure and nonfunctioning if the individual is not awakened to its existence. For most of humankind, it is obscured by delusion in the form of a tendency to discriminate between "self" and "other," by conventional and habitual patterns of interpreting experience, by stereotyped reactions to events, by grasping experience from the perspective of the ordinary self obsessed with fear and craving, by filtering experience through the lens of some philosophical position or ideological perspective, and so on. In short, what passes among us for clear understanding of our experience is, according to Keizan, a clouded, distorted, darkened misunderstanding. When we really become aware of this truth, and at the same time become aware of this clear light within us, we awaken and become Buddhas. If we do not, then, says Keizan, we remain bound to the prison of this world and transmigrate endlessly in the six paths, falling repeatedly into the clutches of "Old Yama," the Lord of the Dead.

This light is none other than wisdom, insight, or the impeccably clear knowing known throughout Buddhist history as *prajna*, a term that Keizan himself uses occasionally in the text. Prajna is not a special, privileged, "correct" way of knowing events but rather is the knowing of events in the total absence of all viewpoints and perspectives. Thus, while it is a mode of knowing, it is a knowing that does not filter experience through a pre-existing set of assumptions about the nature of an experience. So thoroughgoing is the demand to eliminate all perspectives that not even something such as a "Zen position" or "Buddhist perspective" is considered a legitimate filter. Thus, as Nagarjuna insisted in the second century, *all* perspectives and positions must be abandoned so that events are encountered and responded to from what might be called a perspective of no perspective or a positionless position.

Western philosophers in modern times have concluded that such a perspectiveless perspective is impossible and, indeed, the crisis in contemporary philosophy and theology is a result of the growing consensus that all knowledge is necessarily conditioned by culture, physiology, and personality. Thus, it is argued, we can never know events as they truly are, apart from our interpretation of them because we can never transcend those factors that condition our experience of events. We are necessarily and forever locked within our minds, and our minds are conditioned. On the other hand, Buddhism has claimed for well over two thousand years that a pure, unconditioned way of knowing is indeed possible and we can know events just as they are, undistorted by culture or personality. This claim, in fact, is the tacit assumption at the bottom of Keizan's text. Keizan, like all his predecessors, saw without doubt that this way of knowing is innate in all of us, and that although it has been obscured by various conditioning factors, like a precious jewel buried in a heap of excrement, it can be uncovered and found. This assumption is, in fact, the sole rationale for Zen practice.

Zen practice, consisting primarily of zazen and koan study, is a process of digging down through the various layers that cover the light of clear knowing, a kind of spiritual archaeology, so to speak. In human beings, these layers are made up of such things as concepts, symbols, language, categories, habits, ideological presuppositions, and the natural, innate tendency to divide the world into "self" and "not self." Some layers are made up of the acquired, some of the innate, but all are perceived in Buddhism as similar to the layers of excrement that obscure the precious jewel of clear knowing. Once these layers are removed, a way of knowing is recovered that functions without conventional concepts and categories of thought which, according to all schools of Buddhism, superimpose a meaning on events that does not belong intrinsically to them. To experience events as they truly are, one must experience them without the least bit of personal or cultural meaning added to them. This kind of knowing might best be called "no mind," a term favored by some Zen masters. "No mind" is not confusion, uncertainty, or blankness but, rather, an extremely clear knowing freed of all conceptualization and symbolization.

This kind of knowing is said to be innate, basic, and prior to ordinary discriminative, conceptualizing knowing. It is prior because it is the root and origin of the latter, which arises from the more basic, prior consciousness in the form of a bifurcation into a knowing aspect and a known aspect. The consequence of this split is twofold. On the one hand, consciousness becomes *self*-conscious, so that human beings are not only aware of an experience but can also be aware of being aware. On the other hand, what are thought to be events or things "out there," external to the mind, are in reality only the mind's ideas of events. Thus, rather than knowing an event as it truly is in itself, what we know is our idea about the event. This latter is the known aspect of mind, or mind as its own object. Consequently, as Western thinkers admit, we are ordinarily locked within our own minds and have no access to the true and real. Buddhists also admit that this is the case ordinarily, but that the subject/object split can be healed and mind restored to its original form. This is awakening or enlightenment and is the professed objective of Buddhism.

Since this awakening is, by definition, the ability to know events just as they are, apart from interpretation, assumption, and emotional reaction, then it follows that there is really no "correct" way of knowing events that stands in opposition to a "false" way. The religious and existential problem is not a matter of having wrong ideas about events so much as it is having any idea at all. Any interpretive mechanism is, as an interpretation, a distortion, even a "Buddhist" interpretation, and so enlightenment can never be a matter of replacing bad ideas with good ones. Consequently, the kind of pristine knowing that is Keizan's concern should not be mistaken as being a superior "Zen" way of looking at things that replaces a defective way of seeing them. Pristine knowing is not a point of view.

This is the light that Keizan celebrates and appreciates in his *Record* and the kind of knowing that the master looks for in the disciple. The good teacher is one who recognizes it in the student when he sees it, and since it is absolutely essential that teachers possess this form of knowing, the student who convincingly displays it becomes the master's successor through what is considered a transmission. The fifty-three chapters of Keizan's work show clearly that succession is never based on mere mastery of Buddhist doctrine, the displaying of doctrinal correctness, or the adherence to sectarian orthodoxy, but is based on this kind of unconditioned, unprejudiced knowing that Keizan likens to a brightness greater than the sun and moon combined.

Shakyamuni found it and passed it on to Mahakashyapa, who passed it on to Ananda, and so on down the generations to Dogen and then Ejo in Japan. This is Keizan's story and the foundation of his own position as Great Patriarch of Japanese Soto Zen.

I have considered my task to be that of translating this important and interesting text and, in so doing, contributing to a better knowledge of Buddhist teaching and history, particularly the form of Zen founded in Japan by Dogen in the thirteenth century. However, despite my primary concern with translation, and despite the length of my translation, a few words of a critical nature need be said concerning the story told in the *Denkoroku*. Specifically, the reader needs to be aware of the modern, scholarly evaluation of the kind of traditional material that is found in Keizan's *Record*.

It is probably safe to say that few if any reputable modern scholars, and probably not many even within the Soto priesthood itself, believe that many of the central events and characters in the *Denkoroku* are based on historical fact. Probably no one in Japan or the United States doing research in Zen history believes, for instance, that Chinese Zen began with the arrival from India of the monk Bodhidharma, or that there was a transmission from Bodhidharma to Huike, who had cut off his own arm to demonstrate his sincerity. Bodhidharma has, among scholars, now been relegated to the status of a legendary or mythic figure. Likewise, it is now generally agreed that the Sixth Patriarch was not in fact Huineng, and that the *Platform Sutra,* usually attributed to him, was composed by someone else. In fact, the specific circumstances of the real history of Chinese Zen are probably such that there could not have been anything like a "Sixth Patriarch." It is also widely agreed that the kind of transmission of authority that did occur at a later time in China and Japan did not occur in India, and thus could not have been imported by the Chinese. The origins and early development of Chinese Zen are just now becoming clearer, and the gradually emerging picture is very different from the traditional Zen history found in such works as Keizan's *Record*.

It is significant that in the whole vast body of Indian Buddhist scriptural and commentarial literature, there is not a single word of a patriarchal transmission of the kind celebrated in Keizan's work. Great Indian teachers such as Nagarjuna and Dignaga had students who carried on their work in what was, in effect, a school or philosophical tradition, but that was a very different process and could not be called a patriarchal transmission of the Zen type. This latter process of transmission seems to have developed in China. Not only that, but the first genealogies of the sort we find in the *Denkoroku*, which trace the patriarchal line back into India to Shakyamuni, were composed many generations after the emergence of a distinctive form of practice and Buddhology that came to identify itself as "Zen."

The idea of patriarchal succession seems to have originated in China as a result of circumstances unique to Chinese Buddhism. One of these was the development of schools of Buddhism, such as Pure Land and Zen, which had no Indian roots. Leaders of these schools sought ways to give their schools authority and legitimacy, and several devices uniquely Chinese came to be employed. One of these was to insist that the new school really had its roots in Indian Buddhism, India being the Holy Land and therefore an indisputable guarantor of legitimacy. Many Chinese schools argued that Nagarjuna was a patriarchal ancestor and the originator of that Chinese school's ideas, for instance. Zen leaders of a comparatively late date began creating elaborate patriarchal lineages that stretched back into the past in China to a pivotal figure who was linked to India and ultimately to the Buddha himself through a succession of authorities. The effect, as I have pointed out above, is to show that one's own school, and one's own authority and legitimacy, are derived from the Buddha himself—and are therefore beyond question.

Consequently, traditional Zen histories or genealogies are not "true" if by "true"' we only mean that the story is an account of actual historical events. However, there are other ways of defining truth. For instance, literate and thoughtful people would agree that Herman Melville's *Moby Dick* is a story brimming with truth, despite the fact that no Captain Ahab or ship named *Pequod* ever actually existed. Likewise, F. Scott Fitzgerald's most famous character, Jay Gatsby, is animated by a spirit as real as any actual person who ever lived. Fictional works such as these are treasured, read, and reread over the generations precisely because the stories are "true" despite their lack of historical factuality.

Likewise, myth is a form of truth that has no historical basis. There was never a real Garden of Eden with an Adam and Eve, but the story of original innocence and its loss is very meaningful to all who have reflected on human nature and human potential. The stern literalist who insists that the story is meaningless nonsense because it never actually happened is truly missing the whole point and needs to think seriously about the nature and function of myth. Much of the biography of the Buddha is also mythic, intended to present a model of the religious life for later followers. A story does not have to be literally true to be true in terms of religious life. The bodhisattva Guanyin (or Kannon, as she is known in Japan) is not a historical, flesh-and-blood being, but her actions are visible in every manifestation of compassion and clear knowing.

I am suggesting that the *Denkoroku*'s account of patriarchal succession may be read as expressing a genuine truth—although not a historical one—about the survival and spread of the Buddha's teaching down through the generations, about the relationship between one's own awakening and that of the Buddha, and about the essential completeness and perfection of every being. Thus, one may think of the *Denkoroku* as a way of expressing these things that is true in a way unrelated to historical fact. Teachers of Zen might therefore claim with some legitimacy that the patriarchal succession *has* indeed taken place from the time of the Buddha, continues to take place today, and will continue to do so in the future as each individual actualizes within himself or herself that same human completeness and perfection discovered by the Buddha and pointed out to his followers and posterity.

This is the essence of what is conveyed by Keizan's *Record* of patriarchal succession. After all, the heroic life of the Buddha, as it has come down to us after many hundreds of years, is presented to his followers as a model of what is possible for all who undertake the self-discipline of the Buddha way. That human perfection so beautifully exemplified by the Buddha is the same for all, there is not one perfection for the founder and another for the rest of his followers. That perfection is preserved and passed on from one generation to the next, with nothing lost and with no alteration, like water passed completely from one vessel to another. Zen, as an institution and a way of life, stands on the conviction that this is so, and histories such as Zen Master Keizan's *Record of Transmitting the Light* may be seen as ways to express this point.

II. The Author

Authorship of the *Record* is attributed to Zen Master Keizan Jokin, the first patriarch of the Soji-ji branch of Japanese Soto Zen and the fourth patriarch of Japanese Soto Zen. Most older secondary sources list his birth date as 1268, but recent scholars have argued for a date of 1264.[1] Assuming the latter date to be correct, this means that Keizan was born eleven years after the death of the great founder of Japanese Soto Zen, Zen Master Eihei Dogen. Keizan was born in modern-day Fukui Prefecture, known at the time as Echizen Prefecture, and he was a member of the great and powerful Fujiwara family that had been at the center of Japanese politics for many centuries.

His secular history is nonexistent, since he took up the religious life at a very early age, either in his eighth or thirteenth year. Apparently, he was heavily influenced to seek religion by his mother, who had suffered from the time she was quite young and had sought solace and help from the merciful bodhisattva Kannon. At any rate, he seems to have made the short journey to Eihei-ji monastery while still a boy. There, he became a student of the third patriarch in Dogen's line and then current abbot of the temple, Tettsu Gikai. Keizan records that at the age of twelve, he received the precepts from the still living former abbot and second patriarch, Koun Ejo.

At the age of seventeen, he left Eihei-ji to travel from monastery to monastery to meet various teachers and be tested by them, a practice that went back hundreds of years in China and that survived in Japanese Zen circles. His first stop was nearby Hokyo-ji where the abbot was Jakuen, as he was called in Japan, a Chinese monk who had followed Dogen back to Japan when Dogen returned from China in 1227. Jakuen had studied Zen under Dogen and then under Dogen's successor, Ejo, and now he was abbot of Hokyo-ji.

Keizan stayed awhile with Jakuen, impressing the Chinese master so much that even though there were many followers at the monastery, Jakuen made Keizan the *ino* (the head priest who oversees all personal affairs within the monastery), a high honor indeed, since the position is always reserved for monks who had trained a long time and who were recognized as being proficient in all temple matters. However, Keizan only stayed for a short time and then continued his travels, eventually studying with a series of teachers such as Egyo and Kakushin. This was to be fruitful and fateful study, for these teachers were Rinzai masters who combined Zen practice with the esoteric practices found in Shingon Buddhism and the esoteric branch of Tendai Buddhism. This eclectic approach seems to have influenced Keizan, who later incorporated some of these same practices in his monasteries. He even climbed Mount Hiei and studied for a while in the great Tendai monastic complex there.

In the end, he returned to Eihei-ji and his teacher Tettsu Gikai. However, by this time, some historians claim, there was very serious turmoil at the monastery. A dispute had broken out among the monks, and Gikai, the abbot, was at the center of the dispute. Scholars have studied this dispute from several angles and have arrived at differing theories as to the essence of the controversy. The exact nature of the dispute cannot be stated with any degree of certainty, if indeed it actually took place, but what seems to be clear from traditional accounts is that a large faction of monks questioned Gikai's qualifications as abbot. They wanted Gikai out, but Gikai also had his own supporters, and so two factions fought over who would be the abbot. The anti-Gikai faction triumphed, and Gikai was forced to leave Eihei-ji, to be succeeded by the fourth abbot, Gien. Gikai founded a new monastery, Daijo-ji, and became its first abbot, to be followed a little later by his student Keizan. Thus Keizan became the second abbot of Daijo-ji, a monastery with which he would be strongly associated throughout his mature years. However, for the time being, in 1288, at the age of twenty-four, he went back to study awhile with Jakuen.

Eventually, he followed Gikai to Daijo-ji to mature as a Zen student. In 1294, at the age of thirty, he had his great awakening when he heard Gikai use the old Zen phrase, "Ordinary mind is the Way." The following year, he inherited Gikai's Dharma and became his successor. The next few years were spent teaching at Joman-ji, a temple in Tokushima Prefecture. It was about this time that he first met Gasan Joseki, who was to become one of his greatest disciples and his successor. In 1298 he returned to Daijo-ji to assist the aging and ailing Gikai, and it was in this capacity as assistant to Gikai that he began the fifty-three talks of the *Denkoroku* in the winter of 1300. Two years later, he became the second abbot of Daijo-ji. He had granted the seal of approval to Gasan the year before, and the following year, he also granted it to Meiho Sotetsu, thus acquiring his two greatest succes-

sors and thus laying the foundation for the future development of his branch
of Soto Zen.

Keizan was the abbot at Daijo-ji from 1302 to 1311. Gikai died in 1309 at the
age of ninety-one, and two years later, Keizan turned the monastery over to
his disciple and successor Meiho and started a new monastery named Joju-ji.
The final decade and a half of his life was spent establishing a number of new
monasteries, such as Joju-ji, Yoko-ji, and Koko-ji, acting as abbot, and establishing what he considered proper practice at all these places. His biggest
accomplishment, probably, was the founding of Soji-ji, in Noto, through
which in later centuries passed a long succession of illustrious Soto abbots
and scholar-priests. It became the headquarters monastery of Keizan's wing
of Soto Zen, Eihei-ji becoming the other headquarters in a system of dual
headquarters that has lasted until today and makes Soto Zen unique in Japanese Buddhism. This is the heritage of the great dispute at Eihei-ji that resulted
in a dual abbacy. Keizan died at Yoko-ji in 1325 at the comparatively young
age of sixty-one.

His important place in Japanese Soto Zen history is indicated by his title,
Taiso, which means "Great Patriarch." Dogen, the original founder of Japanese Soto is known as *Koso,* or "Eminent Patriarch." The similar titles and the
metaphor of parentage indicate the crucial, if different, role that each played
in the building of a new form of Buddhism in Japan. Without Dogen, there
would have been no Soto Zen. He made the hazardous trip to Sung China and
brought back the new teaching and practice. He found a small group of dedicated students who wanted to learn what he had to teach and, thus, he started
a new religious community. He also founded Eihei-ji and acquired students
such as Ejo who succeeded him and kept his line going.

However, the fact remains that when Dogen died in 1253, Soto Zen had
grown very little in terms of numbers or strength. It is true that Dogen died
very young and thus did not have a long life to build and expand, but the
problem was probably not so much a matter of time as it was of objectives and
motivation. Much of Dogen's energy went into writing and teaching, and he
probably simply was not interested in expanding an empire.

Thus, when Keizan became abbot of Daijo-ji, Dogen's Buddhism was still
a small, localized community with few temples and priests. The later growth
of Soto to the point where it had a very large number of temples and priests

and millions of parishioners, with the corollary power and prestige, was due to Keizan's work and that of his successors. Keizan, himself, founded several new monasteries during his lifetime, including Soji-ji, which was to be the headquarters of his branch of the school, and then he left several inspired followers, primarily Gasan and Meiho, who spread the faith and continued their teacher's work of building temples and monasteries.

However, it would not have been enough to simply build monasteries and temples. It was also necessary to present the faith in such a way as to be attractive to people other than already dedicated monks. Dogen's religious vision had to be translated for the masses. The Zen that Dogen taught at Eihei-ji was severe, demanding, uncompromising, and had a purist streak in it. It was not the kind of Buddhism that was likely to attract many people, and most likely Dogen did not care much if it did not. However, Keizan was a different kind of person, with a different history, and clearly he had a different objective. For one thing, as a young man, he had studied under teachers who flavored their Zen with practices usually associated with other forms of Buddhism, primarily esoteric practices. Their own approach to religion was pragmatic and eclectic, which differed very much from Dogen's much more purist attitude. Keizan remembered his teachers when he had his own monasteries and incorporated some of these same practices. He also instituted the practice of ministering to the mortuary needs of parishioners. This was something the people had a great need for and expected from the priests, and the result was both a closer bond between temples and parishioners and a great deal of income for the temples. All of this in turn was instrumental in the growth of Soto Zen. Thus, by resisting taking a purist approach and by responding to the needs of parishioners, by taking an active role in founding new monasteries and temples, and by acquiring inspired successors such as Gasan and Meiho to continue his work, Keizan was responsible for the eventual spectacular growth of Soto Zen.

Of course, Keizan did not just build new temples and monasteries. He was, primarily, the first patriarch of his own branch of Soto Zen and the fourth patriarch in Dogen's line. With the destructive internal dispute at Eihei-ji in the late 1200s and Gikai's banishment, Soto Zen split into two branches, to be known later as the Eihei-ji branch and the Soji-ji branch. Gien assumed the position of fourth abbot of Eihei-ji when Gikai left, but the damage was great, and supporters abandoned the monastery and the practice declined. Gikai, meanwhile, founded Daijo-ji and became its first abbot, and when Keizan succeeded him as abbot, in effect a new branch of Soto was established that persists to the present day. Thus, the two branches went their respective ways with their own respective succession of abbots. Keizan's title of "Great Patriarch" reflects both his place in the growth of Soto and his position as the founder of the Soji-ji branch of Soto.

Finally, Keizan wrote the *Denkoroku*, regarded in Soto circles almost as highly as Dogen's *Shobogenzo*. He also composed an important work on monastic discipline, the *Keizan Shingi;* a commentary on the Chinese Zen classic, *Xin Xin Ming,* entitled *Shinjin Mei Nentei;* two works on Zen meditation, the *Sankon Zazen Setsu* and *Zazen Yojin-ki;* and a record of his life and achievements, the *Tokikki.* However, none of these is of the quality of the *Denkoroku.* This work is unique in structure and purpose among all similar Zen spiritual genealogies. And while it cannot be said to be the literary equal of Master Dogen's peerless work, it is nevertheless of excellent literary quality. However, equally important, it is a sustained presentation of a remarkable man's understanding of the religious life, a valuable religious document from the Zen past, and a prime source for understanding the nature of Soto Zen Buddhism.

III. Text History

A prefatory statement at the beginning of the text of the *Record* says that Keizan began his series of fifty-three Dharma talks to the Daijo-ji monks on the eleventh day of the first month in the year 1300. From his own remarks,[2] we know that by the end of the ninety-day *ango,* the intensive training period during the following summer, he had concluded his talk on the thirty-third patriarch, Huineng. Given the regularity of the monastic schedule, in which specific days of the month are set aside for such talks, Keizan would have concluded all his talks during the next winter *ango* period. He was thirty-six years old at the time, if he was born in 1264 rather than in 1268 as has been traditionally assumed.[3]

The *Denkoroku* was his major piece of writing, assuming the status in Soto Zen circles of being one of the two shining jewels of Japanese Soto Zen literature, the other being, of course, Dogen's *Shobogenzo.* Like the latter work, it became a kind of esoteric text, hidden in the monasteries away from the eyes of the general public for almost six hundred years, highly venerated as the teaching of the "second founder" of Japanese Soto Zen and the founder of the Soji-ji branch of the Soto tradition. As the considerable number of extant copies of the text indicates, the process of copying the text probably began very soon after its composition, resulting in the presence of copies at many Soto monasteries. However, few if any people outside these monasteries seem to have known of its existence for hundreds of years. Indeed, even the records of important Soto monasteries do not acknowledge its existence in the century following Keizan's death, a matter I will return to below.

Finally, in 1857, after 557 years of obscurity, the *Denkoroku* was edited and published in a two-volume woodblock edition by a monk named Sen'ei (1794–1864). Sen'ei says in his prefatory remarks that he was given a five-volume copy of the text by a wandering monk and that he also consulted and used several other copies he found for his edition: a two-volume copy stored at Daijo-ji, another five-volume copy at Eihei-ji, and "several other" copies, all five-volume copies. Now that the text had seen the light of day, it began to arouse interest among scholars and Soto officials. Annotated editions began to appear, such as Yoshida Gizan's two-volume *Shusho Bokun Keizan Denkoroku*, published in Kyoto in 1886. In 1885 Soji-ji published its own edition, the so-called Honzan edition, based on a manuscript owned by a private collector named Ouchi.

In 1959 the oldest manuscript copy to date was found at Kenkon-in in Aichi Prefecture, where, coincidentally, a seventy-five-chapter manuscript of Dogen's *Shobogenzo* was also found. The Kenkon-in text has been dated as copied in the middle to later fifteenth century on the basis of writing style and other internal evidence.[4] Thus, although a number of manuscripts have been uncovered; the oldest to date is from a period of a hundred or more years after Keizan's death in 1325. No manuscript in Keizan's own hand or one copied by one of his attendants has been discovered so far.

The Kenkon-in manuscript is important as the oldest text discovered so far. However, over the last several decades, a number of newer copies have been found at such monasteries as Eihei-ji, Yoko-ji, and Shozan-ji, and it is known that several private collectors possess copies. A catalog published by Komazawa University in 1962 lists eleven copies.[5] In 1969, in his edition of the Kenkon-in text, Azuma Ryushin listed thirteen texts.[6] Eight years later, six more copies were added to that list.[7] The *Zengaku Daijiten,* published in 1976, lists nineteen manuscript copies.[8] The existence of many of these has been verified, while others known to have once existed no longer exist, the location of some is unknown, and the existence of some is known only indirectly through the testimony of such people as Sen'ei.

The discovery of a manuscript copy in Keizan's own hand, or one dated conclusively from a period very near to his lifetime, would decisively put to rest a lingering doubt, arising in modern times, about Keizan's authorship of the text. While no one seems to have asserted flatly and categorically that Keizan was not the author, some scholars have expressed what they call "misgivings" or "uneasiness" *(fuan)* about the authorship of the text. For instance, the highly respected scholar and editor of the standard edition of Dogen's writings, Okubo Doshu, has expressed serious doubts about the authorship of *Denkoroku,* saying that anachronisms and other problems in the final two chapters of the text cast serious doubt about authorship.[9]

The evidence that Okubo and others point to can be summarized briefly as follows. One problem is that there are discrepancies in time periods. For instance, the author of the text seems to be writing at a time considerably later than 1300, when the text was presumably composed, such as when he mentions the length of time between Dogen's return from China and the composition of the *Denkoroku.*[10] Another problem is that the author refers to Daijo-ji using another name which seems not to have been used in 1300. These are two of several anachronisms of this kind in the last two chapters.

There is also external evidence. If the text really existed in Keizan's lifetime, and if it was really an extremely honored text, it would surely have been mentioned in records of Keizan's accomplishments, but it is not. Likewise, were Keizan the author of such an important text, it would have been widely known in the Soto monasteries associated with the author, such as Daijo-ji, Yoko-ji, and Soji-ji, but there is no mention of the text in their records as late as the early fifteenth century. Finally, there is the fact that the oldest manuscript copy found so far dates only from the mid-to-late fifteenth century. Okubo and others have consequently expressed uneasiness about the text, saying, in summary, that the author does not *seem* to have been Keizan and that the time of composition does not seem to have been 1300.

While some scholars express "uneasiness," no one seems to have said flatly that Keizan was not the author, and thus the consensus remains that Keizan wrote the work, and the scholarly challenge is not to discover a presumed author but to explain the problems in the text. In fact, some of the evidence outlined above has been discussed and argued to be either inconclusive or explainable.[11] Difficulties of the sort mentioned above could easily creep into a text during its transmission history, while copying, and the silence surrounding the text during the hundred or more years after its composition could be explained by historical facts we do not know about. More needs to be learned about the text's transmission history and the events that took place as Keizan's branch of Zen spread in Japan. Finally, while the kinds of problems found in the text are good reason for uneasiness, they are a kind of negative evidence that cannot replace a convincing, positive demonstration that the text was written later by a specific person.

My translation has used as its text the Honzan edition of 1885 as published by Kochi Egaku in four volumes in 1987. This is a very useful and convenient, including not only the original Honzan text but also a modern Japanese translation; helpful notes; a comparison of the material Keizan got from the *Chuan Deng Lu* and *Wu Deng Hui Yuan* with the original sources; and, most important, variant readings from five other texts: the texts of Kenkon-in, Tenrin-ji, Eihei-ji, Muzen, and the Senei. These variant readings have been most useful, because, while Kochi's text presents no great textual problems, I have had to choose a variant reading on occasion. I have discussed my reasons for doing so in the notes to the translation. While there are, occasionally, substantial differences in the form of longer passages either present or absent in one or the other text, it has been my observation that the main differences, recurring over and over, consist of such things as one text substituting a synonym for a term used in the other, one text using either phonetic script or ideographic characters where the other uses the opposite, the occasional elimination or use of an introductory phrase or word. I would estimate that at least ninety-nine percent of the variations are not significant enough to alter meaning significantly. Whatever other problems the text may offer, a corrupt text, lacunae, and widely diverging variants are not among them.

The language of the *Denkoroku* presents few serious problems for the translator. The general literary style is typical of documents of this kind that originated in the Kamakura period. The style, grammar, and so on are of moderate difficulty. Anyone familiar with Dogen's style, particularly in the Shobogenzo, will immediately notice the relatively straightforward, transparent style of Keizan's work. The two styles, like the two men, are as different as night and day. However, some Zen technical terms and traditional phrases will challenge any translator, and while I believe that my translations are correct and otherwise adequate, I am sure others may suggest better, more felicitous ways of translating them. As is the case with Buddhist studies in general, there is little or no agreement on standard translation terms. Finally, probably the one place almost any translator will find his skills taxed is in the *juko* verse at the conclusion of each chapter. Like the introductory koan to each chapter, the *juko* are in Chinese, and as is the case with most Chinese verse, often a tremendous amount of meaning is packed into a little space, and this makes an easy, confident translation doubtful. The challenge to the translator is to (1) try to determine what the verse is saying, (2) try to duplicate the sense in good English, and (3) try to make it sound like verse. This is difficult. I can only hope that I have hit the mark most of the time.

THE RECORD OF

TRANSMITTING
THE LIGHT

SHAKYAMUNI

Case

Shakyamuni Buddha saw the morning star and was enlightened, and he said, "I and the great earth and beings simultaneously achieve the Way."

Circumstances

Shakyamuni Buddha was of the Sun Race in India.[1] At the age of nineteen he leaped over the palace walls in the dead of night, and at Mount Dantaloka, he cut off his hair. Subsequently, he practiced austerities for six years. Later, he sat on the Adamantine Seat, where spiders spun webs in his eyebrows and magpies built a nest on top of his head. Reeds grew up between his legs as he sat tranquilly and erect without movement for six years. At the age of thirty, on the eighth day of the twelfth month, as the morning star appeared, he was suddenly enlightened. These words [in the above case] are his very first lion's roar.

From that time on, for forty-nine years, he did not spend a day alone but preached the Dharma for the assembly constantly. He was never without a robe and begging bowl. During that time, he preached to the assembly more than three hundred sixty times. Later, he transmitted the Treasury of the Eye of the True Dharma to Mahakashyapa, and it has been passed down from Mahakashyapa through generation after generation to the present. Truly, it has been transmitted through India, China, and Japan, where the practice of the True Dharma is based on it.

The practices of his lifetime are the standard for his descendants. Even though he possessed the thirty-two marks and eighty minor marks,[2] he certainly looked like an ordinary old monk and was no different from other people. Therefore, after his appearance in the world, throughout the three times of the True Dharma, Counterfeit Dharma, and the present Collapsed Dharma,[3] those who emulate his teaching and conduct model themselves on his deportment, use what he used, and each moment, while walking about, standing in place, sitting, or lying down, do as the Buddha did. Buddha after Buddha, and patriarch after patriarch have simply transmitted this so that the True Dharma is not extinguished, and this event clearly indicates this. Even though the method of expression—various stories, figures of speech, and words—was different on the more than three hundred sixty occasions during the forty-nine years, they are nothing more than the expression of this principle.

Teisho

The so-called I [in the main case] is not Shakyamuni Buddha, and Shakyamuni Buddha also comes from this "I." Not only does Shakyamuni come from it but the great earth and beings also come from it. Just as when a large net is taken up and all the many openings of the net are also taken up, when Shakyamuni Buddha was enlightened, the great earth and all beings were enlightened. Not just the great earth and beings but all the Buddhas of the past, future, and present were also enlightened.

Since this is so, do not think that it was just Shakyamuni Buddha who was enlightened. You must not see any Shakyamuni Buddha apart from the great earth and beings. Even though mountains, rivers, and their myriad forms flourish in great abundance, none are left out of the pupil of Gotama's eye. All of you here are also established in the pupil of Gotama's eye. Not only are you established in it but, rather, it is enfolded within you. Also, the pupil of Gotama's eye becomes the fleshly body; it becomes the whole body of each person, standing like an eighty-thousand-foot precipice in each. Therefore, do not think that from the past to the present there was an eye's bright pupil and distinct people. You are the pupil of Gotama's eye; Gotama is the entirety of each of you.

If this is the way it is, what do you call this principle of enlightenment? Let me ask you, monks, does Gotama become enlightened with you, or do you become enlightened with Gotama?[4] If you say that you become enlightened with Gotama, or that Gotama becomes enlightened with you, this is not Gotama's enlightenment. Therefore, this is not the principle of enlightenment.

If you want an intimate understanding of enlightenment, you should get rid of "you" and "Gotama" at once and quickly understand this matter of "I." "I" is the great earth and beings as "and." "And" is not "I" as the old fellow Gotama. Examine carefully, deliberate carefully, and clarify this "I" and this "and." Even if you clarify the meaning of "I," but you fail to clarify "and," you lose the discerning eye.

This being so, "I" and "and" are neither identical nor different. Truthfully, your skin, flesh, bones, and marrow are totally "and." The "Lord of the House" is "I." It has nothing to do with skin, flesh, bones, and marrow, nor has it anything to do with the four elements or the five aggregates. Ultimately, if you wish to know the "Undying Person in the Hermitage," how could it be something separate from this present skin bag? Thus, do not think of it as the great earth and beings.

Although the seasons change and the mountains, rivers, and great earth are different over time, you should realize that because this is the old fellow Gotama raising his eyebrows and blinking his eyes, all this is that body standing independently and openly within the myriad things. It brushes aside the myriad things and does not brush aside the myriad things. [Zen Master] Fayan said, "You cannot say whether it brushes aside or does not brush aside."[5] [Zen Master] Dizang said, "What do you mean by 'myriad things'?"[6]

Therefore, practice fully and sufficiently, develop full mastery, and clarify both Gotama's enlightenment and your own as well. You should figure it out by inspecting this case in detail. Let the answer flow from your heart without borrowing the words of former Buddhas or contemporaries. On the next day set aside for explanations, I want you to present your understanding with a decisive word.

Verse

This mountain monk would like to say a few humble words about this case. Would you like to listen?

A splendid branch issues from the old plum tree;
At the same time, obstructing thorns flourish everywhere.

MAHAKASHYAPA

Case

The first patriarch was Mahakashyapa. Once, the World-honored One held up a flower and blinked. Kashyapa smiled. The World-honored One said, "I have the Treasury of the Eye of the True Dharma and Wondrous Mind of Nirvana, and I transmit it to Mahakashyapa."[7]

Circumstances

The Venerable Mahakashyapa's family was Brahmin.[8] In India, he was called "Kashyapa," which in our country means "Most Venerable Light Drinker." When the Venerable One was born, a golden light filled the room and all of it entered his mouth. Therefore, he was called "Light Drinker." His body had a golden color, as well as thirty marks, lacking only the protuberance on top of his head and the tuft of white hairs between his eyebrows.[9]

He met the World-honored One in front of the Stupa of Many Children. When the World-honored One said, "Welcome, mendicant," his hair fell off as a result, he shed his earthly body, and he was [miraculously] clothed in the robes of a monk. Also, he was entrusted with the Treasury of the Eye of the True Dharma [by the Buddha]. He practiced the twelve austerities and never vainly wasted his time during the night or day. Seeing his emaciated body and uncouth clothing, the whole community of monks was struck with wonder. As a result, when the Buddha preached the Dharma, he shared his seat at each assembly with Kashyapa. From then on Kashyapa was the senior among the monks. Not only was he the senior monk at the assemblies of Shakyamuni but he was also the nonregressing senior monk among the assemblies of all past Buddhas.[10] You should know that he was an old Buddha and not think that he was simply one of the Buddha's ordinary disciples.

Also, before an assembly of eighty thousand monks on Mount Grdhrakuta, the World-honored One held up a flower and blinked. None of the assembly understood his mind, and they remained silent. Mahakashyapa alone smiled. The World-honored One said, "I have the Treasury of the Eye of the True Dharma and Wondrous Mind of Nirvana, the Complete Pure Markless Teaching, and I transmit it completely to Mahakashyapa."

Teisho

The so-called holding up a flower of that time has been intimately transmitted from patriarch to patriarch. It has not been indiscriminately transmitted to outsiders. Therefore, it has not been understood by teachers of the scriptures and treatises or even by many meditation teachers. In truth, they did not understand its true meaning. Be that as it may, this koan is not the koan of the assembly at Mount Grdhrakuta but rather the words transmitted at the Stupa of Many Children. It is not a matter of what was said on Mount Grdhrakuta, as claimed by the *Chuan Deng Lu*,[11] the *Bu Deng Lu*, and others. When the Buddhadharma was transmitted the very first time [to Mahakashyapa] there was this kind of etiquette.

If you are not a patriarchal teacher who transmits the seal of Buddha Mind, you do not understand the occasion of his holding up the flower, nor do you understand [the spirit of] his holding up the flower. You must meticulously study and carefully experience it. Understand that Kashyapa is Kashyapa and clarify that Shakyamuni is Shakyamuni, and separately transmit the perfectly pure Way.

Put aside for a while the holding up of the flower and clarify the blinking. There is not a hair's breadth of difference between your ordinary lifting your eyebrows and blinking, and Gotama's holding up of the flower. There is not a hair's breadth of difference between your speaking and smiling and Mahakashyapa's breaking into a smile. However, if you do not know who it was who raised his eyebrows and blinked, then Shakyamuni and Mahakashyapa are in India, and skin, flesh, bones, and marrow are within you. So many flowers in your eyes, so much floating dust! You have not yet been liberated for countless eons, and for eons to come you will be ruined.

If only once you thoroughly know the Lord,[12] then Mahakashyapa will be able to move his toes in your sandals. Don't you know that Gotama completely vanished when he raised his eyebrows and blinked, and that Kashyapa was enlightened when he smiled? Isn't it our own, then? The Treasury of the Eye of the True Dharma has been completely transmitted to yourselves. Therefore, it cannot be called Kashyapa or Shakyamuni.

Never presenting this Dharma to others, never receiving the Dharma from another—this is called the True Law. In order to indicate that, [the Buddha] held up a flower and showed that it was unchanging. [Kashyapa] smiled to show that it was eternal. In this way, Shakyamuni and Mahakashyapa became acquainted and their life pulses intermingled. Perfectly pure complete understanding is not involved with the ordinary discriminating mind, so [Mahakashyapa] sat in meditation and cut out the root of thought. He entered Mount Kukkutapada, where he awaits the future appearance of Maitreya. Even now, Mahakashyapa has not entered nirvana.

Monks, if you intimately study the Way and investigate carefully, not only is Mahakashyapa not extinct but Shakyamuni abides eternally. Therefore, [the Wondrous Mind of Nirvana], which has been directly indicated and intimately transmitted before you were born, has burgeoned and spread everywhere from antiquity to the present. Monks, do not yearn for the antiquity of two thousand years ago. If you just urgently practice the Way today, Kashyapa has not yet entered Mount Kukkutapada but can appear in Japan, Shakyamuni's fleshly body will be warm right now, and Kashyapa's smile will be new again.

If you can reach this place, then you will be a successor to Kashyapa, and Kashyapa will receive [the True Law] from you. Not only does it come down to you from the seven [past] Buddhas, but you will be able to be the patriarchal teacher of the seven Buddhas. Beginningless and endless, annihilating past and present, here is the abiding place of the entrusting of the Treasury of the Eye of the True Dharma.

For this reason, Shakyamuni also received the transmission from Kashyapa, who dwells now in the Heaven of the Satisfied,[13] and you also abide in the assembly of Mount Grdhrakuta unchanging. Are you not familiar with the expression [by Shakyamuni, in the *Lotus Sutra*], "I always abide on Mount Grdhrakuta and other places, and at the time of the great conflagration [at the end of the world], my land is peaceful and calm, filled with celestials and humans"?[14] Mount Grdhrakuta is not the only abode [of the Dharma]. How could India, China, and Japan be excluded? The Tathagata's True Dharma is transmitted and not so much as a hair of it is lost.

If this is so, this assembly [here] must be the assembly of Mount Grdhrakuta, and Mount Grdhrakuta must be this assembly. On the basis of your diligence or lack of diligence, the Buddha either appears or does not appear. Today, also, if you practice the Way incessantly and master it in detail, the Venerable Shakyamuni will instantly appear. It is only because you have not clarified the self that the Venerable Shakyamuni entered nirvana in ancient times. Since you are children of the Buddha, why do you kill the Buddha? Therefore, you must practice the Way at once and encounter your compassionate father promptly.

Daily the old fellow Shakyamuni and you walk about, stand in place, sit, and lie down together, and you have words together without even a moment of separation. If in this life you do not become acquainted with the old fellow, then you will be thoroughly undutiful. Since you are the Buddha's children, then if you are undutiful, not even the hands of a thousand Buddhas will help.

Verse

Today, this descendent of Daijo Monastery [i.e., Keizan successor of Tettsu Gikai, the first abbot of Daijo Monastery] would like to say a few humble words to point to this principle. Do you want to hear them?

Know that in a remote place in a cloud-covered valley,
There is still a sacred pine that passes through the chill of the ages.

ANANDA

Case

The second patriarch was the Venerable Ananda. He asked the Venerable Kashyapa, "Elder Dharma brother, did the World-honored One transmit anything else to you besides the gold brocade robe?" Kashyapa called, "Ananda!" Ananda replied. Kashyapa said, "Knock down the flag pole in front of the gate." Ananda was greatly awakened.[15]

Circumstances

The Venerable Ananda was from Rajagriha and came from a Kshatriya family.[16] His father was King Dronodana. Actually, he was the World-honored One's cousin. In Sanskrit his name was Ananda, which in our country means "Joy." He was born on the night the Tathagata achieved the Way. He was respectable and proper in appearance, and no one in the sixteen great kingdoms [of India] was his equal. Everyone who saw him was filled with joy, hence his name.

He was foremost of those who had heard much [of the Buddha's teaching], and he was wise, with vast learning.[17] He was the Buddha's attendant for twenty years and proclaimed everything the Buddha taught, and he studied the Buddha's deportment. At the same time the World-honored One entrusted the Treasury of the Eye of the True Dharma to Kashyapa, he likewise entrusted it to Ananda, saying, "Help transmit it." For this reason, he also followed Kashyapa for twenty years, and cannot at all be said to have not understood the Treasury of the Eye of the True Dharma.

Teisho

This should be evidence that the Way of the patriarchal teachers is not the same as that of other traditions [outside Zen]. Since Ananda was foremost among those who had heard much and had vast learning, the Buddha must have personally approved him greatly. However, he still did not transmit the True Dharma, nor did he open up and clarify the mind-ground. When Kashyapa was assembling the teachings left by the Buddha at a meeting at the Vipula Cave, Ananda was not allowed to enter since he had not yet acquired the fruit [of being an arhat].[18]

At that time, Ananda secretly entered samadhi and promptly acquired the fruit of being an arhat. When he was about to enter the cave, Kashyapa said, "If you have acquired the fruit, enter by exhibiting paranormal power." Ananda made himself very small and entered the room through the keyhole. The disciples said, "Ananda has heard much as the Buddha's assistant, and his learning is extensive. Just as water is passed from one container to another without a drop being spilled, [so Ananda possesses all the Buddha's teachings]. We pray that you will ask Ananda to repeat the teachings." Kashyapa said to Ananda, "The monks choose you, so ascend to your seat and repeat what the Buddha said."

At the time, Ananda had secretly retained the Buddha's entrustment within him. Receiving this request from Kashyapa, he stood, bowed at the feet of the assembled monks, and ascended to his seat where he proclaimed, "Thus I have heard. At one time the Buddha was at...." He [gradually] repeated all the holy teaching of the [Buddha's] lifetime.[19] Kashyapa asked the disciples, "Is this different from what the Tathagata preached?" The disciples said, "It does not differ by as much as a word from what the Tathagata preached." The disciples were great arhats who possessed the three kinds of spiritual knowledge and the six paranormal powers, and they did not miss hearing anything.[20] With one voice, they said, "We don't know whether the Tathagata has returned or whether this was spoken by Ananda." They praised him, saying, "The great ocean of the Buddhadharma has flowed into Ananda! What Ananda has spoken is the flowing right now of what the Tathagata has spoken."

We understand that this is evidence that this Way does not rely on much hearing or on realizing the fruit [of being an arhat]. Moreover, for twenty years [Ananda] followed Kashyapa and was greatly awakened for the first time on the occasion of this story [recounted in the main case]. Since he was born on the night the Tathagata achieved the Way, he had not heard the *Avatamsaka Sutra* or other scriptures [spoken right after the enlightenment]. Still, he acquired the samadhi of the perfect knowledge of a Buddha and proclaimed what he had never heard. However, as for not entering the Way of the patriarchal teachers, [his inability] is the same as our not entering [when we rely on erudition and intellectual understanding].

Ananda had put forth the thought of the highest, perfect, complete enlightenment at the same time the Buddha did ages and ages ago at the time of the Buddha named "King of the Empty [Eon]." However, Ananda was fond of much hearing and therefore had still not achieved perfect enlightenment. Shakyamuni practiced diligently and consequently achieved perfect enlightenment. Truly, much hearing is an obstacle to the Way, and this is the evidence. Therefore, the *Avatamsaka Sutra* says, "Much hearing is like a poor person who counts another's treasure and hasn't a halfpenny of his own." If you want to be settled intimately in the Way, don't be fond of much hearing but just be courageous and diligent at once.

Ananda persisted in thinking that something was transmitted besides the robe. He asked, "Elder Dharma brother, was anything else transmitted to you by the World-honored One besides the gold brocade robe?" At that time, Kashyapa realized that [Ananda] had arrived [at a crucial stage] and called Ananda." Ananda responded. Kashyapa replied [immediately], "Knock down the flagpole in front of the gate." Responding to the sound, Ananda was greatly awakened and the Buddha's robe spontaneously came down over his head. That robe was the one correctly transmitted by the seven past Buddhas.

There are three explanations concerning this robe. One is that the Tathagata [was born] bearing it from the maternal womb. Another explanation is that he received it from the Celestials of the Pure Abode.[21] Another is that he received it from a hunter [right after making his home departure from the palace]. There are also other Buddha robes. The robe transmitted to Caoxi [i.e., Huineng, the sixth patriarch in China] from Bodhidharma was a blue-black cotton robe with a blue lining. The lining was added after the robe arrived in China. At present it is stored in the Sixth Patriarch's temple and it is considered an important national treasure. In the *Da Zhi Du Lun* it says that "the Tathagata wore a coarse *sanghati* [large robe]," and this is the same one. That gold brocade robe is a wool robe with gold threads [added]. A sutra says, "The Buddha's aunt with her own hands made a wool robe with gold threads added and presented it to the Buddha." These are a few of a number of items.

With regard to supernatural experiences, there are a number of stories in the scriptures. Long ago, the Venerable Vasasita encountered difficulties with a wicked king. He threw the Buddha's robe into a fire where it emanated rays of five colors. When the fire went out, the Buddha's robe was unharmed, and so the king had faith that it was the Buddha's robe. It is the one to be transmitted to Maitreya [at the time when he appears in the world].

The Treasury of the Eye of the True Dharma was not transmitted to two men. Only one person, Kashyapa, received the transmission from the Tathagata. Ananda served Kashyapa for twenty years and [then] held and transmitted the True Dharma. Thus, you should understand that our [Zen] tradition is transmitted apart from the scriptural teachings. However, in recent times, the two are carelessly thought to be identical. If they are identical, how could the Venerable Ananda, who was an arhat with the three kinds of spiritual knowledge and six paranormal powers, receive the Tathagata's transmission and be called the second patriarch?

Could anyone at present surpass Ananda in understanding the sutras? If anyone does surpass Ananda, then we must acknowledge the identity [of the sutra's meaning and the patriarchal teachers' meaning]. If it can simply be said that they are identical, then why did he serve with so much trouble for twenty years and now clarify [the mind-ground] on [hearing the words] "Knock down the flagpole"? You must understand that the meaning of the sutras and treatises are not to be considered as fundamentally the Way of the patriarchal teachers.

It is not that a Buddha is not a Buddha. Even though [Ananda] served [the Buddha] and acted as his attendant, since he did not penetrate to the Buddha Mind [which he possessed innately] how could he transmit the Mind Seal? You must understand that it does not depend on much hearing and extensive learning. Even though you can hear and retain all ordinary writings and sacred teachings because you are bright and have sharp ears, if you fail to penetrate them [to the essential meaning], you are like someone counting a neighbor's wealth. Regretfully, it is not that this Mind does not exist in the sutra teachings but that Ananda did not penetrate to it. How much more do people in China and Japan depend on words for the meaning and fail to acquire the essence of the sutras.

You must understand that you should not make light of the [experience of the] Buddha Way. Ananda, thoroughly versed in the holy teachings of the Buddha's whole lifetime, repeated them as the Buddha's disciple, so who would not go along with him? However, you must understand that he followed Kashyapa and served him. After he became greatly enlightened, he proclaimed the teachings again. It was like fire uniting with fire. Clearly, if you want to investigate the True Way, abandon the [false] view of a self, old emotions, pride, and egotism. Turn your original Mind to acquiring Buddha knowledge.

With regard to this present story, [Ananda] thought that the transmission of the gold cloth robe [to Kashyapa] meant that outside of being a disciple of the Buddha [symbolized by the robe], there was nothing else [to be transmitted]. However, after following Kashyapa and taking care of him so intimately, he thought that something was communicated [between master and disciple]. Kashyapa, knowing that the time was ripe, called "Ananda," and like an echo following a sound, Ananda responded. It was like a spark flying from a piece of flint.

Though [Kashyapa] called "Ananda," he was not calling Ananda, and the response was not an answer. As for the matter of knocking down the flagpole, in India when the Buddha's disciples and non-Buddhists had a debate, both sides put up a flag. When one side was defeated [in debate] their flag was taken down. Defeat was indicated without sounding drums and bells. In the present story, also, it is as if Kashyapa and Ananda had lined up [for debate] and set up their flags. If Ananda wins, Kashyapa should roll up his flag. One comes forth, the other disappears. However, this is not the case in the present story. If Kashyapa and Ananda are flagpoles, the principle [of the original face] is not revealed. When a flagpole is knocked down, a flagpole will be revealed.

When Kashyapa instructed him to knock down the flagpole, Ananda was greatly awakened because master and disciple had become one in the Way. After this great awakening, Kashyapa was also knocked down, and mountains and rivers were all also demolished. As a result, the Buddha's robes spontaneously came down over Ananda's head. However, you should not stop at standing like a ten-thousand-foot cliff in this lump of red flesh. Do not get stuck in purity. You should go further and understand the existence of the echo. All Buddhas have appeared one after another in the world, and patriarchal teachers have indicated it generation after generation. There is only this. Mind is transmitted by Mind, but no one understands this at all.

Even though the revealed lumps of red flesh, Kashyapa and Ananda, are That Person revealed in the world as one or two faces, do not think that Kashyapa and Ananda [alone] are That Person. You monks right now are each the ten-thousand-foot cliff, the thousand changes, and ten thousand transformations of That Person. If you understand That Person, you will all disappear at once. If that is so, do not look for the knocked-down flagpole outside of yourselves.

Verse

Today, this descendent of Daijo [i.e., Keizan, successor of Tettsu Gikai] would also like to add a few words. Would you like to hear them?

Wisteria withered, trees fallen, mountains crumbled—
Valley streams gush forth, and sparks pour out [from the stones].

SHANAVASA

Case

The third patriarch was Shanavasa. He asked Ananda, "What kind of thing is the original unborn nature of all things?" Ananda pointed to a corner of Shanavasa's robe. Again, he asked, "What kind of thing is the original nature of the Buddhas' awakening?" Ananda then grasped a corner of Shanavasa's robe and pulled it. At that time, Shanavasa was greatly awakened.[22]

Circumstances

The master was a man of Mathura. In India he was called Shanaka[-vasa], which here [in Japan] means "Natural Clothing." Shanavasa was born wearing clothes, and later, the clothes became cool in summer and warm in winter. When he aroused the thought [of enlightenment] and made his home departure, his layman's clothes were spontaneously transformed into [monk's] clothes, just like [an incident recounted concerning] the nun "Lotus Color," during the Buddha's lifetime. When he was a merchant long ago [in previous lifetimes], he presented one hundred lengths of woolen cloth to one hundred Buddhas. Since then, [as a result of his acts,] he wore this natural clothing over many lifetimes. The time between when people die and are reborn is called the "intermediate period." During this time, they have absolutely no clothes. In the present case of Shanavasa, he wore clothes even during the intermediate period.[23]

Also, in India *Shanavasa* is the name of a grass called "Nine Branch Splendor." When a saintly person is born, this grass grows on pure ground. This grass grew when Shanavasa was born, hence his name. He was born after being carried in the womb for six years. In ancient times, the World-honored One pointed to a lush, verdant forest and told Ananda, "This grove is called 'Urumanda' and a hundred years after my death, there will be a monk named 'Shanavasa' and he will turn the Wheel of the Wondrous Dharma here." The master was born here after a hundred years. Later, he received the Venerable Ananda's transmission and stayed here at this grove. He turned the Wheel of the Dharma and vanquished a fire dragon. The dragon submitted to him and presented him with the grove. Truly, this was all in accordance with the World-honored One's prediction.

The Venerable Shanavasa was originally a wizard who lived in the Himalaya Mountains. He joined with the Venerable Ananda and so we have this story. This "What kind of thing is the original unborn nature of all things?" is truly a question no one had ever asked. Shanavasa alone asked it. There is no one who is not born with this original unborn nature of all things, but no one knows it and no one asks about it. Why is it called "unborn nature"? Even though the myriad things are born from it, this nature is not something that is born, so it is called "unborn nature." It is wholly the original unborn. Mountains are not mountains and rivers are not rivers. Therefore, Ananda pointed to a corner of Shanavasa's robe.

Teisho

Kesa [i.e., kashaya, the monk's robe] is an Indian word and it means "spoiled color" or "unborn color." Truly, you should not see it as a color. One way to see it is as the color of the mind and body and external environment of all things[24]—from Buddhas above to the ants, mosquitoes, and horse flies below. However, they are not form and color. Therefore, there are no three realms to leave[25] and no fruit of the Way to acquire.

Though he understood in this manner, Shanavasa asked a second time, "What kind of thing is the original nature of the Buddhas' awakening?" Even though from the beginning we are not confused in this matter, if we do not realize its existence one time, we will be vainly obstructed by our eyes. Therefore, [Shanavasa] asked like this in order to clarify the place whence Buddhas come. In order to let him know that [Buddhas] respond to calls and appear in accordance with knocking, [Ananda] showed him by grasping the corner of the robe and tugging it. At that time, Shanavasa was greatly awakened.

Truly, though from the beginning we are not confused about this matter, if we do not experience it one time, we will not realize that we are the mothers of the wisdom of all Buddhas. Therefore, Buddhas have appeared in the world one after another and patriarchal teachers have pointed it out generation after generation. Although one thing [i.e., original nature] is never given to another or received from another, it should be like touching your own nostrils by searching your face.

The practice of Zen must be one's own practice of enlightenment. When you are enlightened, you should meet a person [who is a true teacher]. If you do not meet a person, you will be [like a bodiless spirit] vainly dependent on grasses and adhering to trees.[26] You should use this story to clarify the fact that you must not practice Zen aimlessly and spend your whole life in vain. Do not vainly express naturalistic views or put your own individual views first.

You may think, "The Way of the Buddha patriarchs distinguishes individuals and capacities. We are not up to it." Such a view is truly the stupidest of stupid views. Who among the ancients was not a body born of a mother and father? Who did not have feelings of love and affection or thoughts of fame and fortune? However, once they practiced [Zen], they practiced thoroughly [thereby achieving enlightenment]. From India to Japan, throughout the different times of the True Dharma, Counterfeit Dharma, and Collapsed Dharma,[27] enough holy and wise men to overflow the mountains and oceans have realized the result [of enlightenment]. Thus, you monks who possess sight and hearing are no different from the ancients. Wherever you go, it can be said that you are this [complete] person, and you are Kashyapa and Ananda. There is no difference in the four great elements and five aggregates, so how are you different from the ancients as far as the Way is concerned?

As a result of merely not penetrating this principle and making an effort in the Way, you will not only lose your human body [which is hard to obtain], but you will not realize that it is the [expression of the] Self. Realizing in this way that one should not be negligent, Ananda again took Kashyapa as his teacher, and Ananda also accepted Shanavasa. Thus the way of teacher and disciple was transmitted. The Treasury of the Eye of the True Dharma and Wondrous Mind of Nirvana which has come down to us in this way is not different from when the Buddha was alive. Therefore, do not grieve because you were not born in the land where the Buddha was born, and do not regret not living in the time when the Buddha was alive. In ancient times you planted the roots of good abundantly and you deeply created auspicious conditions for [acquiring] *prajna*. As a result, you are now assembled here at Daijo [Monastery]. Truly, it is as if you were shoulder to shoulder with Kashyapa and knee to knee with Ananda. Thus, while we are host and guest for this one time, in later lives you will be Buddha patriarchs. Do not get blocked by feelings about past and present, and do not get attached to sounds and forms. Do not spend your days and nights in vain. Carefully make an effort in the Way, arrive at the ancients' ultimate realm, and receive the authenticating seal and prediction [to Buddhahood] of the present [master of Daijo-ji, Tettsu Gikai].

Verse

I would like to clarify this story with a humble verse. Would you like to hear it?

> *Sourceless stream from a ten-thousand-foot cliff,*
> *Washing out stones, scattering clouds, gushing forth,*
> *Brushing away the snow, making the flowers wildly fly—*
> *A length of pure white silk beyond the dust.*[28]

UPAGUPTA

Case

The fourth patriarch was the Venerable Upagupta.[29] He attended Shanavasa for three years and then shaved his head and became a monk. Once, the Venerable [Upagupta] asked him, "Did you make your home departure physically or in spirit?" The master replied, "Truly, I made my home departure physically." The Venerable [Upagupta] said, "How can the Wondrous Dharma of the Buddhas have anything to do with body or mind?" On hearing this, the master was greatly awakened.

Circumstances

The master was from the land of Dali[30] and his name was Upagupta. He belonged to the Shudra class [the lowest of the four social classes]. At the age of fifteen he visited Shanavasa, at seventeen he made his home departure, and at twenty-two he acquired the fruit [of practice]. Traveling about and converting others, he arrived at Mathura, and the number of those who became monks was exceedingly great. As a result, the palace of a demon shook and trembled and the demon grieved and was afraid. Each time someone was enlightened, [Upagupta] tossed a tally four inches in length into a stone room. The room was eighteen cubits high and twelve cubits square and it was filled with tallies. One cubit is equal to [about] two feet. [Upagupta] was cremated with the tallies accumulated from a lifetime of encouraging home departure. The number of people who made their home departure was as great as when the Tathagata was alive. Therefore, people called him the "Buddha without the major and minor marks.[31]

The demon, resentful, watched for a time when [Upagupta] entered samadhi. Then, exercising his demonic powers, he tried to harm the True Dharma. The Venerable [Upagupta], while in samadhi, saw what was intended. The demon watched and secretly hung a garland around [Upagupta's] neck. Then, the Venerable [Upagupta] had the idea of subduing him. Rising from samadhi, he took the dead bodies of a human being, a dog, and a snake, and transformed them into a flower garland. Speaking softly, he put the demon at ease, saying, "You offered me a very rare and wonderful garland, and now I have a garland that I want to offer you in return." The demon was very happy and extended his neck to receive it. Then, the garland changed back into the three smelly corpses. Insects and worms crawled from them. The demon detested it and was greatly distressed. He could not get rid of it despite his supernatural powers, nor could he unfasten or move it.

Then, he rose up to the six heavens of [the realm of] desire[32] and spoke to the celestial beings. He also visited the Brahma heavens and sought deliverance.[33] The celestial beings said, "This is a supernatural transformation done by a disciple [of the Buddha] who has the ten powers.[34] We are ordinary beings, so what can we do about it?" The demon said, "Then what can I do?" The Brahma celestials told him to take refuge with Upagupta and then he would be able to get rid of the garland. They recited this verse in order to change his mind:

If you fall down because of the ground,
You must use the ground to get up.
Trying to get up without the ground,
Makes no sense.
"Return and seek liberation from a disciple with the ten powers."

Having received this instruction, the demon left the celestial mansion and, in repentance, paid homage at the feet of the Venerable Upagupta. The Venerable [Upagupta] asked him, "Are you going to ever try to harm the Tathagata's True Dharma?" The demon replied, "I completely take refuge in the Buddha Way and will forever cease what is not good." The Venerable [Upagupta] said, "In that case, you must say that you take refuge in the Three Treasures." The demon king joined his hands and pronounced [the formula for taking refuge] three times, and the garland fell off.[35]

Teisho

In this way, [Upagupta] displayed the powerful effects of the Buddhadharma, just as when the Tathagata was alive. When he was seventeen years old and shaved his head, Shanavasa asked him, "Did you make your home departure physically or in spirit?" For Buddhists, there are basically two forms of departure, which are physical and mental. Leaving home physically means that they cast away love and affection, leave their homes and birthplaces, shave their heads, don monks' robes, do not have male or female servants, become monks or nuns, and make an effort in the Way throughout the twenty-four hours of each day. Whatever the time, they do not pass it in vain. They desire nothing else. They neither delight in life nor fear death. Their minds are as pure as the autumn moon; their eyes are as clear as a bright mirror. They do not seek Mind nor do they hanker [to see] their [original] natures. They do not cultivate the holy truth, much less worldly attachments. In this way, they do not abide in the stage of ordinary folk or cherish the rank of the wise and holy, but more and more become mindless seekers of the Way. These are people who leave home physically.

Those who leave home in spirit do not shave their heads or wear monks' clothing. Even though they live at home and remain among worldly cares, they are like lotuses, which are not soiled by the mud [in which they grow], or jewels, which are immune to [contamination by] dust. Even though there are karmic conditions so that they have wives and children, they consider them trash and dust. They do not entertain love for even a moment or covet anything. Like the moon suspended in the sky, like a ball rolling around on a tray, they live in the noisy city and see one who is tranquil. In the midst of the three realms, they clarify the fact that they dwell beyond time. They realize that exterminating the passions is a sickness, and that aiming for ultimate reality is wrong. They realize that both nirvana and samsara are illusions, and they are not attached to either enlightenment or the passions. These are people who leave home in spirit. [Shanavasa] asked [Upagupta] whether he had made his home departure physically or in spirit. If it is not one or the other, then home departure is not home departure. Hence, the question. However, Upagupta replied, "Truly, it was physical home departure." In this, he did not think about Mind, speak of [original] nature, or discuss the abstruse. He just knew that it was the body composed of the four elements and five aggregates that left home. He attained [enlightenment] spontaneously, and therefore clarified that it was a matter of psychic powers.[36] He acquired it without seeking and, therefore, clarified the fact that it is unobtainable. Since this was the way it was, he said that he had left home physically.

However, from the standpoint of the Buddha's Wondrous Dharma, this is not the explanation. Therefore, Shanavasa explained that Buddhas do not leave home physically or in spirit, nor should they be seen in terms of the four elements and five aggregates, nor seen as the profound mystery of truth. They cannot be seen in terms of wise and foolish, nor are they bound to such things as mind and body. They are like space, which has neither inside nor outside, like the ocean, which has neither surface nor interior. Even though there are many subtle principles and numerous teachings, he spoke only of this.

Do not say that "I alone am honored" is Buddha,[37] and do not say that he either comes or goes. Who can speak of "before my parents were born," or "prior to the empty eon"? Aiming at this place, one transcends birth and no birth, one is liberated from mind and no mind. It is like water conforming to its container, like space, which rests against things. Though you grasp it, your hands are not filled; though you search for it, you cannot find a trace. This is the Wondrous Dharma of the Buddhas. When you reach this place, Upagupta does not exist and Shanavasa does not arise, so you cannot consider them to move or be still, to come or go. Even though there is "is" and "is not," "other" and "self," it is like a sound at the bottom of a stream or like the endlessness of space.

If you do not experience [this place] one time, then even a million teachings and countless wonderful principles will end up uselessly as the flow of ordinary karmic consciousness. In this way, when [Shanavasa] spoke about this and Upagupta was instantly awakened, it was like a clap of thunder in a clear sky, like a raging fire bursting out on the great earth. Once the thunder roared, not only was [it as if] the roots of Upagupta's ears were cut off, but he instantly lost the root of his life. The raging fire blazed suddenly and the Buddhas' teachings and the true face of the patriarchal teachers were completely reduced to ashes. These ashes appeared with the name of the Venerable Upagupta. They were as hard as stone, black as lacquer. Getting rid of the ordinary natures of any number of people and smashing their bodies, he vainly counted emptiness by casting tallies and left behind traces of emptiness by burning emptiness.

Verse

Today, this descendent of Daijo [Monastery] would like to look for the traces beyond the clouds and fix some words to the clear sky. Would you like to hear them?

House demolished, the person perished, neither inside nor outside,
Where can body and mind hide their forms?

DHRITAKA

Case

The fifth patriarch, Dhritaka,[38] said, "Because one who makes his home
departure [and becomes a monk] is a selfless Self,[39] is selfless and possesses
nothing, and because the [original] Mind neither arises nor ceases, this is the
eternal Way. All Buddhas are also eternal. The Mind has no form and its
essence is the same." Upagupta said, "You must become thoroughly awakened and realize it with your own mind." The master was greatly awakened.

Circumstances

The master was from the kingdom of Magadha. When he was born, his
father dreamed that a golden sun appeared from the house and brilliantly
illuminated heaven and earth. In front was a large mountain decorated with
seven jewels. On the top of the mountain there was a spring that gushed
forth, flowing copiously in the four directions. When the master first visited
Upagupta, he recounted this. Upagupta told him the following: "The large
mountain is myself, and the gushing spring is you, arousing prajna-insight
and penetrating the inexhaustibility of the Dharma. The sun appearing from
the house is your present entering the Way. The illumination of heaven and
earth is the preeminence of your prajna-insight." The master was originally
named "Gandhahastin" [Fragrant Elephant] but because of this [dream] his
name was changed. In India he was named "Dhritaka," which in our land
means "Intimate with the Limit of Reality."

Having heard what Upagupta said, the master made this verse:

From the lofty mountain of seven jewels
A stream of prajna-insight gushes always.
It transmits the taste of the True Dharma
And brings deliverance to those who respond.

Then Upagupta replied with a verse:

I transmit my Dharma to you
And you will manifest great prajna-insight.
A golden sun appears from a house
And brilliantly illuminates heaven and earth.

The master paid reverence [to Upagupta] and consequently followed him, requesting to make his home departure.

Upagupta asked him, "Is your intention to make your home departure a home departure of mind or body?" The master replied, "My request for home departure is not for the sake of mind or body." Upagupta said, "If not for mind or body, then who leaves home?" The master replied, "The one who makes his home departure…" and so on [as in the main case], and he became greatly awakened.

Teisho

Truly, this home departure reveals the Self which is a selfless Self. Therefore, it cannot be distinguished in terms of body or mind. This Self which is a selfless Self is the eternal Way. It cannot be fathomed in terms of birth or cessation. It is not the Buddhas, nor is it sentient beings; how much less is it the four great elements, the five aggregates, the three realms, or the six paths [of rebirth]! The Mind has no form. Even though there is hearing, seeing, and perception; in the end, it neither comes nor goes, neither moves nor is still. The fellow who understands in this way, who understands that this is the Mind, still must be said to understand intellectually. Therefore, even though Dhritaka understood in this way, Upagupta pointed out that he had to become greatly awakened and understand it in his own mind. It is like placing the imperial seal on commercial goods. When you see the royal seal, you know it is not poison, not the wrong item, and not something reserved for official use. Therefore, it can be used by people. This is the way it is when the paths of master and disciple coincide. Even though you grasp it as principle and clarify it as the Way, you necessarily get it for the first time when you become greatly awakened. If you are not greatly awakened one time, you will vainly become someone who understands intellectually and never penetrates the mind-ground. If you still do not escape [naive] views of Buddha and Dharma, when will you escape being bound by self and others?

Thus, even if you do not miss a single word of all that was preached during the forty-nine years [of the Buddha's life] and do not get one teaching of the three vehicles or five vehicles mixed up, without being once awakened, it would be hard to call you a true patch-robe monk. Even if you can expound a thousand sutras and ten thousand treatises, make the Buddhas reveal their countenances, make the great earth tremble, and make flowers rain down from the sky, you still have the standpoint of a [mere] lecturer. You are not a true patch-robe monk.

You must not try to understand this in terms of "the three realms are Mind only," "all things are reality," "the whole being is Buddha nature," or "absolutely empty and quiescent."[40] "All things are reality" still has to do with ranking; "all is empty" is the same as [the incorrect view of] nihilism; "the whole being is Buddha nature" resembles a spiritual nature; and "Mind only" does not avoid [ordinary] understanding. Someone who seeks this matter in the thousand sutras and ten thousand treatises is regrettably abandoning his father and running off.[41] When each of you breaks open your own treasure store and carries out the great store of sutras [which is your own Mind], the holy teachings will naturally become your own.

If you do not understand in this way, the Buddhas and patriarchs will become your enemies. It is said, "What wicked demon made you take your home departure? What wicked demon made you wander about [as a homeless monk]? Whether you can express it or not, you will die from my staff."[42] This being so, it is said [previously] that "home departure is not for the sake of body or mind." Even though Dhritaka understood in this way, he was still not a true patch-robe monk. When this was pointed out to him again, he was awakened for the first time and was able to reach [his essential Mind].

Good people, carefully make an effort in the Way and meticulously practice. Do not base understanding on texts, or discern the spiritual on the basis of ordinary understanding. Smash [such distinctions as] heaven and earth, worldly and holy, and personal and environmental karmic consequences.[43] Even if you move back and forth between the past and the future, there will not be a shred of obstruction. Even if you exit and enter above [to enlightenment] and below [in service of living beings], there will not be an atom of difference. Paint divisions on empty space and raise waves on the flat earth. Thoroughly see the Buddha's face and thoroughly experience awakening and your bright [original] Mind. Just as a gourd is entwined with its own vines and a bright jewel is surrounded by a halo, one understands the existence of the Inner Hall of the Buddhas and patriarchs and for the first time acquires it.

Verse

I would like to add some humble words to the above story. Would you like to hear them?

> By acquiring the marrow,
> you will know the clarity of what you found,
> Lunbian[44] still possesses subtleties
> he does not pass on.

MICCHAKA

Case

The sixth patriarch was Micchaka. Once, the fifth patriarch said to him, "The Buddha said, 'Practicing wizardry and studying the small is like being dragged with a rope.' You yourself should know that if you leave the small stream and immediately come to the great ocean, you will realize the birthless." Hearing this, the master experienced awakening.

Circumstances

The master was from central India and was the leader of eight thousand wizards. One day while leading his followers, he respectfully paid reverence to Dhritaka. He said, "In former lives we were both born in the Brahma Heavens. I met the wizard Asita[45] and received the way of the wizard from him. You met a disciple [of Buddhism] who possessed the ten powers and learned to practice meditation. After that, our karmic paths separated and six eons have passed since we went our own ways." The Venerable [Dhritaka] said, "So many eons apart is true, not a lie. Now you must abandon the false and come to the true, and thus enter the Buddha vehicle." The master said, "In former times, the wizard Asita made a prediction, saying, 'After six eons you will meet a fellow student and realize the fruit of purity [which is being an arhat].[46] Isn't meeting you my destiny? I ask the priest to be compassionate now and liberate me." The Venerable [Dhritaka] gave him the complete monastic precepts and made him a monk. The other wizards felt proud of themselves at first, but then the Venerable [Dhritaka] exerted great supernatural powers. As a result, they all aroused the thought of enlightenment

and simultaneously became monks. Eight thousand wizards became monks.
It was right at the time when they decided to become monks and follow him
that the Venerable [Dhritaka] said "Practicing wizardry and studying the
small..." etc. The master [Micchaka] heard it and was enlightened.

Teisho

Even if you study wizardry and learn to prolong your life, or command the
marvelous use of supernatural powers,[47] you can only really perceive eighty
thousand eons into the past and eighty thousand eons into the future, but
you cannot scrutinize anything before or after that. Even if you cultivate the
meditative trances at the stage of neither perception nor nonperception and
enter the trances of no mind or thought, you will unfortunately be born in
the celestial realm of no perception and become a celestial being with long
life. Even though you get rid of a corporeal body, you still will have the functioning of karmic consciousness. Thus, you will not be able to meet a
Buddha or comprehend the Way. And when the results of karmic consciousness are exhausted, you will fall into the Avici Hell. This is like being
bound and dragged with a rope. In the end, there is no liberation.

Although students of the small vehicle attain the first, second, third, and
fourth fruits, and attain [the rank of] pratyekabuddha,[48] still, this is practice
in terms of body and mind, or making an effort in the Way in terms of delusion and enlightenment. For this reason, saintly ones with the first fruit pass
through eighty thousand eons and then become bodhisattvas [who arouse]
the first thought [of enlightenment] for the first time. Those with the second
fruit pass through sixty thousand eons and then become bodhisattvas with
the first thought [of enlightenment]. Those with the third fruit pass through
forty thousand eons and arouse the first thought of enlightenment. The
pratyekabuddha passes through ten thousand eons and enters the path of
the bodhisattva. Even though he comes [to the bodhisattva path] as a result
of good conditions [in the past], unfortunately, as a result of this, the turning
of the wheel of karma does not end. This also is like being dragged with a
rope. One is not truly liberated.

Even though you destroy the eighty-eight defilements of views and concepts, the subtle defilements,[49] and countless delusions, so that not an atom
of them remains, this is a conditioned effort and finally not the undefiled

result, Buddhahood. Such efforts in the Way as returning to the root, going back to the source, waiting for enlightenment, and making these your standard, are all in this category.

Good people, do not get caught up even in nothingness. You may become like non-Buddhists who fall into an empty nothingness [by missing one whole side of the teaching of emptiness]. Do not stop in an emptiness like the empty eon before the beginning of the universe. This is like being a corpse from which the spirit has not completely departed. Do not think about putting an end to false illusions and trying to reach true essential nature. This is like saintly people who destroy ignorance and attain the middle way. You produce clouds where there are no clouds, and produce imperfection where there is none. It will be as if you left your own home to wander in a foreign land, an impoverished guest drunk on the wine of ignorance and delusion.

Think! How can you think you are somebody and speak of "before birth" and "after death." What past, future, and present can you be aware of? For vast eons, there has been no discrepancy even for a second. From birth to death it is only "this." Be that as it may, if you do not intimately experience it one time, you will become deluded by your senses and their objects and will not know this Self. This is being estranged from what is right in front of you. Therefore, you will not understand the source of your body and mind or the source of the myriad things, and you will want to brush away [delusion] for no good reason and seek [enlightenment] for no good reason. This being the case, you made the Buddha take the trouble to appear in the world, and you made the patriarchal teachers courteously extend their admonitions. Even though they extend their admonitions in this way, you are still deluded in your own views, either saying that you do not grasp it or do not understand.[50] Truly, you are not ignorant, nor are you intimately in touch with the truth, but you dwell vainly in thoughts and calculations, discriminating between right and wrong.

Don't you realize that when someone calls, you respond, and when someone points with a finger, you follow? This does not occur through discriminating judgment or through a conscious effort; it is [the working of] your Lord. This Lord has neither face nor bodily characteristics; however, He never stops moving. Because of this, this Mind arises and is called "body." When the body appears, the four great elements, the five aggregates, myriad pores, and three hundred sixty bones come together and you are a body. It is like a jewel having light, or a sound having an echo. From birth to death, you lack nothing and have nothing in excess. With such a birth and death, though you are born, your birth has no beginning; though you die, your death leaves no traces. It is like waves rising and falling on the ocean and leaving no traces. Even though [the waves] disappear, they do not go to any particular place. Because the ocean is what it is, large or small waves appear and disappear.

Your own mind is the same. It moves without ever stopping, and, therefore, appears as skin, flesh, bones, and marrow. It functions as the four great elements and five aggregates. It also appears in the form of peach blossoms and verdant bamboo. It realizes enlightenment in the form of acquiring the Way and enlightening the Mind. It divides into sounds and forms and is different in the forms of seeing and hearing. It functions as wearing clothes and eating food, and as speech and action. Dividing and dividing, it is [nevertheless] not separated itself; appearing and appearing, it is not limited by physical characteristics. It resembles a magician performing various magical illusions, like producing images in a dream. Even though ten thousand images go through a thousand changes and ten thousand transformations in the face of a mirror, it is still just this single mirror. If you do not know this, and vainly cultivate wizardry or study the trivial, there is no chance for liberation.

Monks, you are not in bondage, so how can you become newly liberated? Delusion and enlightenment are originally nonexistent. You are free of bondage and liberation from the beginning. Isn't this non-birth [and non-extinction]? Isn't it the great ocean? Where are there any small streams? Lands [as numerous] as grains of dust or atoms are all the ocean of the universe. The flowing of valley streams, cascading waterfalls, and swirling rivers are all the lively turning of the great ocean. So, there is no small stream to leave, no great ocean to seize. This being so, all [of Micchaka's] difficulties went away of themselves, and his former views were taken care of in one blow, and he gave up wizardry and made his home departure. This is an expression of karmic conditions.

What is more, when you practice and practice in this way and there is agreement between thoughts and words, it will truly be like intimate friends meeting, or self nodding to self. You will all swim together in the ocean of [essential] nature and never be separated for even an instant. If you are influenced in this way, it must be the manifestation of karmic conditions. Don't you see? The Great Master Ma [i.e., Mazu Daoyi] said, "No sentient being for countless eons has ever left the samadhi of Dharma nature. In the samadhi of Dharma nature they wear clothes and eat food, talk together and reply. The functioning of the six [sense] bases and the carrying out of activities is nothing but Dharma nature." Hearing this, do not take it as meaning that sentient beings exist within Dharma nature. Whether you say "Dharma nature" or "sentient beings," it is the same as saying "water" and "waves." Therefore, we may use words like "water" and "waves," but how can there be much difference?

Verse

This morning, in order to say something definitive about this story, I have a humble verse. Do you want to hear it?

> *Even with purity like an autumn flood reaching to the heavens,*
> *How can it compare with the haziness of a spring night's moon?*
> *Many people desire to find purity in their lives,*
> *But though they sweep and sweep, their minds are not yet empty.*

VASUMITRA

Case

The seventh patriarch was the Venerable Vasumitra. He placed a wine vessel before the Venerable Micchaka, bowed, and stood. The Venerable [Micchaka] asked him, "Is this my vessel or yours?" The master thought about it. The Venerable [Micchaka] said, "If you think it is my vessel, it is your intrinsic nature; if you think it is your vessel, you will receive my Dharma." Hearing this, the master was greatly awakened concerning the unborn intrinsic nature.

Circumstances

The master was from northern India, of the Bharadvaja family. He always wore clean clothes. He wandered about in the village carrying a wine vessel, and he would sometimes sigh or howl. People thought he was crazy. He did not let anyone know his name. Now, the Venerable Micchaka was traveling about teaching people and arrived in northern India, where he beheld a golden cloud rising up over the wall [of the town]. The Venerable [Micchaka] said to his followers, "This is the energy of a great man who will inherit my Dharma." He had hardly finished speaking when the master arrived and asked him, "Do you know what I have in my hand?" The Venerable [Micchaka] replied, "It is an impure vessel, not a pure one." The master then placed the wine vessel in front of the Venerable Micchaka, and so on, and became greatly awakened concerning the unborn intrinsic nature. Then, the wine vessel suddenly disappeared.

The Venerable [Micchaka] said, "Try and tell me your own name, and I will tell you something about past conditions [which brought you to this place]." The master replied in verse:

For innumerable eons up to my birth in this land
My family name has been Bharadvaja, my given name Vasumitra.

The Venerable [Micchaka] said, "My teacher, Dhritaka, said that the World-honored One was traveling in northern India and told Ananda, 'Three hundred years after my death, there will be a holy man in this land whose family name will be Bharadvaja and whose given name will be Vasumitra. He will become the seventh patriarch of the Zen lineage.' The World-honored One made a prediction about you. You should make your home departure." The master replied, "As I reflect on my lives [in the past], I was once a donor and presented a Tathagata with a jeweled seat. That Buddha made a prediction about me, saying, 'You will become a patriarch in the lineage of Shakyamuni Buddha during the Fortunate Eon.'"[51] For this reason, he attained the status of seventh patriarch.

Teisho

Prior to arriving where the Venerable [Micchaka] was, the master carried a wine vessel around with him day and night, never letting go of it. In truth, it was a symbol. This vessel was important in the morning and in the evening, and he used it freely. Truly, it represented himself as a vessel. Therefore, at the beginning of his practice, he asked, "Do you know what I have in my hand?" Even if you realize that the mind is the Way and clarify the fact that the body is the Buddha, it is still an impure vessel. In that case, it violates purity. Even if you understand that it existed in the past and the present, and realize that it is fundamentally complete,[52] it nevertheless remains an impure vessel. What past can you speak of? What present? What beginning can you speak of, or what end? Such views as these necessarily violate purity. Hearing the superiority of this principle, the master put down the vessel, symbolizing his conversion by the Venerable [Micchaka]. [Micchaka] asked, "Is this vessel mine or yours?" Since this is already no longer a question of past or present, it has nothing to do with going or coming. At this time, can you ask whether it is "mine" or "yours"? As [Vasumitra] thought about whether it was "mine" or "yours," [Micchaka] said, "If you consider it my vessel, it is your intrinsic nature." Thus, it is not Micchaka's vessel. "If it is your vessel, you will receive my Dharma." Therefore, it is not Vasumitra's vessel. Since it is neither my vessel nor yours, the vessel is also not a vessel. As a result, the vessel disappeared.

Truly, this story makes no sense to people today. Though you practice and practice, and arrive at the place where not even Buddhas and patriarchal teachers can reach, this still must be an impure vessel and necessarily violates purity. One who is truly a pure person does not establish purity, and for that reason also does not establish a vessel. The paths of teacher and disciple coincide because there is no obstacle on the path. You will receive my Dharma because it is your intrinsic nature. Not one thing is received from someone else, and not one thing is given to another. When you get to the bottom of this matter in this way, then you can speak of "teacher" and "disciple." Therefore, the disciple rises up on the teacher's head, and the teacher comes down to the disciple's feet. At this time, there are no two things, no separation. Therefore, it is difficult to speak of a vessel; the vessel has disappeared.

Today, too, if you can reach this realm, there is no former body and mind. It is therefore difficult to speak of existing in the past or present. How much less can you speak of birth and death, or going and coming! How can you be aware of skin, flesh, bones, and marrow! It is a realm where the sky congeals into a single mass, admitting neither of front nor back, neither inside nor outside.

Verse

Today I want to take up this story and add a humble verse. Do you want to hear it?

> *Just as an echo follows when a bell sounds on a frosty morning,*
> *So, here, from the first there is no need for an empty cup.*

BUDDHANANDI

Case

The eighth patriarch was Buddhanandi. He met the seventh patriarch, the Venerable Vasumitra, and said, "I have come to discuss the truth with you." The Venerable [Vasumitra] said, "Good sir, if you discuss, it is not the truth; truth is not discussed. If you intend to discuss the truth, then in the end it is not a discussion of truth." The master realized that the Venerable [Vasumitra]'s truth was superior and was awakened to the principle of the unborn.

Circumstances

The master was from Kamala,[53] and he belonged to the Gotama family. He had a fleshy protuberance on his head. In debate he was unstoppable. The seventh patriarch, the Venerable Vasumitra, came to Kamala to convert people and he promoted Buddhism extensively. The master stood before the sitting [Vasumitra] and said, "I am named Buddhanandi, and right now I want to discuss truth with you." The Venerable [Vasumitra] said, "Good sir, if you discuss, it is not the truth; truth is not discussed."

Teisho

Real truth cannot be discussed, and real discussion has nothing to do with truth. Therefore, when there is discussion, it is not truth; when there is truth, it is not discussion. That is why it was said that "If you intend to discuss truth, then in the end it is not a discussion of truth." In the end, there is not a single thing to be considered truth, nor a single thing to be called discussion. Moreover, [the Buddha] did not have two kinds of speech. For that reason, experiencing the Buddha's words is seeing the Buddha's body; seeing the Buddha's body is bearing witness to the Buddha's tongue. Even if you say that mind and objects are not two, this is not a discussion of reality. If you say that nothing changes [or that everything changes], this is not truth. If you say that words cannot be uttered or that the principle cannot be revealed, this still does not penetrate reality. If you say that essential nature is real, or that mind is the absolute, what sort of discussion is this? If you say that subject and object are both forgotten, this is still not a real discussion. Even if subject and object are not forgotten, this is not the truth. Though you speak of guest and host, one or identical, again, this is not a discussion of truth.

With this in mind, even Manjushri's speaking of no words and no speech is not an announcement of reality. Neither is Vimalakirti's sitting in silence [refusing to say anything] a discussion of truth.[54] It is as if both Manjushri and Vimalakirti were confused. Even less have Shariputra, who was foremost in wisdom, and Maudgalyayana, who was foremost in supernatural powers, ever seen this truth even in a dream. It is like someone who is born blind never seeing objects or colors. Moreover, the Buddha said that Buddha nature was something shravakas and pratyekabuddhas had never known even in a dream. (In the chapter on "The Nature of the Tathagata," in the *Mahaparinirvana Sutra*, [the Buddha] says, "O, good sons, only a Buddha knows such a Buddha nature as this. It is not something known by shravakas and pratyekabuddhas.") Bodhisattvas on the [stage of the] ten abodes[55] seeing cranes in the distance are confused as to whether it is water or cranes. Even though after reflecting on it they conclude, well, it is cranes, they are still not sure.[56] (In the same sutra, same chapter, the Buddha says, "Good sons, to give an illustration, it is like a thirsty man wandering in a wilderness and in his agony and delusion is unable to distinguish between water and trees. After he has got a better look, he sees that it is white cranes in a grove of trees. Good sons, the bodhisattva in the ten abodes being able to see a small part of Buddha nature is like this.") The bodhisattva in the ten abodes does not clearly see that this is Buddha nature. (In the same sutra, same chapter, the Buddha says, "Even though the bodhisattva in the ten abodes has seen the nature of the Tathagata within his body, in the same way, it is not clear.") Moreover, on the basis of what the Tathagata preached, [bodhisattvas] understand a little that their own [true] nature exists, and they say, happily, "We have transmigrated in samsara for countless eons and our inability to grasp the fact of this eternal existence [of Buddha nature] is due to perplexity about the absence of self." (In the same sutra, same chapter, the Buddha says, "In the ten abodes they are unable to see Buddha nature." Once the Tathagata has explained it, they see a little. Once these bodhisattvas, great beings, have seen it, they cry, "Wonderful, O World-honored One! We have transmigrated in samsara for countless eons and have always been perplexed about the absence of self.")

Moreover, though you say that you have extinguished seeing and hearing, forgotten body and mind, shunned delusion and enlightenment, and avoided impurity and purity, you cannot see the truth even in a dream. Therefore, you should not seek it in emptiness or in forms. How much less should you seek it in Buddhas and patriarchs!

Good people, for vast numbers of eons up to the present, how many [cycles of] birth and death have you passed through? How many times have body and mind arisen and ceased? You may think, "This birth and death, coming and going, is all a dream, a delusion." I have to really laugh. What kind of theory is this? Is there someone who is born and dies, who comes and goes? What do you mean by "True Self?' [And if you speak of "True Self,"] what do you mean by "a dream, a delusion"? [From the standpoint of a True Self] you cannot understand in terms of emptiness. [From the standpoint of birth and death] you cannot understand it as truth. If you think in terms of empty and false or true, then by arriving at this situation, the whole thing is wrong. Therefore, you will only grasp this whole matter for the first time when you carefully and exhaustively experience [the truth]. Do not vainly think that such a place is reached by making your object emptiness or the absolute. Even if you clarify the fact that it is as still and pure as level water or as unadulterated with stain as the sky, will you be able to clarify this situation?

Priest Dongshan studied with Guishan and Yunyan.[57] Although he was one with the myriad things and [understood that] the whole of existence preaches the Dharma, still, he thought that this was not enough. For this reason, Yunyan continued to encourage him, saying, "You must be careful in experiencing this matter." However, some doubt remained. Leaving Yunyan for a while and going away, he was crossing a stream, and when he saw his reflection [in the water] he suddenly grasped the matter. He said, in a verse:

> *Avoid seeking Him in someone else*
> *Or you will be far apart from the Self.*
> *Solitary now am I, and independent,*
> *But I meet Him everywhere.*
> *He now is surely me,*
> *But I am not Him.*
> *Understanding it in this way,*
> *You will directly be one with thusness.*

Understanding in this way, [Dongshan] became the root of the Caodong tradition as an heir to Yunyan.[58] Moreover, he not only understood that the whole of existence preaches the Dharma but also that temple pillars, votive lanterns, every particle, is thus, every second is thus, and everything is thus. Even though he understood that everything in the three times preaches, there was something he still had not reached, and so he was encouraged [by Yunyan].

How much more do people today understand "the Mind is Buddha"' or "the body is Buddha" in dependence on opinions. They do not understand what sort of thing the Buddha Way is. They see that it is nothing but the opening of blossoms in spring or the falling of leaves in autumn, or they think that everything abides in its dharma state.[59] They are laughable. If this were the, why did Shakyamuni appear in the world, or why did Bodhidharma come from the West [to China]? However, from the Venerable Shakyamuni, the highest, to the patriarchal teachers in China, there has been no distinction [in terms of enlightenment]. Who [of them] was not greatly awakened? If every one of them understood the truth on the basis of words and, thus, considered truth to be discussion, how many Buddha patriarchs would there be? Therefore, if you abandon that [approach] and thoroughly experience this place [i.e., the True Self], you will be able to become Buddha patriarchs.

If you are not, above all, greatly awakened to the ultimate degree in the Way of the patriarchal teachers, you are not that person [to succeed as a patriarchal teacher]. Therefore, do not dwell either in total purity or in the clarity of emptiness. Priest Chuanzi said,[60]

> There must be a place without traces for concealing your body,
> But do not conceal your body in this place without traces.
> I was at Yao Mountain for thirty years and only understood this:
> Total purity is not the place to conceal your body.

Even though you say you have forgotten both subject and object, still, [Chuanzi] says that you must not conceal your body in this place. There is no need to discuss past and present or delusion and enlightenment. When you thoroughly experience [the truth] in this way, there are no walls in the ten directions and no gates in the four quarters. Everywhere it is clear and obvious. Therefore, work carefully and do not be hasty.

Verse

I have some humble words this morning to express this situation. Would you like to hear them?

> The discussions by Subhuti and Vimalakirti did not reach it;
> Maudgalyayana and Shariputra saw it as if blind.
> If you wish to understand the meaning of this intimately,
> When is some seasoning not appropriate?

BUDDHAMITRA

Case

The ninth patriarch was the Venerable Buddhamitra. He heard Buddhanandi say:

> *Your speech is one with your [intrinsic] Mind,*
> *And not even your mother and father can compare [in closeness].*
> *Your actions are one with the Way,*
> *And this is what the Mind of Buddhas is.*
> *If you search externally for a Buddha with form,*
> *He will not resemble you.*
> *If you want to know your intrinsic Mind,*
> *You are neither one with it nor separate.*

[Upon hearing this] the master was greatly awakened.

Circumstances

The master was from the kingdom of Daigya and belonged to the Vaishya class.[61] Buddhanandi was going around teaching and came to a Vaishya house in the city in Daigya. Seeing a white light rising above the house, he said to his followers, "There must be a holy man in this house. No word escapes his mouth, so he must be a vessel of the Mahayana. His feet never tread the ground, because he knows that touching it will only soil them. So, he will be my successor." When he had finished speaking, an elder [of the house] appeared, saluted him, and said, "What do you want?" The Venerable

[Buddhanandi] replied, "I am seeking an attendant." The elder said, "I have only one son. He is now fifty years old and he has never spoken or walked." The Venerable [Buddhanandi] said, "If it is as you say, truly, he will be my disciple." When the Venerable [Buddhamitra] saw him and heard these words, he suddenly got to his feet, bowed, and said in a verse:

> *Father and mother are not close to me;*
> *With whom am I most intimate?*
> *The Buddhas are not my Way;*
> *With what Way am I most intimate?*

The Venerable [Buddhanandi] then replied in the verse [in the above[62] case]. When the master heard this wonderful verse, he took seven steps. The Venerable [Buddhanandi] said, "This person met a Buddha in ancient times and made vast, great vows of compassion. He has never spoken or walked because he was thinking of the difficulty of turning his back on the love of father and mother."

Teisho

Truly, father and mother are not close to me, and the Buddhas are not my Way. So if you want to know what intimacy really is, you cannot compare it with father and mother. If you want to know what the Way really is, you cannot learn it from Buddhas. If you want to know why, your seeing and hearing do not require someone else's eyes and ears, nor do your hands and feet need someone else to move them. Sentient beings are sentient beings; Buddhas are Buddhas. That one studying this one, or this one studying that one, is not intimacy. How could that be the Way? Because [Buddhamitra] was guarding and maintaining this principle, for fifty years nothing escaped his mouth and he did not take a step. He was truly a vessel of the Mahayana and simply did not dwell within the defilement of contact.

[Buddhamitra] said, "Father and mother are not close to me." These are "your words." It is at once "one with your [intrinsic] Mind." He said, "The Buddhas are not my Way," and never took a step [on this Way]. Thus, seeking a Buddha with form outside yourself is wrong. Bodhidharma's followers proceed [in the Way] by not depending on words and letters, directly pointing [to the Mind] intimately transmitting this, seeing their [essential] nature, and achieving Buddhahood.[63] Therefore, there is nothing to do but show people this direct pointing and transmit it intimately. They proceed by just getting people to cut off discriminating thought processes through zazen and letting mold grow around their mouths. This does not mean avoiding speech and esteeming silence. It is getting you to realize that your Mind is what it is.

[Mind] is like still water and like space, pure and still, interpenetrating [with all things], and free. Therefore, there is not a single thing revealed outside one's own Mind, not a particle to obstruct your spirit. [The Mind's] brilliant clarity outshines jewels, so do not compare it to even the brilliance of the sun and moon, nor compare the brilliance of a blazing jewel to the brilliance of your own eyes. Aren't you aware of the saying, "People's own brightness is like that of a thousand suns"? He who is in darkness [in a room] looks outside [where it is bright], but he who is in bright light does not even look outside. Think quietly about this: inside is not close, and outside is not separate.

Though it has been thus in the past and present, you must not become arrogant or willful. The patriarchal teachers just met each other in this way, and there was nothing unusual about it. The preceding situation makes this quite clear. This does not mean that Mind is reached by means of practice and realization, or that it is mastered by means of practical study. It just means that your [original] Mind is close to you. You are the Way right now, and you do not look externally for a Buddha with form or a Buddha without form. With whom are you in union? From whom are you separated? In the final analysis, it is neither union nor separation. Though you say that [essential nature] is the body, they are not separate. Though you say that it is Mind, they are not united. Even though you arrive at such a realm, do not seek for Mind outside the body. Even though we are born and die, come and go, this is not the doing of the mind and body [as ordinarily understood].

All buddhas take responsibility [for the truth] in this way and always bear witness to it in the three times. All the patriarchs take responsibility in this way and appear in the three lands [of India, China, and Japan]. You also take responsibility for it, but do not act from external truth. There is not, in the end, any confusion throughout the day and night, and the twelve conditions [of suffering] are ultimately the turning of the wheel of the Dharma.[64] When you reach this realm, transmigration in the five paths [of rebirth] is nothing but the revolving axle of the Mahayana. Karmic recompense in the four forms of birth[65] is truly the activity of the Self. Whether you speak of sentient or insentient [beings], these are just different expressions for the same reality, just as both *me* and *manako* mean "eye" [in Japanese]. Even though you speak of [Buddhas and] ordinary beings, it is like *kokoro* and *i* [both of which mean "mind" in Japanese]. Do not think that *kokoro*, is superior and *i* is inferior. How can you devalue *me* and value *manako*? This place is not the realm of senses and their objects, nor the realm of mind and its objects. Therefore, everyone is without exception the Way, and there is nothing that is not Mind.

Verse

This morning, again, I have a few humble words concerning this situation. Would you like to hear them?

> *Do not say that speech and silence are involved*
> *with separation and concealment;*[66]
> *How can senses and their objects defile one's own nature?*

PARSHVA

Case

The tenth patriarch was the Venerable Parshva.[67] He attended the Venerable Buddhamitra for three years without ever sleeping [lying down]. One day, the Venerable [Buddhamitra] was reciting a sutra and he expounded on the birthless [nature of all things]. Hearing this, the master was awakened.

Circumstances

The master was from central India and his original name was Durjata [Difficult Birth]. Just before he was born, his father dreamed of a white elephant with a jeweled seat on its back. On the seat was a bright pearl, the light of which illuminated the four communities [of monks, nuns, laymen, and laywomen]. When he awakened from the dream, [Parshva] was born.

The Venerable Buddhamitra was teaching in central India where there was an elder named Kogai.[68] He arrived carrying his son. He bowed to the Venerable [Buddhamitra] and said, "My child was in the womb for sixty years and for that reason was named 'Difficult Birth.' I met a wizard who told me that this old person is no ordinary man and he will become a vessel of the Dharma. Now that we have met the Venerable [Buddhamitra], please make him a monk." The Venerable [Buddhamitra] had his head shaved and gave him the precepts. [Parshva] first aroused the thought [of enlightenment] after being in the womb for sixty years and then aging another eighty years, a total of one hundred forty years. He had grown old after already being old, so that when he aroused the thought [of enlightenment], everyone admonished him, saying, "You are already so old, why do you want to waste your

time being a monk? There are two kinds of monk: Those who practice meditation and those who chant sutras. You are not up to either."

When Parshva heard these worldlings criticizing him, he made a pledge:
"I am a monk, and until I gain complete knowledge of the three stores [of
Buddhist sacred texts][69] and acquire the three kinds of spiritual knowledge,[70]
my ribs will not touch the mat [in sleeping]." Vowing in this way, he studied and chanted the sutras by day, and meditated and contemplated by night,
and all the while he never slept. When he first became a monk, an auspicious light illuminated his seat [where he meditated] and he had the impression of twenty-one grains of relics in front of him.[71] From then on he
progressed diligently and practiced for three years, never paying any attention to weariness. Finally, he mastered the three stores [of sacred texts] and
developed the three kinds of spiritual knowledge. One day, the Venerable
[Buddhamitra] was chanting a sutra, and when [Parshva] heard him expound
the birthless [and deathless], he was awakened. In the end, he attained the
rank of tenth patriarch.

Teisho

You should understand that in his practice to become a Buddha patriarch, he
diligently progressed and forgot fatigue, studied and chanted sutras, and
peacefully meditated and contemplated in this way. Subsequently, the master always recited sutras and expounded the supreme [Way]. The "sutra"
mentioned here means genuine Mahayana sutras. Even if it was the
Buddha's preaching, if it was not a Mahayana sutra, he would not chant it,
and he would not rely on a sutra that was not the complete truth. These
Mahayana sutras do not speak of sweeping away the dust [of defilement] or
of getting rid of erroneous thoughts. Sutras of complete truth do not necessarily just completely discuss the absolute and the subtle but also exhaustively discuss concrete matters. "Exhaustively discuss concrete matters"[72]
means that they discuss everything from the Buddhas' first arousing the
thought of enlightenment up to their arriving at awakening and nirvana,
their preaching of the three vehicles and five vehicles,[73] the eons [of establishing purified lands], the lands, the names [of Buddhas], the names [of the
lands] and other details. This is what "complete truth" means. Thus, you
should understand that this is what Buddha sutras are like.

Even though you can express a phrase or grasp some principle, if you do not complete a lifetime of study, then it would be hard to call you a Buddha patriarch. Thus, you [like Parshva] must proceed diligently and forget fatigue, surpass others in your aspiration for enlightenment and in your practice, investigate and clarify carefully, examine in detail, continue night and day, establish your resolve, and awaken your powers. The Buddha patriarchs' reason for appearing in the world and the preeminence of your own responsibility will be thoroughly clarified. By not failing to get to the very bottom of both the absolute and concrete matters, you will become Buddha patriarchs. The Way of the patriarchal teachers has fallen into disuse in recent times, and there is no genuineness of practice, so it is believed that it is sufficient to grasp a phrase or a principle. These people are probably the same type as those arrogant ones [in the Lotus Sutra who left the assembly during the Buddha's preaching].[74] Be careful!

Don't you know the expression, "The Way is like mountains because they get higher as you climb, and merit is like the ocean because it gets deeper as you go farther into it"? Entering the depths, you penetrate to the bottom; climbing the heights, you reach the summit. Then, for the first time, you will be a disciple of the Buddha. Do not vainly throw away body and mind. Everyone without exception is a vessel of the Dharma. Every day is a good day.

Accordingly as you practice carefully or not, you will be either one who has gone to the very end or one who has not. It is not necessarily a matter of who the person is, or a matter of time, as the present situation [concerning Parshva] shows. He was old, more than one hundred forty years old, but because his resolve was beyond comparison, because he went ahead vigorously and forgot fatigue, ultimately he concluded the practice and study of a lifetime. Even with his pitiful old body, they say that he attended [Buddhamitra] in all things for three years without ever sleeping [lying down]. People these days become negligent, especially when they get old. Remember those early worthies in the ancient past [such as Parshva], and do not think of the discomfort of cold as the discomfort of cold, or of the burning of heat as the burning of heat, or that you might die, or that you may not be up to it mentally. If you can do this, then you will be one who searches out the ancient Way and who acquires the Way. If you search out the ancient Way and become one with it, who will not become a Buddha patriarch?

It is said that [Parshva] recited sutras. "Recited sutras" does not necessarily consist of oral recitation, or holding a sutra in the hands and turning [pages silently and rapidly].[75] It means dwelling carefully within the house of the Buddha patriarchs and not vainly doing your work within form and sound or within the womb of ignorance. Reading sutras must mean arousing prajna-insight everywhere and illuminating the mind-ground at all times. When you come to practice like this day and night, as if you were not dependent on anything, then this will be the experience of your birthless [and deathless] intrinsic nature.

Don't you realize that although we are born, there is no place to come from, and though we die and depart, there is no place to go to? We are born according to conditions, we die according to conditions. This rising and ceasing never stops for even a moment. Therefore, birth is not [simply] birth, death is not [simply] death. However, in your practice and study, do not dwell on birth and death [as ordinarily conceived], or block yourselves through ordinary understanding. Ordinary understanding though it becomes, sounds and forms though it becomes, it is your own treasury of brilliant light. When you emit this light from your eyes, you adorn [the world] with color and forms, and when you emit this light from your ears, you hear the sounds [of things] that are Buddha. Emitting light from our hands, we change ourselves and others; emitting light from our feet, we advance and withdraw.

Verse

Today, I have some humble words that concern this principle. Would you like to hear them?

> Turning, turning —so many sutra scrolls!
> Born here, dying there—nothing but chapters and phrases.[76]

PUNYAYASHAS

Case

The eleventh patriarch was Punyayashas. He stood with folded hands before the Venerable Parshva, and the Venerable [Parshva] asked him, "Where did you come from?" The master replied, "My mind does not go [or come]." The Venerable [Parshva] asked, "Where do you dwell?" The master replied, "My mind does not stop [or move]." The Venerable [Parshva] asked him, "Aren't you undecided?" The master replied, "All Buddhas are also like this." The Venerable [Parshva] said, "You are not 'all Buddhas' and 'all Buddhas' is also wrong." Hearing this, the master practiced unremittingly for twenty-one days and acquired patience with regard to the non-origination of things.[77] [Then,] he said to the Venerable [Parshva], "'All Buddhas' is wrong, and they are not the Venerable [Parshva]." Parshva acknowledged him and transmitted the True Dharma to him.

Circumstances

The master was from the kingdom of Kashi (Magadha). His family name was Gotama and his father was Ratnakaya. When the Venerable Parshva first arrived in Kashi, he paused beneath a tree, pointed to the ground with his right hand, and said to the monks, "When this ground turns a golden color, a wise man will appear and join our congregation." As soon as he finished, the ground turned a golden color. At the same time, someone named Punyayashas, the son of a rich man, appeared before Parshva and stood with folded hands [as in the main case]. The Venerable Parshva said in verse:

This ground has turned a golden color,
Showing the appearance of a wise man.
He will sit at the tree of awakening
Where enlightenment will flower and reach completion.

Punyayashas replied in verse:

The master sits on the golden earth
Always preaching the genuine truth.
The light [of his wisdom] turns around and illumines me
And makes me enter samadhi.

The Venerable [Parshva] understood his thoughts, made him a monk, and gave him the complete precepts.

Teisho

In this story, Punyayashas was originally a wise man. For that reason he said, "My mind does not go, my mind does not stop, and all Buddhas are likewise so." However, this is a dualistic view and the reason is that he understood "my mind is thus," and "all Buddhas are thus." Therefore, the Venerable Parshva "drove off the plowman's ox and snatched away the hungry man's food." Even those who try to attain the Way are unable to help themselves, so how much less can one depend on [some external reality called] "all Buddhas"? Therefore, Parshva said, "You are not all Buddhas."

This cannot be understood through reason, nor can it be discerned through [such concepts as] "the formless." It cannot be understood through the wisdom of all Buddhas, nor can it be figured out through your own intelligence. After hearing these words [uttered by Parshva], he practiced for twenty-one days without letup. Finally, one day he was enlightened and forgot "my mind," and was liberated from "all Buddhas." This is called "being enlightened in patience with regard to the non-origination of all things." In the end, he grasped this principle and experienced boundlessness and the absence of subject and object. He expressed what he had experienced with the words, "'All Buddhas' is wrong and they are not the Venerable [Parshva]."[78]

The Patriarchal Way cannot be grasped by means of reason nor can it be discerned with the mind. Therefore, you cannot consider "Dharma body," "Dharma nature," or "the myriad things are One Mind" to be ultimate. You cannot speak of it as non-change, or as purity. How much less can you understand it as empty cessation or supreme principle! When the wise of all traditions arrived fully at this place, they reversed their original thinking, opened and clarified the realm of Mind, directly passed onto the entry road, and promptly blocked their own views. This is clear from the present story. Because Punyayashas was already a wise man, the earth turned a golden color when he arrived. His virtue was like wind that has the power to create a stir among things. However, he still practiced for twenty-one days before he reached this place. Good people, clarify and discern carefully and do not settle the essential point by using small virtue, small wisdom, your own views, or old attitudes. Be extremely careful and you will acquire it for the first time.

Verse

This morning, I gratefully use a few humble words to help you understand this matter. Would you like to hear them?

> *My mind is not the Buddhas, nor is it you.*
> *Coming and going abide herein as always.*

ASHVAGHOSA

Case

The twelfth patriarch was the Venerable Ashvaghosa.[79] He asked the Venerable Punyayashas, "I wish to know the Buddha; what is Buddha?" The Venerable [Punyayashas] replied, "You wish to know the Buddha, but he who does not know is the Buddha." The master said, "Since Buddha is not knowing, how can I know that it is Buddha?" The Venerable [Punyayashas] said, "Since you do not know Buddha, how can you know that it is not Buddha?" The master said, "It is like a saw." The Venerable [Punyayashas] replied, "It is like wood. Now I ask, what does 'saw' mean?" The master said, "The Venerable [Punyayashas] and I are lined up evenly [like the teeth in the saw]. What does 'wood' mean?" The Venerable [Punyayashas] replied, "You are cut through by me." The master was suddenly awakened.

Circumstances

The master was from Benares, and he also had the name of "Superior in Virtue."[80] He was so named because he was superior in all virtues, both mundane and supra-mundane. He visited the Venerable Punyayashas and the first thing he asked was, "I wish to know the Buddha; what is Buddha?" The Venerable [Punyayashas] replied, "You wish to know the Buddha, but he who does not know is Buddha."

Teisho

The very first thing one must seek in one's study is Buddha. All Buddhas of the past, present, and future, as well as generations of patriarchal teachers, are referred to as people who study Buddha. If you do not study what Buddha is, you are called "non-Buddhists." Therefore, there was no need to seek in sounds or try to understand through forms, and it was not enough to think of Buddha in terms of the thirty-two marks and the eighty minor marks.[81] Consequently, [Ashvaghosa] asked, "I wish to know the Buddha; what is Buddha?"

In saying, "You wish to know the Buddha, but he who does not know is the Buddha," "he who does not know" points to the Venerable Ashvaghosa himself, and not to anyone else. Whether it is known or not, it has no particular way to be or other appearance. Therefore, from the past to the present, it is just this. Sometimes [the Buddha] bears the thirty-two marks and possesses the eighty minor marks, or he bears three heads and eight arms,[82] or is subject to the five signs of decay and the eight forms of suffering.[83] Sometimes he is covered with horns and hair, or wears iron shackles and chains.[84] But he is always in the world, taking responsibility for the way he appears, coming and going within his own mind, putting on different faces.

When [Buddha] is born, we don't know who that is. When [Buddha] dies, we don't know who that is. Even though we try to give him a form, he is not something that can be constructed. Although we try to pin a name on him, he is not something that can be captured in a name. Therefore, from eon to eon, he is not known, and though he follows me and keeps me company, he is totally unknown.

Hearing this story, many interpret it as meaning that when there is any kind of knowing, this is different from Buddha, and that not knowing and not discriminating must be Buddha. If you understand "not knowing" in this way, why did Punyayashas take such pains to explain the way he did? [Believing in this way] is like entering darkness from [another] darkness. But this is not the way it really is, so Punyayashas directly pointed out that "He who does not know is Buddha." Ashvaghosa was still not clear about it and understood what had been said as meaning ordinary "not knowing." Therefore, he said, "Since Buddha is not knowing, how can I know that it is Buddha?" The Venerable [Punyayashas] replied, "Since you do not know Buddha, how do you know that it is not Buddha?" He did not seek for Buddha externally. "He who does not know is Buddha"—how can you say that this is not correct? The master [Ashvaghosa] said, "It is like a saw," and the Venerable [Punyayashas] replied, "It is like wood." Punyayashas then asked, "What does 'saw' mean?" The master replied, "We are lined up evenly [like saw teeth]. What does 'wood' mean?" The Venerable [Punyayashas] answered, "You are cut through by me," and the master was suddenly awakened.

Truly, you are thus and I am thus [in being Buddha]. There is no difference between us, and our hands are filled with it. Neither you nor I receive a speck; neither do you and I borrow the least morsel. We are like a saw, because we are lined up evenly like the teeth of a saw. The master [Ashvaghosa] explained it by saying, "It is like a saw," and the Venerable [Punyayashas] said, "It is like wood." The reason this is so is that in boundless darkness, nothing is to be known. Not a speck is added, not one fragment of knowledge is borrowed. One is like a log or a pillar in being without mind. So in the end there is nothing to discriminate. Because this was the way he understood it, [Punyayashas] therefore said, "It is like wood."

However, [Ashvaghosa] still had some moral and cognitive faults remaining and thus did not understand what [Punyayashas] meant. Because the Venerable [Punyayashas] was compassionate, he asked, "What does 'saw' mean?" The master [Ashvaghosa] replied, "We are lined up evenly [like saw teeth]." Then he spoke again on his own and asked, "What does 'wood' mean?" Punyayashas gave him a hand by saying, "You are cut through by me." In this, the paths of teacher and disciple merged, emotions and thoughts that had existed from ancient times were demolished, a road was paved within a dream, and they walked along it within emptiness. Punyayashas said, "You are cut through by me," and [Ashvaghosa] was thereupon freed from the stiff bonds of no-mind. He emerged from the cavern of brilliant clarity, and was suddenly awakened. Finally, he attained the rank of twelfth patriarch.

The Venerable [Punyayashas] told the monks assembled there, "This great man was the king of Vaishali in ancient times. In that kingdom there was a kind of people who went about naked, like horses. The king exerted his supernatural power, divided his body, and turned the parts into silkworms so the people could have clothes. The king was later reborn in central India, and the horse people missed him and cried. For that reason, the master was named 'Horse Voice' [i.e., Ashvaghosa]. The Tathagata made a prediction, saying, 'Six hundred years after my death, there will be someone named Ashvaghosa who will triumph over non-Buddhists. He will liberate humans and celestials far and wide, and they will be beyond number. He will succeed me and carry on the teaching."' Saying, "Now is the time," Punyayashas conferred [upon Ashvaghosa] the Treasury of the Eye of the True Dharma.

Do not be deluded and think that this whole story means that we do not know anything or sense anything anytime or anywhere. We say, "not knowing," but if we inspect carefully and calculate carefully [in a state of no-mind] as if we had not yet been conceived, even if we grope about for a Buddha's face or a patriarch's face, we don't succeed. Even if we search for the faces of humans, demons, or animals, we can't find them. It is neither non-change nor change, nor emptiness, nor a matter of inside or outside, nor absolute or relative. If you truly understand that it is your original face, then even if it is manifested as an ordinary person or a wise person, or divides into the two forms of karmic results [consisting of the environment and the body-mind], these things come and go within it, appear and disappear within it. It is like waves on the ocean; they appear and appear, but there is not a drop of increase in the water. And it is like the subsiding of the waves; they subside and subside, but not a drop is lost.

Among humans and celestials, it is provisionally called "Buddhas," or it is called "demons," or "animals." It is as if many faces were temporarily displayed on one face. But if you think that it is a Buddha's face, this is wrong. If you think that it is a demon's face, this is also wrong. In the light of setting up a method of instruction, there is knocking [or questioning by the disciple] and answering [by the master]. One cultivates the samadhi which is like a fantasy and performs the actions of a Buddha in a dream. For this reason, Indian methods of conversion and arts of illusion continue down through the present, flowing through India, China, and Japan, turning ordinary people into sages. If you can change yourselves and cultivate [the Way] in such a manner, then you will be neither careless about your faults nor be deluded about your own life and death. You will be true patch-robed monks.

Verse

Today, I have a few humble words concerning the story I have presented. Would you like to hear them?

> *The red of the rustic village is unknown to the peach blossoms;*
> *Yet, they instruct Lingyun to arrive at doubtlessness.*[85]

KAPIMALA

Case

The thirteenth patriarch was the Venerable Kapimala. One time the Venerable Ashvaghosa spoke of the ocean of Buddha nature, saying, "Mountains, rivers, and the great earth appear in dependence [on Buddha nature]. The three kinds of spiritual knowledge and the six paranormal powers[86] appear as a result of it." The master, hearing this, was awakened.[87]

Circumstances

The master was from the kingdom of Kashi. In the beginning when he was a follower of non-Buddhist teachings, he had three thousand followers and he studied all the different theories. The Venerable Ashvaghosa was preaching the wonderful Dharma in Magadha when all of a sudden an old man collapsed to the ground in front of [Ashvaghosa's] seat. The Venerable [Ashvaghosa] told the assembly, "This is no ordinary man. There must be something different about him." No sooner had he spoken than the old man disappeared and a man of golden color popped out of the earth. Then he changed into a female. Pointing to Ashvaghosa with her right hand, she recited this verse:

> I bow deeply to the venerable elder.
> In accordance with the Tathagata's prediction,
> You must expound the highest truth
> Right here, now, in this place.

As soon as she finished speaking, she disappeared. The Venerable [Ashvaghosa] said, "A demon will appear and test his powers against mine." After a while, the wind rose, rain poured, and heaven and earth were darkened. Ashvaghosa said, "This proves that a demon is coming. I will get rid of it." Then, he pointed to the sky and a huge golden dragon appeared, displaying great powers and making the mountains tremble. But the Venerable Ashvaghosa sat solemnly [in meditation], and the demon's acts consequently ceased.

Seven days later, a small insect appeared, no larger than a speck, and it concealed itself beneath Ashvaghosa's seat. The Venerable [Ashvaghosa] grasped it in his hand and said to the assembly, "This is the transformation of the demon. He just wants to eavesdrop on my teaching." He released the insect, but it was unable to move. The Venerable [Ashvaghosa] spoke to it, saying, "If you will just take refuge in the Three Treasures, you will regain your powers." The demon at once resumed his former shape, bowed, and repented. The Venerable [Ashvaghosa] asked him, "What is your name? How many followers do you have?" The demon replied, "I am Kapimala, and I have three thousand followers." [Ashvaghosa asked,] "What can you do when you use all your powers?" The demon replied, "I consider changing the great ocean to be very easy." The Venerable [Ashvaghosa] asked him, "Can you transform the ocean of [Buddha] nature?" The demon asked, "What do you mean by 'ocean of [Buddha] nature'? I still do not completely understand." The Venerable [Ashvaghosa] then told him about the ocean of [Buddha] nature, saying, "Mountains, rivers, and the great earth all appear in dependence on it. The three kinds of spiritual knowledge and the six supernatural powers appear as a result of it." The master, hearing this, aroused faith and was awakened.

Teisho

From the time the old man fell to the ground up to the moment when he became a tiny insect, [the demon] manifested spiritual powers countless times. He said that transforming the great ocean was very easy. Even though he could change the ocean into mountains or change mountains into an ocean, thus manifesting spiritual powers without end, he still did not even know the name of "ocean of nature." How much less could he transform it! Nevertheless, since he did not know what mountains, rivers, and the great earth were transformations of, Ashvaghosa said that these are the transformation of the ocean of [Buddha] nature. Not only that, but the three kinds of spiritual knowledge and the six supernatural powers appear because of it.

As for samadhi, there are innumerable samadhis, such as the *shuramgama*,[88] and there are the six supernatural powers, such as the celestial eye and the celestial ear.[89] These are beginningless and endless and beyond number.[90] When mountains, rivers, and the great earth appear, samadhi becomes earth, water, fire, and wind, and transforms into mountains, rivers, grass, and trees. It also changes into skin, flesh, bones, and marrow, and it changes into head and four limbs. Not one event, not one thing comes from elsewhere. Therefore, throughout the twenty-four hours, no effort is vainly cast aside, and no features that appear during innumerable births and deaths are manifested in vain. Seeing with our eyes and hearing with our ears is limitless, and perhaps not even the wisdom of a Buddha can fathom it. Are these not the transformation of the ocean of [Buddha] nature?

Everything, even the smallest atoms, are all boundless things, not at all subject to number or limit. They are like this because they are the ocean of nature. Moreover, to see this present body is to see the [original] Mind; to know the Mind is to witness the body, because body and Mind are not at all two things. How can nature and characteristics be divided?[91] Even though [the demon] revealed supernatural powers while a member of a nonbuddhist tradition, and that was not apart [from Mind, or the ocean of nature], he did not realize that it was something called "ocean of nature." Therefore, he doubted both himself and others. Moreover, since he did not understand these realities, he was not one who had reached the fundamental. When he matched powers [with Ashvaghosa], he was not equal to it. He just exhausted his demonic powers and found it difficult to make transformations. In the end, he turned away from himself and took refuge in another, putting an end to contention and displaying the correct [faith].

Even if you understand [the true nature of] mountains, rivers, and the great earth, do not get uselessly entangled with sounds and forms. Even if you clarify your original nature, do not settle down in ordinary knowledge. Yet, even ordinary knowledge is nothing other than one or two Buddha faces or patriarch faces, as are hedges, walls, tiles, and pebbles. Our original nature is different from the ordinary knowledge of seeing and hearing, and it is not dependent on movement or stillness. However, once the ocean of nature is established, movement and stillness, and coming and going are necessarily connected with it, and skin, flesh, bones, and marrow are manifested when it is time. Speaking from the standpoint of the basis, its appearance as seeing and hearing, sights and sounds, can be nothing else. When emptiness is struck, it makes an echo, and thus all sounds are manifested. When emptiness is transformed, all things are manifested and, therefore, forms are distinguished. Do not think that emptiness is not forms, or think that emptiness is not sounds. When you investigate carefully and reach this realm, you will not think that it is emptiness or that it is being. You will not think that it is something that is concealed or revealed, or that it is oneself or another. What do you mean by "self" and "other"? It is like the absence of anything in emptiness, or like large and small waves appearing in the great ocean. This has never changed in the past or present. Can going and coming be anything other than what they [truly] are?

Therefore, when [Buddha nature] is manifested, not a speck is added, and when it is concealed, not a hair is lost. When the various things are put together, it becomes this body; when the myriad things are obliterated, we refer to it as "One Mind." Clarifying the Way and arousing this Mind should not be sought outside of it. But when the scenery of one's own original realm is manifested, it is called "human," "demon," or "animal." [Zen master] Xue-feng[92] said, "If you want to understand this matter, it is as if there were an ancient mirror inside me. When a Mongol appears [before it], a Mongol is reflected, and when a Chinese appears, a Chinese is reflected." [All manifestations] are wholly the fantasy-like samadhi,[93] and have no beginning or end. Therefore, when the mountains, rivers, and the great earth appear, they all [appear] dependent on it; when the three kinds of spiritual knowledge and six supernatural powers appear, they depend on it. You should not see even an inch of the great earth as something outside your own Mind. Do not put even a drop of water outside of the ocean of [Buddha] nature.

Verse

This morning I would like to say a few humble words about this situation. Would you like to hear them? [After a while, he said:]

> Even though the huge waves flood the heavens,
> How can the pure ocean water ever change?

NAGARJUNA

Case

The fourteenth patriarch was the Venerable Nagarjuna. Once the thirteenth patriarch paid a visit at the request of a Naga king and received a wish-fulfilling jewel.[94] The master [Nagarjuna] asked, "This jewel is the best in the world. Does it have a form or is it formless?" Kapimala replied, "You just understand having form and not having form, but you do not understand that this jewel neither has form nor is formless, nor do you understand that this jewel is not a jewel." Hearing this, the master was deeply enlightened.

Circumstances

The master was from western India and was also named Naga Greatness and Naga Excellence.[95] At this time, the thirteenth patriarch, having become a monk and having been transmitted the True Dharma, traveled to western India. There was a prince named Megheshvara. He respected Kapimala and invited him to his palace, where he made offerings to him. Kapimala said, "The Tathagata taught that a [Buddhist] mendicant cannot approach the dwellings of a ruler, his ministers, or other powerful people." The prince said, "There is a big mountain north of this city and on the mountain there is a cave. Would the master like to practice meditation there?" Kapimala said that he would like it. After a few miles he reached the mountain and there he encountered a huge snake. The Venerable [Kapimala] continued ahead without paying any attention, and the snake approached and wrapped itself around him. Thereupon, the Venerable [Kapimala] conferred the Triple Refuge on the snake, and when the snake heard this, he left.

As the Venerable [Kapimala] was about to enter the cave, an old man wearing plain white clothes appeared from the cave and greeted him with folded hands. The Venerable [Kapimala] asked him, "Where do you live?" The old man answered, "Long ago, I was a monk who enjoyed solitude very much and lived obscurely in mountain forests. Occasionally, a novice monk would come asking for instruction, but I felt that it was a nuisance to answer and got angry. When I died, I was reborn as a huge snake. I have lived in this cave for a thousand years since. Now I have met the Venerable [Kapimala] and have been able to take the Triple Refuge, so I have come to thank you."

Hearing this, the Venerable [Kapimala] asked, "Do any other people live in these mountains?" The man replied, "Several miles north from here there is a big tree that shelters five hundred great Nagas. The name of their leader is Nagarjuna. He is always preaching the Dharma to the Nagas and I listen." The Venerable [Kapimala] finally visited him with his followers. Nagarjuna appeared and greeted Kapimala, saying, "The deep mountains are lonely and still, a place where great serpents dwell. Why does the great sage, the most venerable one, turn his venerable feet [in this direction]?" Kapimala replied, "I am not the most venerable. I have come here to visit a virtuous man." Nagarjuna thought to himself, "Has this teacher attained certainty and clarified his Dharma eye? Is he a great sage who perpetuates the Mahayana?" The Venerable [Kapimala] said, "Even though you are just thinking this, I already know what you mean. Just be discriminating about making your home departure. Why worry about whether I am or am not wise!" Hearing this, Nagarjuna apologized and made his home departure. The Venerable [Kapimala] liberated him from his layman's body and made him into a monk. The five hundred Nagas also received the full precepts as a group.

Subsequently, [Nagarjuna] followed [Kapimala] for four years and [as in the main case] a Naga king gave Kapimala a wish-fulfilling jewel for visiting him. The master [Nagarjuna] said, "This, is the best jewel in the world" and so on, becoming deeply awakened. Later, he ranked as the fourteenth patriarch.

Teisho

Nagarjuna studied non-Buddhist methods and possessed supernatural powers. He often visited the palaces of the Nagas and saw the scriptures of the seven past Buddhas. Just by seeing the titles, he knew what the scriptures were all about. He also taught five hundred Nagas. The Naga kings, Nanda and Upananda and others, were [really] enlightened bodhisattvas. They had received a request from former Buddhas and enshrined various scriptures [in their palaces]. Even though the present Great Master Shakyamuni's scriptural teachings have not exhausted their transforming work among humans and celestial beings, they must be stored in the palaces of the Nagas. Even though [Nagarjuna] had such great and awesome powers and often visited the great Naga kings and carried on conversations with them, he was not a true man of the Way; he just studied non-Buddhist ways. Once this man was given the precepts by the thirteenth patriarch, he became someone with a great, clarified vision.

However, people think, "Nagarjuna was not only the fourteenth patriarch of the [Zen] patriarchal lineage but he was also the patriarchal teacher of various other traditions. Shingon and Tendai[96] also consider him to have been their original patriarch, as do yin-yang diviners, silk producers, and others." These are all arts he had practiced in the past. When he became the fourteenth patriarch, he abandoned them all, but students of these arts say that Nagarjuna was their original patriarch. These are demons and animals who are confused about truth and falsity and who cannot distinguish between jewels and stones. Only Nagarjuna's Buddhadharma was correctly transmitted to Kanadeva [the fifteenth patriarch]; the rest were traditions he abandoned. You can understand this on the basis of the present story.

Even though Nagarjuna taught the five hundred Nagas, still, when Kapimala arrived, he [Nagarjuna] appeared and greeted him, paid reverence to him, and tried to test him. The Venerable [Kapimala] was secretive for a while and did not disclose the true teaching. Nagarjuna reflected silently, "This is a great sage who has inherited the true vehicle," and he tried mentally to figure [Kapimala] out. The Patriarch said, "Just be discriminating about home departure and don't worry about whether I am wise or not wise." When he said this, Nagarjuna was ashamed and [eventually] came to succeed the thirteenth patriarch. You should clarify this through the present story.

[Nagarjuna] asked, "This is the best jewel in the world. Does it have form or is it formless?" In fact, Nagarjuna understood right from the beginning. Considering it to have form or not have form is just attachment to the extreme views of existence and nonexistence. It was for precisely this reason that the Patriarch [Kapimala] spoke as he did. In fact, even though it is an ordinary jewel, when you speak from the standpoint of truth, it neither has form nor lacks form; it is just a jewel. How much less is the jewel suspended from the wrestler's forehead, the jewel wound in the ruler's turban, the jewel [under the chin of the] dragon king, and the jewel [hidden] in the clothes of the drunken man connected with what people think the jewel is.[97] It is difficult to decide whether they have form or lack form. However, the above-mentioned jewels are ordinary jewels and not at all the supreme jewel of the Way. How can anyone know that this jewel is also not a jewel? This must be clarified carefully.

Xuansha[98] said, "The entirety is a jewel; who should I inform?" He also said, "The whole universe in the ten directions is one bright jewel." Truly, this cannot be discriminated with the views of humans and celestials. However, though it is an ordinary jewel, it does not come from outside but rather appears totally from the human mind. Therefore, Shakra, Lord of the Heavens, uses it as a wish-fulfilling jewel or *mani*-jewel. If you use this jewel when you are ill, the illness is cured. If you wear this jewel when you are worried, the worry will dissipate on its own. Using this jewel, one also manifests supernatural powers and magical transformations. There is a *mani*-jewel among the seven treasures of the Wheel-turning Monarch.[99] All treasures appear from this jewel, and it is said that no matter how much it is used, it is inexhaustible. In this way, there is superior and inferior and distinctions in [karmic] results for humans and celestial beings.

The wish-fulfilling jewel among humans is also called a grain of rice, and this is thought to be a precious jewel. When compared with a heavenly jewel, it is thought to be something created, but we still call it a jewel. Also, when the Buddhadharma is extinguished, the Buddha's relics[100] will become *mani*-jewels, rain down on everything, and turn into rice and benefit living beings. Even though it is revealed as a Buddha's body, as a grain of rice, as the myriad things, or as one brightness, when one's own [original] Mind is revealed, it becomes this fathom-long body, a figure with three heads, [animal] forms with horns and hair, and an infinite variety of other forms. Nevertheless, you must discern this Mind-jewel.

Do not seek solitude and hide yourselves in mountain forests like monks long ago. People who were not fully enlightened made this mistake in earlier times. People who are not fully enlightened still make this mistake. People think that being around others and being involved in various activities prevents them from becoming tranquil, so they want to live alone in mountain forests and do zazen, practicing the Way quietly. Saying this, many live in obscurity in mountains and valleys, mistakenly cultivating and polishing themselves, and thus many enter into false paths. The reason for this is that they do not understand what the truth is and vainly put themselves first.

They also say, "Zen Master Damei Fazhang did zazen in a pine forest with a [miniature] iron pagoda on top of his head, and Guishan Dayuan cultivated [the Way in the mountains] in the clouds and mists with tigers and wolves for companions.[101] We, too, should practice in the same way." This is truly laughable. You must realize that these ancients all experienced enlightenment and received authentication from a true teacher. For a while they practiced in this way in order to mature their understanding while awaiting the [right] circumstances for offering their teaching. It was after Damei received the true seal from Master Ma[-zu] and Guishan obtained the transmission from Baizhang [that they practiced in this way]. It was not as the deluded think. Ancients such as Yinshan and Luoshan[102] never lived alone prior to complete enlightenment. They were clear-eyed, true men of great sagacity who had become enlightened; they displayed meritorious conduct and left their fame to posterity. If you live in mountains and valleys while neglecting to practice what should be practiced and not reaching what you should reach, you will be like monkeys. You could not be more lacking in the Mind of the Way.

If their Dharma eyes are not clear and bright, these people who practice alone to regulate [mind and body] become shravakas and pratyekabuddhas and destroy the seed [of Buddhahood].[103] "Destroyed seeds" are scorched seeds. Therefore, people, train carefully in a monastery, practice a long time with a spiritual teacher, completely clarify the great matter [of life and death], and finish clarifying the [true] Self. As for deepening the roots later for a while and solidifying your attainment, even though you become a successor of former generations of patriarchs, in our own [Soto] lineage, our founder Eihei [Dogen] has admonished us against living alone. This was so that people would not stray onto the wrong path. In particular, our previous master in the second generation [Koun Ejo][104] said, "My disciples should not live alone. Even though you have attained enlightenment, you should train in a monastery. How much less should those still engaged in practice live alone. Those who ignore this admonition do not belong to our tradition."

Also, Zen Master Yuanwu[105] said, "After the ancients had acquired the essence, they went to live in huts and caves in the deep mountains and ate food cooked in pots with the legs missing, forgetting the human world for ten or twenty years, forgetting the false world. Nowadays, we cannot hope to do this." Also, Huanglong[106] [Hui]nan said, "After you have become old and bent over, living in the mountains guarding your own practice, how will you compare with others who bring people into the monastery?" None of the masters of recent times has enjoyed solitary living. How much weaker are their faculties than those of the ancients! [For this reason,] you should simply remain in a monastery and make an effort in your own practice. [As in the above story] that person of long ago was careless and enjoyed peace and quiet. When a monk new to practice came and requested to be taught, [the recluse] did not answer what ought to be answered and became resentful. You should understand that if mind and body are still not regulated, you should not dwell alone away from a spiritual teacher. Even if you preach the Dharma just as Nagarjuna did, you will only end up someone who will suffer the results of [bad] karma.

Monks, because [in the past] you abundantly planted good roots, you can surely hear the Tathagata's True Dharma, which is to not approach the rulers of kingdoms or their ministers. [But] you should not enjoy solitary living; rather, continue your effort in the Dharma diligently and concentrate on penetrating to the source of the Dharma. These are the Tathagata's true, secret words.

Verse

Today, I have some humble words to say concerning this story. Do you want to hear them?

> The orphan light, marvelously vast, is never darkened;
> The wish-fulfilling mani [-jewel] shines everywhere.

Kanadeva

Case

The fifteenth patriarch was the Venerable Kanadeva.[107] He had an audience with the Great Being, Nagarjuna, in the hope of becoming a follower. Nagarjuna knew he was a man of great wisdom. First he sent his assistant for a bowl full of water and had it placed before him. The Venerable [Kanadeva] saw it and thrust a needle into the bowl of water and presented it [to Nagarjuna]. They met each other and joyfully realized that they were of like minds.

Circumstances

The master was from southern India and belonged to the Vaishya class. In the beginning, he sought worldly benefits and enjoyed argument. The Venerable Nagarjuna had obtained the Way and was in southern India to teach. Many there believed in worldly benefits. When they heard him preach the Dharma, they said, "Worldly benefits are the best thing for people. He speaks pointlessly about Buddha nature. Who can see it?" Nagarjuna replied, "If you want to see Buddha nature, you must get rid of self-pride." The people asked, "Is Buddha nature large or small?" Nagarjuna answered, "It is neither wide nor narrow, it has no blessings or recompense, and it is not born and does not die.'" When the people heard how superior this principle is, they totally changed their former thinking.

Among the people, there was a man of great wisdom, Kanadeva. He had an audience with the Great Being, Nagarjuna, and so on [as in the above case] and finally they joyfully realized that they were of like minds. [Nagarjuna] shared his seat with Kanadeva, just as the Buddha shared his seat with

Mahakashyapa on Mount Grdhrakuta. Then, Nagarjuna preached the Dharma to the people. Remaining seated, he showed himself in the form of the full moon. The master [Kanadeva] explained to the people, "This is the Venerable [Nagarjuna] showing us the very form of Buddha nature by manifesting it. When you think about it, the shape of the formless samadhi[108] is like a full moon. The meaning of Buddha nature is clarity and empty brightness." When he finished speaking, the disc vanished. Nagarjuna, assuming his original form, made this verse:

> The body manifested in the shape of the full moon
> Represents the body of all the Buddhas.
> When they preach the Dharma, no form is seen,
> Thereby showing that it is not form or sound.

Because this is the way it is, it is difficult to distinguish master and disciple, and their life lines merge.

Teisho

This story is not ordinary. From the first, [Kanadeva] was one with the Way. Nagarjuna does not say a word, nor does Kanadeva hear a word. Therefore, it is hard to say that they are master and disciple. How can guest and host be distinguished? As a result, Kanadeva promoted the tradition and in the end it was known all over India as the Deva Tradition. It is like the saying, "Heaping snow in a silver bowl, concealing a crane in bright moonlight."[109] Because this is the way it was, when they first met, a bowl filled with water was placed before them. How can you say that water has inside or outside? Since the bowl is full, none [of the water] is missing, and the water is deep and clear. It is pure right to the bottom and wondrously bright in its fullness. Therefore, [Kanadeva] thrust a needle into it and they experienced a oneness [of minds]. It must have pierced the bottom and pierced the top. Here, there is neither absolute nor relative. At this point, it is hard to distinguish master and disciple. Even though they are similar, they are not the same, and even though they become mixed, there is no trace [of mixture].

This matter was [first] manifested in the raising of an eyebrow and the blinking eyes [by Shakyamuni], and it was represented in the seeing of forms [of peach blossoms by Lingyun] and the hearing of sounds [of a bamboo being struck by a pebble by Xiangyan].[110] There is nothing you can call sounds and forms, and no seeing or hearing to be abandoned. [One's own mind] is round and bright and without form, like the transparency of pure water. It is like seeking the sharp point when you get to the bottom of the spiritual principle. You display the sharp point everywhere; ever so bright, it pervades the mind. Water, too, flows and pervades everything, boring through mountains and inundating the heavens. A needle, also, penetrates a [thick] bag and pierces a mustard seed. Moreover, water is not overcome by anything, and even less does it leave traces. A needle is also harder than a diamond.

Can such a needle and water be other [than your body and mind]? They are your own bodies and minds. Swallowed completely, it is just a needle [with nothing else left]; when vomited out, it is just pure water. Therefore, the paths of master and disciple merge, and there is no self and other at all. When their lifelines merge, and there is truly transparency, [this realm] cannot be concealed anywhere. It is like gourd vines wrapping around gourds. Climbing here and climbing there, [like the vines] it is just your own mind. Nevertheless, although you can understand the pure water, you must fully experience it and clarify [the existence of] the needle lying at the bottom. If you make a mistake and swallow it, it will end up sticking in your throat.

Though this is so, do not think dualisticly. You must try to think about it carefully by swallowing totally and vomiting totally. Even though you are aware of purity and transparency and pervasiveness, you will surely be vast and firm [like a diamond]. The three calamities of water, fire, and wind will not touch you, and you will remain undisturbed throughout the cosmic eons of formation, continuation, extinction, and nonexistence.[111]

Verse

I have some humble words concerning this story. Would you like to hear them?

A needle fishes up all the ocean water;
Wherever fierce dragons go, it is hard to conceal themselves.

RAHULATA

Case

The sixteenth patriarch was the Venerable Rahulata. He was serving Kanadeva, and when he heard about [karmic] causes in former lives, he experienced awakening.

Circumstances

The master was from Kapilavastu. As for this matter of causes in former lives, the Venerable Kanadeva was traveling around teaching. after experiencing awakening, and arrived in Kapilavastu. There was a householder there named Brahamashuddhaguna. One day, [something resembling] a big ear grew on a tree in the garden. It was like a fungus and its flavor was exceedingly fine. Only the householder and his son Rahulata took any of it and ate it, but whenever they picked some, more grew again, and when it was all gone, it re-grew. No one else in the family could see it. At that time, the Venerable Kanadeva knew about causes in their previous lives. He went to their house, where the householder asked about the reasons [for the fungus]. The Venerable [Kanadeva] told him, "Long ago, a monk was given alms by your family. The monk, however, had not yet completely opened the eye of the Way and consumed the alms of the faithful in vain, so [when he died] he became a tree fungus as recompense. Since only you and your son have made offerings with pure hearts, you have been able to eat [the fungus], while others have not." Then he asked, "How old are you?"' The householder answered, "I am seventy-nine years old." Then the Venerable [Kanadeva] spoke this verse:

Because [the monk] entered the Way but failed to reach the truth,
He changed his body into alms for the faithful.
When you are eighty-one years old,
The tree will no longer bear the ear [fungus].

When the householder heard this, his respect and admiration grew, and he said, "Your disciple is old and weak and I cannot take you for my teacher. But I promise that my second son will become a monk and follow you." The Venerable [Kanadeva] said, "Long ago, the Tathagata predicted that your son [Rahulata] would become a great teaching master during the second five hundred years [of the Dharma].[112] Our present meeting is a result of causes in previous lives." So, [Kanadeva] shaved [Rahulata's] hair, and eventually he became the sixteenth patriarch.

Teisho

Many people in the past and present who studied the Way have referred to this story in admonishing against vainly entering the pure stream [of monkhood] without shame or conscience and vainly accepting the alms of the faithful without understanding or discrimination. They should truly be ashamed. Once you have left home as a monk and entered the Way, your dwelling place is not your own nor is the food you eat at all yours. You do not at all make your own clothing, nor can a drop of water or blade of grass be taken and used as your own. The reason this is so is that you monks were totally conceived by this land [as if by a pregnant woman]. There is no land or water between heaven and earth that does not belong to the emperor. And what is more, if you remain at home, you serve your parents; if you serve the nation, you serve the sovereign. At such a time, heaven and earth protect you, and you receive the blessings of yin and yang naturally. However, if you thoughtlessly claim to seek the Buddhadharma and do not serve parents who ought to be served or do not serve the sovereign who ought to be served, how will you ever requite the kindness of parents who gave you life and fed you? How will you requite the kindness of the emperor's land and water? Entering the Way and not having the eye of the Way is like being a traitor.

It is said, "Since I have abandoned mundane sentiments and entered into the Unconditioned, I have left the triple world."[113] Moreover, now that you have made your home departure, you no longer pay homage to parents or sovereign. You have changed your appearance and become a child of the Buddha and you shelter your body in the pure stream [of the monks]. Even if you receive alms from your [former] wife and children, it is not like receiving them as a layman. You cannot say that they are not at all the alms of the faithful. However, someone long ago said, "If you have not yet clarified your Dharma eye, it is hard to bite into a single grain [of rice]. But once your Dharma eye is clear, even if the sky becomes a bowl and Mount Sumeru is rice, and you consume it night and day, you will not be faulted for receiving the alms of the faithful."

Regardless of the completeness of your Dharma eye, if you think of becoming a monk and receive offerings from people thoughtlessly, then when alms are scarce, you will seek them in vain from the laity. You ought to remember that when you left your family and left your birthplace, you wandered about without a grain of rice or a shred of clothing. You should consign your body to [the search for] the Dharma eye and abandon your life for the sake of the Dharma. How could you vainly arouse the thought [of enlightenment] for fame and fortune or for food and clothing? Thus, it is pointless to ask others. Just recall your own very first arousing of the thought and examine yourself as to whether or not this is so. It has been said, "It is harder later to be as careful as in the beginning." Really, if you proceed in the spirit of that first thought, who will not become a man of the way?

For this reason, even though you all became monks or mendicants, you become traitors [when you forget that first intention]. That mendicant in ancient times had not clarified his Dharma eye, but he was diligent in his religious practice and so, in repayment, he became a tree fungus. When monks who are like him die nowadays, Yama will be unable to pardon them.[114] Their rice gruel will turn into molten iron or iron pellets and when they swallow it, their bodies will become red with inflammation. Zen Master Yunfeng [Wen-]yue[115] said, "Don't you see, a patriarchal teacher said that if you enter the Way and do not attain the truth, then you ought to become alms for the faithful in your next life." This matter is completely settled and there is no doubt about it. Senior monks, you must not waste time; time waits for no one. Don't wait for death to find you; the light in the eyes fails in a second. If you don't turn over a single spadeful in the field of monkhood,[116] you will succumb to the misfortune of a hundred penalties in the ring of iron [mountains].[117] Don't say I didn't warn you! Monks, you have been fortunate to encounter the Tathagata's true Dharma Wheel. This is rarer than encountering a tiger in the city, rarer than the blooming of the Udumbara tree.[118] Be cautious, practice carefully, and clarify your Dharma eye.

Don't you see! You should not say that this story [about the ancient monk] is about sentient beings or insentient beings, nor should you think about such things as karmic results as environment, or karmic results as bodily form. A monk in a former life became a tree fungus in a present life. When he became a tree fungus, he did not know "I was a monk," and when he was a monk, he did not know "I was manifested as [one of] the myriad things." Thus, though you are now sentient, possess some awareness, and can discriminate between pain and tickle, you are no different from a tree fungus. Why? Isn't ignorance not knowing that the tree fungus is you, and not knowing that you became a tree fungus? Thus, you see sentience and nonsentience as different, and the two kinds of karmic result [mentioned above] as [separate] things. If you clarify the Self, then what can you call "sentient" or "insentient"? [The True Self] is not in past, present, or future, nor is it the [six sense] bases, the [six] objective realms, or the [six] sense consciousnesses. It neither cuts off [in the form of enlightenment] nor is cut off [as delusion]. It is neither your own effort nor someone else's effort. You must practice exceedingly carefully and see by dropping off body and mind.

Do not be vainly proud of assuming the appearance of a monk and do not deludedly stop at home departure. Even if you have escaped the calamity of water, you may still be afflicted with the calamity of fire. Even though you have abandoned mundane worries and abide with the Buddha, [karma] is hard to escape. How much more so are [ordinary] people, who pursue things and are deluded by others, like gossamer hairs and drifting dust galloping off east and west, rising and falling in the court and countryside, feet never stepping on the real ground, minds never reaching the real place. They not only miss out in this one life but vainly pass through many lives. Don't you realize that from the ancient past to the present no one has been mistaken and no one has been separated [from the True Self]? You still do not know of its existence, and are therefore like hairs or dust. If you do not exhaust [your ignorance] today, when will you?

Verse

I have some humble words concerning this story. Would you like to hear them?

> *What a pity his Dharma eye was not clear.*
> *Deluded about Self, repaying others, the retribution never ends.*

SANGHANANDI

Case

The seventeenth patriarch was the Venerable Sanghanandi. Once, Rahulata said in verse:

> *Since I am without a self,*
> *You should see the Self.*
> *Because if you make me your master,*
> *You will understand that the self is not the Self.[119]*

When the master heard this, his mind opened and he sought liberation.

Circumstances

The master was the son of King Ratnavyuha of Shravasti. He could speak as soon as he was born and he always praised matters concerning the Buddha. When he was seven, he lost interest in worldly happiness and said to his parents in verse:

> *I prostrate myself to my greatly loving father*
> *And to the mother of my flesh and bones.*
> *For now I wish to make my home departure*
> *And ask you to pity me.*

The parents firmly objected to this, after which he refused to eat. So, they permitted him to make his home departure while still living at home. He was named Sanghanandi. The parents had the monk Zenrita[120] be his teacher. By the time he turned nineteen, he still had not lost interest [in becoming a real monk]. The master always said to himself, "How can I be a monk as long as I continue to live in the royal palace?" One night, a celestial light shined down revealing a flat road, and, without thinking, he started out on it. After several miles he arrived at a huge cliff with a cave in it. He went in, and at once entered samadhi.

Since the king had lost his son, he sent Zenrita from the kingdom to make enquiries about his son's whereabouts, but he could not find out where his son was. Ten years passed and the Venerable Rahulata was going about teaching and arrived at Shravasti. There was a river there named Hiranyavati and its water tasted particularly fine. The images of five Buddhas appeared in midstream. The Venerable [Rahulata] said to the assembly, "The source of this river is about five hundred *li* from here[121] and a wise man named Sanghanandi lives there. The Buddha predicted that after a thousand years this person would inherit the rank of sage." When he finished speaking, he led his followers up the stream to its source. When they arrived there, they saw Sanghanandi sitting peacefully in samadhi and so the Venerable [Rahulata] and his followers waited [for Sanghanandi to finish]. Twenty-one days later, Sanghanandi emerged from samadhi. The Venerable [Rahulata] asked him, "Are you in samadhi physically or mentally?" The Master answered, "Both body and mind are in samadhi." The Venerable [Rahulata] asked, "If both body and mind are in samadhi, then how can there be entering or leaving [samadhi]?"

Teisho

If body and mind are in samadhi, how can there be entering and leaving? If you practice samadhi aimed at both body and mind, this is not true samadhi. If it is not true samadhi, then there will be entering and leaving. If there is entering and leaving, then it must be said that it is not samadhi. Do not look for body and mind where there is samadhi. From the beginning, the practice of Zen has been the dropping off of body and mind, so what can be called "mind"? What can be called "body"?

The master [Sanghanandi] said, "Although there is entering and leaving, the characteristics of samadhi are not lost. It is like gold in a well [being put in and taken out]; the gold remains gold." The Venerable [Rahulata] replied, "If the gold is in a well or leaves the well, but you say there is no motion in the gold, what kinds of things would 'entering' and 'leaving' be? If there is no motion in gold, but it enters and leaves, it is not real gold." Still not grasping the meaning, Sanghanandi said, "You say that if gold moves, what kinds of things are entering and leaving? I say that gold enters and leaves but not that there is motion." Saying that there is no motion in gold but that there is still entering and leaving is a dualistic view. Therefore, the Venerable [Rahulata] said, "If the gold is in a well, how can what emerges be gold? If gold leaves the well, what is it that remains?" What is outside does not enter, nor does what is inside emerge. If [body and mind, or "gold"] leaves, there is total leaving; if they enter, they enter totally. How can they be in a well and also leave it? Therefore, [Rahulata] said, "That which leaves is not gold. What do you call that which remains?"

Not grasping the meaning, the master said, "If the gold leaves the well, what remains is not gold. If the gold stays in the well, what leaves is not anything." These words truly display ignorance of the nature of gold. Therefore, the Venerable [Rahulata] said, "The meaning is otherwise." Really, although it seems as if [Sanghanandi] was in samadhi and grasped the meaning, he still entertained a [dualistic] view of things and self. Therefore, he said, "Your meaning is not clear." However, there is no truth in this, because it was like a gossamer hair being blown about by the wind. The Venerable [Rahulata] said, "Your meaning misses the point." He was referring to the master's words. The master said, "Your meaning cannot possibly stand." With great compassion and pity, the Venerable [Rahulata] continued, "Since your meaning will not stand, then my meaning does." Because he still understood the nonexistence of self falsely, the master said, "Even though my meaning stands, it is because things are not selves." The Venerable [Rahulata] said, "My meaning already stands, because I have no self. Truly, even though you intellectually understand that all things are without self, you still do not know the truth." The master said, "Because I have no self, then what meaning can be established?" In order to make him understand intimately, the Venerable [Rahulata] said, "Because I have no self, I establish your meaning."

The four great elements are completely without self, and the five aggregates originally do not exist.[122] [Sanghanandi] slightly grasped the fact of the existence of the [true] Self where there is no self in a conceptual and discriminating manner and so he asked, "With what wise man as a teacher did you obtain this [knowledge of] no-self?" The Venerable [Rahulata] replied, "I proved the nonexistence of self with the Great Being Kanadeva for a teacher." The master said,

> I prostrate myself to your teacher, [Kana-]Deva,
> And go forth [as a monk] to you.
> Because you have no self,
> I wish to make you my teacher.

The Venerable [Rahulata] replied,

> Since I am without a self,
> You should see the Self.
> Because if you make me your master,
> You will understand that the self is not the Self.

For those who thoroughly see the True Self,[123] the [ordinary] self does not exist. How can the myriad things obstruct their vision? Experience and understanding are finally not separate, nor is there any separation from a single event or thing. Therefore, there is no separation between ordinary and wise, and master and disciple are united. When you thoroughly see this principle, then this is what is meant by encountering the Buddha patriarchs. Oneself is the master, and the master is oneself. Not even a sword or ax can cut the two apart. [Sanghanandi] was suddenly enlightened to this principle and for this reason he sought liberation. The Venerable [Rahulata] told him, "Your mind is free, not bound by me."

Having spoken, the Venerable [Rahulata] then raised up a golden bowl with his right hand and went up to the palace of the Brahma gods. There, he received some wonderful, fragrant rice and [returning] tried to present it to the assembled monks. However, the monks immediately took a dislike to it. The Venerable [Rahulata] said, "I am not to blame. This happened because of your own actions [in previous lives]." Then he had Sanghanandi sit with him and share the food. The monks wondered about this. The Venerable [Rahulata] told them, "This is the reason you cannot eat the food. You should understand that he who shares this seat with me was the Tathagata Shalaraja in the past. He pitied beings and so he has appeared in the world. Even though you men had already attained the third fruit [of practice of the Way][124] during the past eon, you had not yet realized the extinction of defilements."

The monks replied, "We have to believe in the supernatural powers of our teacher, but when you say that Sanghanandi was a Buddha in the past, we have to doubt it." The master, realizing that the monks were filled with pride, said, "When the World-honored One was in the world, the world was flat and there were no hills, and the water in streams and rivers was sweet and fine, grass and trees flourished abundantly, the soil was rich, the eight kinds of suffering did not exist, and people cultivated the ten good [actions].[125] More than eight hundred years after the Buddha died between the twin Shala trees, the world is covered with hills and valleys, and trees are withered. There is no supreme faith in people, and right mindfulness is weak and flimsy. There is no faith in suchness but only hankering after spiritual powers."

So saying, he slowly pushed his right hand down into the earth and drew up some sweet water from the sphere of diamond at the very bottom of the earth.[126] He put it in a bowl made of lapis lazuli and exhibited it before the monks. Seeing this, all the monks repented of their transgressions and took refuge [with the master].

What a shame that eight hundred years after the time of the Tathagata it had come to this. How much more [is it a shame] in these final five hundred years,[127] when even though the name of the Buddhadharma is somewhat known, people are unaware of what the meaning must be. Because there is no one whose body and mind have reached [the realm of the Buddhas], no one asks what it is. And even when the meaning is grasped, no one comes to guard and maintain it. Even though there are intelligent people who understand a little because of great compassionate teaching, they are overwhelmed with laziness, and there are none with true faith and comprehension. When there are no true people of the Way, no one truly arouses the thought [of supreme enlightenment]. We have reached this time of the decline of the Dharma as a result of unskillful actions during the final age, and it is worse than shameful and regretful.

It is truly regretful, good people, that you were not born during the period of the true Dharma and counterfeit Dharma,[128] whether as a teacher or as a disciple. But you should consider the fact that the Buddhadharma did come east [from India and China] and reached its final days, and it has been no more than fifty or sixty years since one could hear the Tathagata's True Dharma in our own land.[129] You should think of this as the beginning and that the True Dharma flourishes wherever it goes. You have expressed your resolve with great bravery and diligence, and you do not believe that your self is the [true] Self. Truly, by quickly proving the nonexistence of the self and speedily attaining [the realm of no-mind], not being caught up in the working of mind and body, not being restricted by feelings about delusion and enlightenment, not being detained in the cave of life and death, not getting snared in the net of [ideas of] ordinary beings and Buddha, you will understand the existence of the Self which has been unchanging for incalculable eons in the past and will be unchanging into the eternal future.

Verse

Here are my capping words:

> Mind's activity smoothly rolling on is the form the mind takes;
> How many times has the Self appeared with a different face!

GAYASHATA

Case

The eighteenth patriarch was the Venerable Gayashata. He served the Venerable Sanghanandi. One time, he heard the sound of the wind blowing the bronze bells in the temple. The Venerable Sanghanandi asked the master, "Are the bells ringing or is the wind ringing?" The master replied, "It is neither the bells nor the wind; it is my Mind that is ringing." The Venerable [Sanghanandi] asked, "And who is the Mind?" The master replied, "Because both are silent."' The Venerable [Sanghanandi] said, "Excellent, excellent! Who but you will succeed to my Way?"

Circumstances

The master was from Magadha. He belonged to the family of Udrarama [putra].[130] His father was "Celestial Canopy" and his mother was "Everywhere Virtuous."[131] Once she had a dream of a great spirit holding a round mirror and, as a result, she became pregnant. In seven days [Gayashata] was born, and his body shined like lapis lazuli. Even without being washed, he was naturally fragrant and clean. After he was born, a round mirror appeared and followed the young boy around. The boy was always fond of quiet places and he was not at all contaminated by worldly matters. The so-called round mirror was before his face when he was sitting, and all matters pertaining to the Buddhas were reflected in this mirror. It was brighter than one's mind illuminated by the holy teaching. If the boy went someplace, the mirror followed him like a halo [behind him]. However, the boy's form could be seen through it. When he went to bed, the mirror hung over his bed like a celestial canopy. In short, the mirror never failed to follow him whether he was walking about, standing still, sitting, or lying down.

Sanghanandi was traveling around preaching and arrived in Magadha. Suddenly, a cool breeze arose, and everyone was delighted in body and mind, but no one could understand why it had happened. The Venerable [Sanghanandi] said, "This is the wind of the virtue of the Way. Some wise person has left the [secular] world and he will perpetuate the patriarchal lamp." So saying, he used his spiritual powers and gathered up the whole assembly of monks and carried them over mountains and valleys. After a while, they arrived at the foot of a mountain and [Sanghanandi] said, "On the top of this peak there is a purple cloud, like a canopy, and a wise man lives there." He wandered around with the monks for a while and finally he saw a hut with a young boy in it who, bearing a round mirror, approached the Venerable [Sanghanandi]. The Venerable [Sanghanandi] asked him, "How old are you?" [The boy] replied, "One hundred years old." The Venerable [Sanghanandi] asked him, "You seem young, how can you be one hundred years old?" [The boy] said, "I do not know the reason; it's just that I am one hundred years old." The Venerable [Sanghanandi] asked, "Are you skilled in functioning [in the manner of a Buddha]?" [The boy] replied, "The Buddha said that even if a person lives one hundred years but does not understand the functioning of the Buddhas, it is not as good as living a single day and being capable of settling the matter."

The Venerable [Sanghanandi] asked, "That thing you hold in your hand, what does it represent?" The boy replied,

> The great round mirror of all the Buddhas
> Has no blemish either inside or outside.
> All alike can see the mirror
> Because their minds' eyes are all the same.

When his parents heard this, they surrendered him and had him make his home departure. The Venerable [Sanghanandi] took him back to where he started from, and when he finished giving him the complete precepts, he named him Gayashata. Once, [Gayashata] heard the sound of the wind blowing some bells in the monastery, and so on, [as in the main case] and [Sang-

hanandi] transmitted the Dharma Treasury to him. Later, he became the
eighteenth patriarch. When the young boy made his home departure, the
round mirror suddenly disappeared.

Teisho

The minds' eyes of all are completely alike, like the present round mirror
which is without blemish inside or out. From the time the young boy was
born, he always praised matters concerning the Buddhas. He did not get
mired down in mundane matters. In the bright mirror he saw things concerning the Buddhas of the past and present. Even though he understood
that minds' eyes of all are the same, he thought that he still did not understand the functioning of the Buddhas. Therefore, he spoke of being one hundred years old. Even if for a single day one understands the functioning of all
the Buddhas, he will not only transcend one hundred years, he will transcend innumerable lives.

For this reason, [the boy] abandoned the round mirror when he realized
this. We can understand from this situation that the one great matter of all
the Buddhas is not something fast or easy. Truly, when one understands the
great round mirror of all the Buddhas, what else is left? Still, this is not the
ultimate truth, for what must the great round mirror of all the Buddhas be?
And what must "all alike see it" be? And what must "no blemish inside or
outside" be? And what is meant by "blemish"? And what in the world are
"minds' eyes"? How are they "the same"? Therefore, he lost the round mirror. Did not the young boy also lose his skin and flesh? Even though what he
saw was this lack of difference of minds' eyes, and he saw that all see it
equally, in fact, this is a dualistic view, and it still is not really thoroughly
clarifying the Self.

Monks, do not form the view of a circle. You should investigate this in
detail, quickly get rid of [views of] karmic results [in the form] of body and
environment, and realize that the Self is incomprehensible. If you do not
reach this realm, you are nothing but sentient beings [subject to] karmic
results, and you do not understand the functioning of all the Buddhas yet.
Thus, [Gayashata] repented, and finally made his home departure, receiving the complete precepts. Later, he spent years serving Sanghanandi.

One time, he heard the sound of the wind blowing the bronze bells in the temple. The Venerable [Sanghanandi] asked the master, "Are the bells ringing or is the wind ringing," and so on. This story should be carefully investigated. Although the Venerable [Sanghanandi] never saw any bells or perceived wind, he still tried to show what this [Mind] is. So he asked, "Are the bells ringing or is the wind ringing?"

What is this [Mind]? You cannot understand it by means of wind bells. These are not ordinary wind bells, they are the bells suspended from the corners of the temple halls. They are called *reitaku*. They are hung everywhere in Nara these days in temples, towers, and so on. This is how temples are distinguished from the houses of people. Even though after the capitol was moved to Kyoto [in 797] the bells were hung in temples at first, nowadays this native custom has been abandoned and is meaningless. However, this is the significance of the bells in India. When the wind blew there, this koan occurred. The master replied by saying, "It is not the wind, it is not the bells, it is just my Mind ringing." You must understand that none of them [wind, bells, etc.] produces the outline of even a single grain of dust. For this reason, "It is not the wind ringing, it is not bells ringing, and if you think that it is ringing, then it is ringing." Such a view is also still not the stillness of the Mind. For this reason, [Gayashata] said, "It is my Mind that is ringing."

People hearing this story all get it wrong, saying, "It is certainly not the wind ringing, it is only the Mind ringing, and this is why Gayashata answered the way he did." When the universe was still in its primordial, undivided state, can you say that it is not the ringing of bells? Therefore, [Gayashata] said, "It is my Mind that is ringing." From the time of Gayashata to the time of the Sixth Patriarch [of Chinese Zen, Huineng] is a very long time, and yet it is not so long. Therefore [Huineng said], "The wind is not moving, the flag is not moving, your Mind is moving." All of you now, too, when you thoroughly attain this realm, will make no distinction among the three times. Realization in past and present will be continuous, and there will be no discrimination of difference. Do not discriminate with ordinary views. You will understand for the first time by means of "not wind ringing, not bells ringing." If you want to understand what this [Mind] is, you must understand, "It is my Mind ringing." The form of this ringing is as lofty as soaring mountains and as deep as the ocean. The luxuriant flourishing of grass and trees, and the clarity of your eyes are all forms of the Mind's ringing. Therefore, do not think that it is a sound ringing; the sound also is the Mind ringing. The four great elements, the five aggregates, and the myriad things are all the ringing of the Mind. There is never a moment when this Mind is not ringing. In the end, it is not accompanied by an echo. Also, it is not something heard with ears. The ear is ringing [also], and so it is said to be silent as well.

When you can see it in this manner, none of the myriad things appears. The mountains are formless, the ocean is formless, and not a single thing exhibits a form. It is like sailing an elegant boat in a dream and traveling about on the ocean. Even though you part the waves with a pole and learn of the power of waves by stopping the boat, there is no boat to sail on, no depths to sink into. Moreover, how can there be any mountains or ocean externally? What self can there be to float in a boat? Therefore, it is shown in this way. Even though there are eyes, there is no hearing; even though there are ears, there is no seeing. You should not say that the six senses are merged into one. You cannot be bound to the six senses. They are all silent. There are no six senses to grasp, nor are there any six objects to abandon. The six senses and their objects are all liberated; both Mind and its objects are forgotten together. If you look carefully, there are no six senses and their objects to be liberated, no Mind and its objects to be obliterated. In truth, being silent, there is no question of their being the same or different, internal or external.

When you reach such a realm, you will receive and hold the Dharma Treasury of all the Buddhas and find yourself in the ranks of the Buddha patriarchs. If you do not become this, then even though you understand that the myriad things are not mixed, you still make a distinction between self and other, and in the end you separate thing from thing [in the same way]. If you separate them, how can you become one with the Buddha patriarchs? This is like building boundary walls in the sky. How can the sky be obstructed? It is just you, yourselves, who create obstructions. Once the boundaries are smashed, what can be considered outside or inside? When you reach this [realm] Old Master Shakyamuni does not begin and you people do not end. [Because all are the One Mind,] there are no distinctions of Buddha faces and ordinary shapes. At such a time, just as still water becomes waves, you all appear as Buddha patriarchs. Even though [water] neither increases nor decreases, the currents bring waves. Thus, if you investigate carefully, you will reach this realm.

Even though for eons in the past and for eons into the future you have cre-ated and will create boundaries, and separate time into past, present, and future, from eon to eon it is all just this [One Mind]. In order to understand this bright, intrinsic nature, you do not have to trouble yourselves by using skin and flesh, nor do you have to distinguish by means of the movement or stillness of the body. This realm cannot at all be known by means of body and mind, nor can it be distinguished by means of movement or stillness. By investigating carefully and putting an end to your own self-inflicted confu-sion, you will be able to experience this for the first time. If you do not clar-ify it in this way, you will uselessly bear the burden of body and mind throughout the twenty-four hours of the day. Like carrying a heavy burden on your shoulders, body and mind will in the end never be put to rest. If you cast away body and mind, the mind will become empty and silent and you will have a most peaceful life. However, even though you do so, if you are unable to clarify and express the ringing of Mind in this story, you will not understand either the appearance of all the Buddhas or the enlightenment of all beings.

Verse

I have some humble words to try to express the ringing of the Mind. Would you like to hear them?

> Silent, still, the Mind rings and echoes in ten thousand ways—
> Sanghanandi, Gayashata, and wind and bells.

KUMARATA

Case

The nineteenth patriarch was the Venerable Kumarata. Once, the Venerable Gayashata said to him, "Long ago, the World-honored One predicted, 'One thousand years after my death, a great being will appear in Tokhara who will inherit and promote the profound teaching.' You have now met with this good fortune by encountering me." Hearing this, the master acquired the knowledge of former lives.

Circumstances

The master was from Tokhara[132] and his family was Brahmin. Long ago, when he was a celestial being in the Paranirmita-vashavartin celestial realm (the sixth celestial realm in the realm of desire),[133] he saw a bodhisattva's necklace of precious stones and suddenly felt attachment. [As a result of the attachment] he fell [from that realm] and was born in the celestial realm of the *Trayastimshas*[134] (the second of the celestial realms in the realm of desire).[135] He heard Indra preaching the *Perfection of Wisdom [Sutra]* and, thanks to [realizing] its superiority, he ascended to [the celestial realm of] the Brahmadevas (in the realm of form). Being quite bright, he was skillful in preaching the essentials of the Dharma, and the celestial beings honored him by making him their teacher. Because the time had arrived for succeeding to the rank of patriarch, he finally descended [from the celestial realms] and was born in Tokhara.

The eighteenth patriarch was preaching and arrived in Tokhara. Seeing a strange atmosphere around a certain Brahmin house, he started to enter it.

The master [appeared and] asked him, "What kind of followers are these?"
The Venerable [Gayashata] replied, "These are followers of the Buddha."
When the master heard the name of the Buddha, he shut the door in awe. The
Venerable [Gayashata] paused a little and struck the door. The master said,
"There is no one in the house." The Venerable [Gayashata] replied, "Who is
it that says 'no one'?" When the master heard this, he realized that this must
be an unusual person. He opened the door quickly and greeted him. The
Venerable [Gayashata] told him, "Long ago, the World-honored One pre-
dicted…" and so on, and Kumarata acquired the knowledge of former lives.

Teisho

You should consider this story carefully. Even if you clarify the way of
names and words,[136] and clarify that the coming and going of birth and
death are the True Person, if you do not clarify the fact that your own intrinsic nature is empty, bright, marvelous, and vast, then you do not understand
[the Mind] that the Buddhas express. Therefore, [Kumarata] was amazed
to see bodhisattvas emitting light, and he had feelings of attachment when
he saw the [thirty-two] marks and [eighty] minor marks on the bodies of
Buddhas. The reason is that he had still not gotten rid of the three basic poisons of craving, hatred, and delusion. When we now look at Kumarata's
past, he retrogressed and fell from the celestial realm of the Trayastrimshas
due to craving. However, due to causes in former lives, he ascended to the
realm of the Brahmadevas when he heard Indra preaching the Dharma and,
finally, he was born in Tokhara. Accumulated merits [from the past] were
not in vain, [and so] finally he met the eighteenth patriarch and acquired
knowledge of former lives.

When "knowledge of former lives" is mentioned, it is thought that this
refers to knowing the past or future as we ordinarily use the terms. What in
the world would be the value of that? If you can simply see that one's original, unchanging Self-nature is neither saintly nor ordinary, neither deluded
[nor enlightened], then hundreds of thousands of teachings and incalculable
numbers of subtle principles all abide in the Mindsource. Therefore, both
the delusions of ordinary beings and the enlightenment of all the Buddhas
abide within one's square inch [of mind]. It is not at all the senses and their
objects, nor the mind and its realm. At this point, what can you consider

"ancient"? What can you consider "present"? Who are "all the Buddhas"? What are "sentient beings"? Not a single thing obstructs the eye [here]; not a speck of dust touches the hands. Being simply a bit of empty brightness, it is vast and boundless. That is, the eternal, truly perfected Tathagata is sentient beings who are enlightened from the beginning. Thus, when there is understanding, there is no increase; when there is no understanding, there is no decrease. Being enlightened to the fact that it has been thus for long eons is what is meant by "acquiring knowledge of former lives."

If you do not reach this realm, you will be agitated by feelings about delusion and awakening. You will be moved about by signs of past and future, and, in the end, you will not understand that there is a [true] Self, nor will you clarify the fact that the fundamental Mind is not mistaken. Therefore, you make the Buddhas take all the trouble of appearing in the world, and you make the patriarchal teacher [Bodhidharma] come from the West long ago. The original meaning [of the Buddha] appearing in the world, and the original intention of coming from the West was for this and nothing else. You should take care and realize that [this original Mind] is very intelligent, not deluded, very bright and unhidden. Understanding that it is the original bright light is the meaning of "acquiring knowledge of former lives."

Verse

Today, also, I have a few humble words and I would like to try to penetrate this principle a little. Would you like to hear them?

> In past lives he cast off one body after another;
> Right now, he encounters the Old Fellow.

JAYATA

Case

The twentieth patriarch was the Venerable Jayata. Once, the nineteenth patriarch said, "Although you already have faith in the karma of the three times, still, you have not yet clarified the fact that karma is produced from delusion, delusion exists as a result of consciousness, consciousness results from ignorance, and ignorance results from mind. Mind is originally pure, without origination or cessation, without doing or effort, without karmic retribution, without superiority or inferiority, very still, and very intelligent. If you accept this teaching, you will become the same as all the Buddhas. All good and evil, conditioned and unconditioned, are like dreams and fantasies." Hearing this, the master grasped the deep meaning of these words and aroused the wisdom he had possessed since time immemorial.

Circumstances

The master was from northern India. His wisdom was exceedingly deep and there was no limit to his [ability in] converting and guiding. At the time, he met the nineteenth patriarch in central India and asked him, "Although my parents have always had faith in the Buddha, his Teaching, and the Community, they have always been in poor health. For the most part, whatever they have done has not worked out as they wished. However, my neighbors have always been engaged in the cruel practices of declaring outcastes, but they have always been in good health, and all their efforts have been successful. Why are they lucky, while my family has bad luck?"

The Venerable [Kumarata] answered, "What is there to doubt? There are three times for good and bad karmic retribution. Generally, people see the kind and compassionate die young, the cruel live a long time, the wicked prosper, and the good find only misfortune. They conclude that there is no cause and effect, and [words such as] misfortune and blessings are empty. In particular, they do not understand that [the result follows the cause] as shadow and echo follow [forms and sounds] without a hair's breadth of confusion. Even after the lapse of millions of eons, there is no break [in the cause and effect relationship], and the causal conditions will have an effect." When the master heard this, his doubt was suddenly cleared up. The Venerable [Kumarata] said, "Although you already have faith in the karma of the three times, [etc.]"— and the master aroused the wisdom he had possessed since time immemorial.

Teisho

As students of the Way, you should look at the above story very carefully. Jayata said, "Although my parents have always had faith in the Buddha, his Teaching, and the Community, they have always been in poor health. For the most part, whatever they have done has not worked out as they wished. However, my neighbors have always been engaged in the cruel practices of outcastes, but they have always been in good health and all their efforts have been successful." Under these circumstances, he thought, "For a long time, I have taken refuge in the Buddhadharma. Relying on the power of the Dharma, I should be in good health, and matters ought to work out satisfactorily, but they don't work out well at all, and my health is not good. What is my offense? The outcaste family has always engaged in evil conduct and they do not cultivate good roots, but they have luck in whatever they do and they are in good health. What is their blessing?" People these days think the same way. Even those who have made their home departure think this way, not to even mention lay followers. [Kumarata] said, "What is there to doubt? There are three times for karmic retribution. Generally, people see the kind and compassionate die young, the cruel live a long time, the wicked prosper, and the good find only misfortune. They are not clear about the past [and its causal conditions], nor do they understand the future. They are just deluded about the present and think that there is no cause and effect and that [words such as] misfortune and blessing are meaningless. This is the ultimate of stupidity. They are like this because they are foolish about practicing the Way."

As for the karma of the three periods, the first is karma that bears results in the present life. When good and bad karma is performed in the present life, then one will receive the results in the present life. The second is karma that bears consequences in the next life. The five unpardonable transgressions and the seven deadly transgressions[137] necessarily bear their consequences in the following life. The third is karma that bears its consequences in some life after the next one. If one accumulates karma in the present life, the results are experienced in the third or fourth lifetime or even during innumerable lifetimes in the future.

Thus, even though one receives good [results] in the present because of good karma in a past life, the result may not be identical because of ancient karma [prior to the last lifetime]. People with so-called unmixed good or bad karma experience either good or bad results accordingly in the present, and those with mixed good and bad karma receive mixed good and bad results. Also, as a result of the power of practicing the Buddhadharma, grave [results] are converted to light ones, and light ones become nonexistent in the present.

This means that evil causes in past eons ought to be experienced in the future as severe suffering, but sometimes they are experienced lightly because of the power of practicing [the Dharma]. One may be ill, things may not work out well, and people make fun of what you say. These are all [examples of] receiving lightly in the present [what would be] severe suffering in the future. Thus, the power of practicing the Buddhadharma should be relied on more and more. Results [of bad karma] in the distant past can all be made light only if you are courageous and energetic. Even though as students you understand the Way very well, you may have a bad reputation, you may fail in your efforts, or your health may be bad. If you realize that these are [examples of] grave [results] changing and being experienced lightly, you will not bear a grudge against malicious people. Even though people slander and injure, do not blame them. Even though these slanderers are venerated and respected, do not hate them. The karma of [practicing] the Way grows daily and the [bad] karma of former lives decreases. But you should practice carefully and thoroughly.

Even though you already have faith in the karma of the three times, you still do not know the root of karma. Karma has good and bad consequences, and there are different categories such as ordinary and saint, and there are karmic results such as the three realms, six destinies, four kinds of birth, and the nine existences.[138] This karma is born from delusion. "Delusion" is hating and desiring what ought not be hated and desired, affirming and denying what should not be affirmed or denied. Delusion consists of thinking that what is not a male is a male and what is not a female is a female, and distinguishing oneself from others. "Non-enlightenment" means not knowing one's origins, not knowing the birthplace of the myriad things, missing wisdom in all situations; this is what is meant by "non-enlightenment." This Mind originally pure, without thought, without an objective realm, is unsoiled by other conditions. We call this Mind's one transformation "non-enlightenment." When one becomes aware of this non-enlightenment, one's own Mind is originally pure, one's Self-nature is spiritual and bright. If you clarify it in this manner, then non-enlightenment is destroyed and the twelve conditions [of conditioned co-arising] are finally empty. The four kinds of birth and the six destinies are forgotten at once. The original Mind of all people is like this; there is no distinction of generation and extinction, no such things as making and doing. Therefore, there is no hating or craving, no increase or decrease. It is nothing but great stillness, great intelligence.

If you try to experience original Mind, you cast away the myriad affairs and still the many conditions. Without thinking of good or evil, just lower your gaze to the tip of your nose and look at the original Mind. When you become single-mindedly still, all characteristics [of things] are exhausted. Because the root of ignorance is destroyed, the branches and leaves of karma and its results no longer exist. Therefore, you are not bound by non-discrimination [or discrimination], nor are you concerned with non thinking [or thinking]. It is neither permanence nor impermanence, neither ignorance nor purity. There is no separation from the Buddhas, no separation from ordinary beings. Arriving at this pure, perfect realm, you will be true patch-robe monks. If you are thus, then you are no different from the Buddhas. At this point, all the conditioned and unconditioned are exhausted, like dreams and fantasies. If you try to grasp it, your hands are empty; if you try to see it, your eyes cannot detect it. If you arrive at this realm, you clarify the deep principle that all the Buddhas have not yet appeared in the world, and you arrive at a place where ordinary beings have not become confused. If your practice has not reached this realm, then even if you pay reverence to the Buddhas twenty-four hours a day and regulate mind and body while standing, sitting, walking, and lying down, this only results in excellent karmic results in the world, or defiled karmic results. It is like chasing shadows; they exist, but they are not real. Therefore, people, practice energetically and clarify your original Mind.

Verse

As usual, I have a few humble words. Would you like to hear them?

The camphor tree, as always, is born in the sky;
Its limbs, leaves, roots, and trunk flourish beyond the clouds.

VASUBANDHU

Case

The twenty-first patriarch was the Venerable Vasubandhu.[139] One time the twentieth patriarch said, "I do not seek the Way, yet I am not confused. I do not venerate the Buddhas, yet I am not conceited. I do not meditate for long periods of time, yet I am not lazy. I do not restrict myself to just one meal a day, yet I am not attached to food. I do not know what is enough, yet I am not covetous. When the mind seeks nothing, this is called the Way." When the master heard this, he aroused the undefiled wisdom.

Circumstances

The master was from Rajagriha and his family name was Vaishakha. His father was Canopy of Light; his mother, Foremost of Adornments.[140] The family was wealthy but there were no children. The parents sought descendants by praying at the stupa of the Buddha. One night the mother had a dream of drinking two jewels, one bright and one dark, and became pregnant. Seven days later, an arhat named Assembly of the Wise[141] appeared at the house. Canopy of Light paid reverence to him and he received [the reverence] while remaining seated. Foremost of Adornments appeared and paid reverence, and the arhat stood up, saying, "I bow to the Great Being who is the Dharma-body." Canopy of Light did not understand the reason for this. He took a precious jewel and, in order to test the arhat, presented it to him. The arhat received it without any special display of humility. Canopy of Light could not put up with this, and he said, "I am the master of the house and you did not pay any attention to my reverence. What virtue does my wife have that the Venerable [arhat] stands up [to receive her respects]?" The arhat said, "Receiving your veneration and accepting the jewel was only to bring you good luck. Your wife bears a wise son in her womb. His birth will be a lamp to the world and the sun of wisdom. That is why I stood up, not because I value females particularly." And he continued, "Your wife will bear two sons. One will be named Vasubandhu, and he is the one I venerate. The other will be named Suni (which means 'Magpie').[142] Long ago, when the Tathagata was practicing the Way in the Himalaya Mountains, a magpie built a nest on top of his head. When the Buddha became enlightened, the magpie was reborn as a king of Nadi as the consequence of his act. The Buddha predicted, 'During the second five hundred years [of the Dharma], you will be born in the Vaishakha family in Rajagriha, as the twin brother of a holy person.' This prediction is now coming true." A month later, the two sons were born.

When the Venerable Vasubandhu turned fifteen, he paid reverence to the arhat Kodo[143] and made his home departure. The bodhisattva named Vipaka[144] gave him the precepts. The twentieth patriarch, the Venerable Jayata was traveling around teaching and went to Rajagriha, spreading the teaching of suddenness.[145] There was a group of students [of Buddhism] there who valued only debate. They considered Vasubandhu (which means "Total Practice") to be their leader. He always ate just one meal a day [at the proper time], and he never lay down [to rest]. Day and night, he paid reverence to the Buddha. He was pure and desireless, and much trusted by the group.

The Venerable [Jayata] wanted to liberate him. First, he asked the group, "This ascetic, Vasubandhu, cultivates purity very well, but can he acquire the Buddha Way?" The group replied, "Our teacher is diligent, so why can't he?" The Venerable [Jayata] answered, "Your teacher is far from the Way. Even if he practices asceticism for countless eons, they are the roots of vanity and falseness." The group asked, "What virtuous practices has the Venerable [Jayata] accumulated that enable him to slander our teacher?" The Venerable [Jayata] replied, "I do not seek the Way..." and so on [as in the main case], and the master aroused the undefiled wisdom. [Vasubandhu] was overjoyed and praised [Jayata]. Then, the Venerable [Jayata] spoke to the group again, saying, "Do you understand what I am saying? The reason I said what I did is because of the importance of the mind that seeks the Way.

If you pluck a string [on an instrument] too hard, it snaps. Therefore, in order to get [Vasubandhu] to abide in the realm of tranquillity and happiness and enter the wisdom of all the Buddhas, I did not praise [the ascetic practices]."

Teisho

This story contains the greatest secret for learning the Way. Why? If you think that you have to become a Buddha or acquire the Way, and that in order to acquire the Way you have to abstain from food [except once a day], live a life of purity, meditate for long periods, never lie down, venerate the Buddha, and chant the scriptures and accumulate all the virtues—this is [like] making flowers rain down from a sky where there are no flowers, or making holes [in the ground] where there are none. Even though you spend eons and eons [doing these things], you will not find liberation. When there is nothing to want, this is called the Way. Thus, even wanting to know what is enough is the root of desire. Even in enjoying meditating for a long time there is the blame of being attached to the body. If you attempt to eat just once a day, you become obsessed with food. Also, if you try to honor the Buddha and chant the scriptures, these are flowers in the eyes.[146] All these practices are meaningless, not at all your own original nature. If you think that sitting in meditation for a long time is the Way, then sitting in the womb for nine months would be the Way, so what would there be to seek later? If abstaining from eating except once a day [at the approved time] is the Way, then does this mean that if you are ill and cannot fix a definite time for eating that you are not practicing the Way? This is really a big laugh!

The establishing of monastic regulations among the Buddha's disciples and indicating the proper conduct by Buddha patriarchs is like this. If you go to extremes and become attached to what is proper, this becomes a passion instead. However, if you hate the coming and going of birth and death and try to seek the Dharma [in externals], you will not be able to put an end to this dying here and being born there that has continued from beginningless time. What situation do you think is the time to acquire the Way? However, seeking the Way by concerning yourself with these things is completely confused thinking. Again, what Buddha do you see that needs to become awakened? What sentient beings do you see that can be deluded? There is not a single person who is deluded, not a single thing that has to be awakened.

For this reason, though you say that delusion is turned into awakening, and ordinary people are turned into wise people, these are all nothing but the words of people who are not yet awakened. What ordinary persons are there who need to be awakened? What delusion is there that needs to be awakened? Jiashan said,[147]

> Clearly there is no thing called awakening;
> Instead, awakening deludes people.
> I stretch out both legs and take a long nap;
> And here there is neither true nor false.
> Truly, such is the essence of the Way.

Though this is the way it is, those who are just beginning to practice or starting out later in life must practice carefully and arrive at such a calm, peaceful realm. The reason is that, if you have never understood this true realm, you can be deluded by others' words. Therefore, if you try to see [this realm] by raising your eyes [to externals], you will be disturbed by a buddha-demon. Even though today you hear things like this being said, and realize that there is nothing to be obtained, still there may be a teacher who says that there is something to be obtained, or a buddha-demon appears who says that there is something to be practiced. The result will be that you will become agitated and confused. Indeed, you have received the true instruction of the Buddha. You should practice carefully and reach the realm of peace and happiness yourselves. Once a person reaches this realm of tranquillity and happiness, he will be like someone who has eaten his fill. Even though they say that there is a royal feast, he will not be interested. Therefore, it is said, "Exquisite food has no appeal for someone who is full." The ancients said, "Once you have been afflicted, you will be relieved shortly."

Once you see carefully, your own original Mind sees no Buddhas, no sentient beings. How could you hate delusion and seek awakening [after that]? Ever since the Patriarchal Teacher [Bodhidharma] came from India in order to make people see directly, Zen masters[148] have not spoken of having wisdom or not having wisdom, or of ancient learning and new learning. They have just made people alike sit up straight and calmly abide in the Self. This itself is the great teaching of tranquillity and happiness. Therefore, people, from incalculable eons in the past to the present, you have thought that not being confused is confusion. Do not vainly become concerned with the [glittering] frost on someone else's gate and forget your own treasure. A close friend [I, Keizan] now meets you. Do not wait expectantly for a later day to become enlightened. You just must stir yourselves and turn [inward] to your own square inch [of mind]. Search there and do not seek elsewhere. If you do such a thing, hundreds of thousands of teachings and boundless matters concerning the Buddhas will all flow out of this and fill heaven and earth. It is important to avoid seeking the Way [externally]; it is nothing but trusting the Self.

Fetching and carrying away for countess eons, never for an instant being apart from the Self, still, if you do not know of its existence, you are like someone bearing it in their hands and looking for it east and west. However much confusion this may seem to be, it is nothing but forgetting the Self. Today, when we see it fully, the wonderful Way of the Buddhas and the separate transmission of the patriarchal teachers consist in only this, so never doubt it. People, when you reach such a realm, you will never doubt the words of the world's old priests. It says above [in the main case] that "Having heard this, he aroused undefiled wisdom." If you want to arouse undefiled wisdom, you just have to trust in the Self. If you want to trust the Self, then from birth to old age, you have to understand that it is only This One. In summary, there is not a speck of dust to be abandoned, not a single thing to receive, so do not think about arousing undefiled wisdom.

Verse

Today, as usual, I have some humble words to address to this story. Would you like to hear them?

The wind blows through the great sky, clouds appear from the mountain caverns;
Feelings for the Way and worldly affairs are of no concern at all.

Manorhita

Case

The twenty-second patriarch was the Venerable Manorhita.[149] He asked Vasubandhu, "What is the *bodhi* of all the Buddhas?" The Venerable [Vasubandhu] said, "It is the original nature of Mind." The master again asked, "What is the original nature of Mind?" The Venerable [Vasubandhu] said, "It is the emptiness of the six sense bases, the six objects, and the six kinds of consciousness.[150] Hearing this, the master was awakened.

Circumstances

The master was the son of King Eternally Sovereign of Nadi.[151] When he was thirty years old, he visited Vasubandhu, the teacher. Vasubandhu was traveling about teaching and arrived in Nadi. Its king was Eternally Sovereign. He had two sons, one named Makara[152] and a second named Manorhita. The king asked Vasubandhu, "What is the difference in local customs between Rajagriha and here?" Vasubandhu replied, "Formerly, three Buddhas appeared in that land. In your kingdom, there are two teachers who convert and guide." The king asked, "Who are these two?" The Venerable [Vasubandhu] answered, "The Buddha predicted, 'During the second five hundred years [of the Dharma], a great being of great spiritual power will make his home departure and succeed to [the rank of] patriarchal teacher.' That is, the king's second son, Manorhita, is the one, and, though my merits are slight, I venture to say that I am the other." The king said, "Really, if it is as the Venerable [Vasubandhu] says, I will let this son go at once and become a monk." The Venerable [Vasubandhu] said, "Excellent! The great king complies with the Buddha's intention very well." Then he gave Manorhita the complete precepts. After that, [Manorhita] served Vasubandhu. Once he asked, "What is the *bodhi* of all the Buddhas?" The Venerable [Vasubandhu] replied, "It is the original nature of Mind."

Teisho

This question is the first that must be asked in the study of the Way. *"Bodhi"* means "Way." Therefore, this question ["What is the *bodhi* of all the Buddhas?"] means "What is the Way?" People's minds, nowadays, are blank and they do not ask about the Dharma. Because they do not have beginners' minds when they encounter a teacher, they do not ask this question. When they have true thoughts about the Way, this cannot be so. The first thing to be asked is "What is the Buddha?" The next to be asked is, "What is the Buddha Way?" Here [in the main case] the question arose and Vasubandhu replied, "It is the original nature of Mind." Moreover, because [Manorhita's] aspiration was genuine and not a speck [of other thoughts] entered his head, he asked, "What is the original nature of Mind?" The answer was, "It is the emptiness of the six sense bases, six objects, and six kinds of consciousness." At that time, [Manorhita] was awakened.

"Buddha" refers to the original nature of Mind. Original nature, finally, is unknowable and unseeable, and this is the Supreme Way. Thus, in the Mind there is no form and no standpoint, much less a Buddha or a Way. These are all nothing but names. Buddha is not something to know, the Way is not something to be cultivated, and Mind is not something to understand. This realm [of Mind] has no objects, and it has no sense [consciousness]. Consciousness cannot be established anywhere, and so it was said that, "It is the emptiness of the six sense bases, six objects, and six kinds of consciousness." Thus, do not speak of this realm as mind and its objects and do not discern it as conscious knowing. When you arrive at this realm, Buddhas do not reveal any shapes, and the wonderful Way does not have to be cultivated and maintained. However, even though seeing, hearing, and ordinary understanding are nowhere to be found, sounds, forms, and movements also cannot be established. Therefore, it was said [by Master Sanping Yizhong]:

This seeing and hearing is not seeing and hearing,
And there is no sound or form to disclose to you.
If you thoroughly understand that in these there is nothing at all,
What is the point of discriminating or not discriminating substance and function?

Do not think of sound as do-re-mi-fa-so. Do not think of forms as blue, yel-
low, red, and white. Do not think of seeing as conditioned[153] by the eye's
brightness. Do not think of hearing as the ear's sense base. In short, people,
the eye is not opposed to forms, nor does the ear deal with sounds. If you say
that the ear is opposed to sounds or that the eye is conditioned by forms, then
there is no clarity in sound and there is darkness in the eye. If you say that
there is something opposed [to the senses] or something held [by the senses],
how can sound enter the ear, and how can forms enter the eye? Therefore,
if it is not like sky merging with sky or water merging with water, there is no
hearing, there is no seeing; but because this is so, the eye merges with forms
and the ear merges with sound. They are joined together without any separation; they are joined together with nothing remaining.

Because it is thus, even though it is a [huge] sound that reverberates
throughout heaven and earth, it enters the small square inch of the ear. Isn't
the supremely large the same as the small? One illuminates the whole earth
with the small square inch of the eye, so isn't the supremely small the same
as the large? Isn't the eye, form? Isn't sound, ears? Understanding it in this
way, discerning it thus, this Mind is boundless and limitless. Therefore, the
eye originally does not grasp, and forms cannot be separated. Aren't all these
divisions [of sense base, object, and consciousness] empty? Therefore, when
you reach this realm, you can speak of sounds, speak of eyes, speak of consciousness, and speak of "thus" and "not thus." Not a speck comes from the
outside; there is not the slightest separation. When you speak of sound, hearing and speaking are distinguished within sound. When you speak of forms,
both perceiver and perceived are discerned within forms. Still, they are
absolutely not outside oneself.

Not versed in this truth, you people may think that sounds and forms are
empty, false things to be located in unreality, but you must banish this
thought. [You think,] "Original Mind is eternal from the beginning and cannot at all be changed." This is most laughable. In this situation, what can

change or not change? What can be real or not real? If you do not become clear in this matter, then not only are you ignorant about sounds and forms, you also fail to grasp seeing and hearing. Therefore, you think that you will not see by averting your gaze, or you think that by blocking your ears you will not hear. This is binding yourself with nonexistent ropes and falling into nonexistent holes. It will be hard to escape the many passions and delusions. If you practice carefully and reach [this realm], get to the very bottom of it and see clearly, then, even when you get to the summit, your arrival will be unobstructed.

Verse

I also have some humble words to try to express something about this story. Would you like to hear them?

> *The spirit of shunyata is neither inside nor outside;*
> *Seeing, hearing, forms, and sounds are all empty.*

HAKLENAYASHAS

Case

The twenty-third patriarch was the Venerable Haklenayashas. Once, the Venerable Manorhita said, "I have the unexcelled great Dharma treasure. You must hear it, accept it, and teach it in the future." Hearing this, the master experienced awakening.

Circumstances

The master was from Tokhara and he was from the Brahmin class. His father was Thousand Victories and his mother was Golden Light. Because she was childless, she prayed to a golden banner of the thousand Buddhas, and she dreamed of a divine youth on top of Mount Sumeru. He held a golden ring and said, "I have arrived." When she awoke, she was pregnant. When the child was seven, he wandered to a village and saw the wanton sacrifices of the people, and he entered the shrine and shouted to them, "You are deluding people by awarding calamity and fortune. Year after year, your waste and injury of sacrificial animals is terrible." When he finished speaking, the shrine collapsed suddenly. As a result of this, the people called him "Holy Youth." When he was twenty-two, he made his home departure. At the age of thirty, he visited Manorhita. The Master was called "Haklena." "Lena" is Sanskrit, and "Ha" [Crane] is Chinese. "Haklena" results from combining the Sanskrit and Chinese.[154] He got this name because a flock of cranes followed him.

Many miracles occurred in the beginning when he visited Manorhita. I should mention them all, but I will mention just this one story. The master asked the Venerable [Manorhita], "Why does this flock of cranes follow me?" The Venerable [Manorhita] replied, "Formerly, during the fourth eon,[155] you became a monk. In going to the Naga palace, it so happened that all of your disciples wanted to go along with you, but in your group of five hundred, there was not one person worthy of the wonderful offering [of the Nagas]. At that time, a number of the disciples said, 'When the master preaches the Dharma, he always says, "He who is impartial with regard to food is also impartial about things." Now, since this is not so [because we cannot go with you], what wisdom can there be in this?' So, you took the group along with you. Although you were reborn [as a human] and converted many lands, those five hundred disciples were reborn as birds because their virtue was meager. Now they feel your benevolence and, therefore, follow you as a flock of cranes." Hearing this, the master asked, "What can I do to liberate them?" The master replied, "I have the unexcelled Dharma treasure," etc.

Teisho

There is no distinction of holy and ordinary [persons] in the principle of impartiality with regard to food and with regard to things. Nevertheless, this principle shows that, although both master and disciples obeyed the request of the Naga palace [to come to a feast], the disciples were deficient in virtue and undeserving of receiving offerings, so they became birds. This story should be a particular warning to students. I think that in preaching about things, there should be no distinctions, and the same should be so regarding food. Nevertheless, there are some who can digest the alms of the faithful and some who are injured by the alms of the faithful, whereupon this does not seem to be equal and, furthermore, must be said to be discrimination. The reason is that if you see food or see things, even though you see them as being equal and understand them as identical, there is the separateness of seeing things and the separateness of seeing food, so you do not escape a dualistic view. As a result of being deluded by thoughts of seeing food and following after the master, [the five hundred disciples] became birds. You must understand that they failed to grasp the principle of impartiality with regard to things and were simply bound to names and forms.

In this "unexcelled great Dharma" which was spoken of, what can be called "food," and what can be called "things"? What is "saintly," and what is "ordinary"? It is not something that can be reached with form and shadow. It is difficult to call it even the nature of Mind. This Dharma is not received from Buddhas, not received from patriarchs, not given to children, not transmitted to fathers, not something you can call "self" or "other." Where could the names "food" and "thing" come from? How much less can there be a palace to go to by request, and how much less could [monks] become birds. Therefore, if you meditate wholeheartedly and observe carefully, you will first understand the purity, vastness, and wonderful brightness of the original nature of your own Mind. If you maintain it well and deeply purify and mature it, you will understand the existence of the lamp transmitted by the Buddha patriarchs. Then for the first time, you will acquire it.

Even though you have clarified the meaning of your own original nature and are already the same as the patriarchs in liberation, still, there is an unexcelled great Dharma Treasure, which you must hear, accept, and teach well in the future. It is not the principle of original nature, much less the realm of seeing and hearing. It transcends ancient and recent circumstances by far. From the beginning it is not limited to [distinctions such as] ordinary beings and Buddhas. Therefore, you cannot call this person [who has reached this realm] "Buddha," nor can you call him "ordinary." [He is like someone who,] if he does not have to sit in the proper place in the meditation hall, is not limited to one side or the other [of the hall].156 Though you seek his shadow, you cannot find it; though you ask about his whereabouts, you cannot find him. If you reach this realm, then what is "nature of Mind"? What is "awakening"? One vomit and you vomit everything; one shit and you shit it all. At such a time, you are a great person who has put an end to calculating thoughts. If you do not reach this place, then you are still a deluded person and, in the end, an ordinary being caught up in rebirth. Therefore, people, examine [this point] carefully and try to take responsibility for this unexcelled great Dharma treasure. Then, old master Shakyamuni's fleshly body will still be warm. Do not get attached to mere names [such as "Buddha" and "things"] and get entangled with forms. In practicing and studying the Way, you must distinguish what is real and true.

Verse

I have some humble words concerning this principle. Would you like to hear them?

A white precipice—snow of a great peak sticking through the clouds.
Its purity annihilates all details and contrasts with the blue sky.

ARYASIMHA

Case

The twenty-fourth patriarch was the Venerable Simha. He asked the twenty-third patriarch, "I want to seek the Way. What concerns should I have?" The Patriarch said, "If you want to seek the Way, there is nothing to be concerned about." The master said, "If I have no concerns, who carries out Buddha activities?" The Patriarch said, "If you have some business, these are not merits. If you do nothing, this is Buddha activity. A scripture says, 'The merits I have achieved are not mine.'" Hearing these words, the master entered the wisdom of the Buddhas.

Circumstances

The master was from central India, and his family was Brahmin. In the beginning, he studied non-Buddhist teachings and was well versed in them. He had an excellent memory. Later, he visited the twenty-third patriarch and this exchange of questions and answers occurred. Immediately upon hearing this "nothing to be concerned about," he suddenly entered the wisdom of the Buddhas. Then, the twenty-third patriarch pointed to the northeast and said, "What is that shape in the air?" The master replied, "When I look at the air, it is like a white rainbow penetrating heaven and earth, and there are five black lines running through it." "What is this omen," asked the Patriarch. The master answered, "I do not understand it." The Patriarch said, "Fifty years after my death, there will be difficulties in northern India and they will involve you. Though this is the way it is, you will transmit and maintain my Dharma treasure and teach it in the future."

At this time, the master received this intimate prediction and went to teach in the land of Kubha.[157] There, he encountered [his successor,] Basiasita, and he told him, "My teacher made an intimate prediction about the distant future. He said that there would be difficulties and that they would involve me. They can by no means be avoided, so I will stay here. You shall preserve my Way and go to other lands to teach it." He gave [Basiasita] both the robes [of a monk] and the Dharma.

At the time, the king of Kubha took refuge in the Buddhadharma and had a deep respect for it, but he still was attached to externals. There were two non-Buddhists there in the kingdom also, one named Mamokuta, the other, Torakusha.[158] They studied the arts of illusion and plotted rebellion. Accordingly, they stole some monks' robes and secretly entered the palace saying, "If we get caught, we will blame it on the Buddhists." The plot failed. The king was angry, and he said, "I have taken refuge in the Three Treasures from the beginning, so why has this trouble come to me?" He decreed that all the Buddhist monasteries were to be destroyed and that the monks should be driven away. Then he, himself, took a sword and went to where the Venerable Aryasimha was. He asked him, "Has the master grasped the emptiness of the aggregates?" The master answered, "I have already grasped the emptiness of the aggregates." The king asked, "Have you abandoned life and death?" The master answered, "I have already abandoned life and death." The king said, "If you have abandoned life and death, then you must donate your head to me." The master replied, "Since this body is not mine, how can I begrudge the head?" Then the king swung the sword and decapitated the master. A white milk gushed out many feet in the air, and the king's right arm twisted around and fell to the ground. Seven days later, the king died. This was the beginning and end of the master.

Teisho

When the master [Haklenayashas] and disciple [Aryasimha] met the very first time, [Aryasimha] asked, "I want to seek the Way. What concerns should I have?" The patriarch said, "If you want to seek the Way, there is nothing to be concerned about." Truly, when you seek the Way, how could the Way have anything to do with concerns? We die here and are born there. Even though we aspire to the Way and seek it everywhere, the fact that we do not make this truth our own is a result of using this mind. Nevertheless, if you suddenly try to become worthy of the Buddha's wisdom, not only do you leave the four perverted views and three poisons,[159] but you will also leave behind the three bodies and four kinds of wisdom.[160] When you roam about [freely] in this way, the result is that it is hard to settle down in the realm of ordinary people, and it is hard to revere the status of Buddha, for you transcend the limits of ordinary and wise by far, and you speedily separate yourself from considerations of difference and sameness. Therefore, this so-called profound, subtle place is still hard for Buddha patriarchs to reach. It is not only hard for Buddha patriarchs to reach, but, of course, when you speak of such a realm, ultimately Buddha patriarchs do not exist. Reaching such a realm is the true meaning of seeking the Dharma.

If you have still not done this, then even if you make it rain flowers from the sky and make the earth tremble, speak about the nature of Mind and discuss the profound and subtle, as far as the true wonderful Way is concerned, you have not glimpsed so much as a hair of it. Therefore, Zen worthies, you must experientially reach such a profound place and clarify this matter that successive generations of patriarchs have shouldered.

Verse

In order to say something about this principle, I have some humble words, as usual. Would you like to hear them?

> *If you want to reveal the sky, do not cover it up.*
> *It is empty, tranquil and originally bright.*

BASIASITA

Case

The twenty-fifth patriarch was the Venerable Basiasita.[161] The twenty-fourth patriarch said, "I now transmit the Tathagata's Treasury of the Eye of the True Dharma to you. You must guard it and benefit all in the future." The master uncovered the [karmic] causes of previous lives and received the Mind Seal.

Circumstances

The master was from Kubha and his family was Brahmin. His father was Calm Conduct; his mother, Eternal Peace and Joy. In the beginning, his mother dreamed of receiving a divine sword, and the result was that she became pregnant. The Venerable Simha was traveling about and arrived in Kubha. There was someone there named Parika and from the first he practiced Zen contemplation. There were five groups: those who practiced samadhi, those who practiced intellection, those who grasped signs, those who abandoned signs, and those who avoided [improper] speech. The Venerable [Aryasimha] collected the five groups together and his fame was spread far and near. Seeking a Dharma successor, he visited a householder. [The householder] introduced his son and asked, "My son's name is Sita; when he was born his left hand was clenched. Although he is grown now, he still cannot unclench it. Will the Venerable [Aryasimha] please reveal the causes of this in former lifetimes?" The Venerable Aryasimha] looked at [the boy], stretched out his hand, and said, "Return the jewel to me." The young boy immediately opened his hand and presented a jewel [to the Patriarch].

Everyone thought this strange. The Venerable [Aryasimha] said, "In a former life I became a monk. There was a young man named Basia. Once I went to a feast [for monks] in the region of the Western Ocean and received a jewel as a gift. I handed it to Basia. Now he is returning the jewel to me and the reason is evident." The householder finally released his son and had him make his home departure, and the Venerable [Aryasimha] gave him the complete precepts. As a result of the earlier situation [in the former lifetime] the Venerable [Aryasimha] named him Basiasita [thus combining the two names]. Finally, he passed on the succession, saying, "I now transmit the Tathagata's Treasury of the Eye of the True Dharma to you. You must guard it and benefit all in the future."

Teisho

"Uncovered the [karmic] causes of previous lives" means that in a previous lifetime he was the young man, Basia. He received the jewel from the Venerable [Aryasimha], entered his mother's womb in the present [life and] was born in the householder's family, still held on [to the jewel] and guarded it, and finally turned it over to the Venerable [Aryasimha]. You should realize as a result of this that the story does not mean that the fleshly body is destroyed and that there is only a true [indestructible] body. If you think that this is a destructible body, then how could he [still] hold the jewel now? You should realize as well that it is not the destructible body that receives life and loses life. You cannot say at this point that all the bones break up and scatter, and that one thing is an eternal spirit that is everlasting.[162] What kind of thing could an eternal spirit be? It is the appearance of leaving a body and the appearance of receiving a body, and nothing else. It must be said that the former [Basia] and the latter [Sita] are not two, and past and present are not different. Therefore, you cannot speak of body, nor can you speak of mind. If it cannot be divided into body and mind, then you cannot divide it into past and present. Therefore, it is thus.

It is not this way just with regard to Basiasita, but, to speak the truth, everyone is like this. There is nothing that is born and dies. It is just renewing heads and changing faces in accordance with time [and conditions]. It certainly is not a matter of renewing the four great elements or renewing the five aggregates. There is never any arrival covered with a lump of flesh or arrival supported by even a gossamer hair of bone. Even though there are a thousand kinds of forms and myriads of types, they are all the original Mind light. Not knowing this principle, we think that this person is young and that that person is old but, in summary, there are no old bodies and there is originally no youth. If this is the way it is, then on what basis can you divide life and death, and how can you divide before and after? Consequently, pointing out that Basia from a former life and Sita in the present are not two bodies is the meaning of "causes from previous lives." [Grasping this,] Basiasita received the Tathagata's Treasury of the Eye of the True Dharma and benefited the future.

Therefore, you must understand that all Buddhas and all patriarchs are fundamentally unawakened, and all ignorant people are ultimately undeluded. Sometimes they practice, sometimes they arouse the thought [of enlightenment]. *Bodhi* and the thought [of enlightenment] are totally beginningless and endless. Sentient beings and the Buddhas are fundamentally not deficient or superior [respectively]. It is nothing but thusness everywhere. Thus, it is just holding and guarding it for many eons, and not forgetting causes from previous lifetimes.

Verse

This morning, as usual, I have some humble words to explain this story.

> *At the time blooming flowers and falling leaves are displayed at once,*
> *The king of medicine trees still has no distinct flavor.*

PUNYAMITRA

Case

The twenty-sixth patriarch was the Venerable Punyamitra. When he was a crown prince, the twenty-fifth patriarch asked him, "You wish to make your home departure. What thing must you do?" The master replied, "When I make my home departure, I will not do any particular thing." The Patriarch asked, "What thing will you not do?" The master answered, "I will not do any ordinary thing." The Patriarch asked, "What thing must you do?" The master answered, "I must do Buddha work." The Patriarch said, "The crown prince's wisdom is naturally excellent; you must be a successor of various sages." Then, the Patriarch permitted him to make his home departure.

Circumstances

The master was the crown prince of King Gaining Victory in southern India. The twenty-fifth patriarch went to southern India after humbling the non-Buddhist Aryanatman. At that time, the king of the land was Devaguna. He invited Basiasita and welcomed him and made offerings. The king had two sons, one who was brutal and very strong [Gaining Victory] and another [Punyamitra] who was peaceful and who had been ill a long time. The Patriarch explained [the law of] cause and effect, and the king was suddenly relieved of doubt.

After King Devaguna died, the [incumbent] crown prince, Gaining Victory, became king. He believed in non-Buddhist teachings and, subsequently, caused trouble for the Patriarch [Basiasita]. Punyamitra [the second son of Devaguna] was arrested for admonishing him. The king asked the Patriarch,

"I eliminated the supernatural from this kingdom long ago. What teaching is it that the master transmits?" The Patriarch replied, "Truly, there has been no false teachings in this kingdom for a long time. What I transmit is the teaching of the Buddha." The king said, "The Buddha died twelve hundred years ago, so from whom did the master receive [the teaching]?" The Patriarch replied, "The Great Being Kashyapa intimately received the seal of the Buddha. For twenty-four generations it was passed on up to Aryasimha, and I received it from him." The king said, "I heard that the monk Simha could not escape execution. How could he transmit the Dharma to a successor?" The Patriarch replied, "Before difficulties arose, the Venerable [Aryasimha] intimately conferred the robe and a Dharma verse, indicating transmission." The king asked, "Where is the robe?" The Patriarch produced the robe from his bag and showed it to the king. The king ordered it to be burned. Five colors blazed vividly [from the robe] and when the firewood was all burned up, [the robe] was just as it was before. The king subsequently repented and paid reverence [to the Patriarch], and the fact that [Basiasita] was Simha's true Dharma heir was made clear. Then, he pardoned the crown prince [Punyamitra] and finally the crown prince asked to make his home departure. The Patriarch asked the crown prince, "You wish to make your home departure. What thing must you do?" and so on, and the Patriarch allowed him to make his home departure.

Teisho

After that, he served [the twenty-fifth patriarch] for six years. Later, in transmitting the Tathagata's Treasury of the Eye of the True Dharma to him, [Basiasita] said, "It has been transmitted generation after generation up to now. You must guard and transmit it, and teach sentient beings." When the master received this intimate sign, he became free of mind and body. The above story shows that he did not make his home departure for any ordinary [thing]. Therefore, [Basiasita] asked, "You wish to make your home departure, so what thing must you do?" And he replied, "I must do Buddha work."

"Thing" means "ordinary thing." You must understand through this that, from the beginning, home departure has not been for the sake of some ordinary thing. A thing is not one's own or another's, so he said, "I will not do any ordinary thing." Even if you shave your head and dye your clothes [black] so that you look like a follower of the Buddha, you will not avoid views of self and other. If you do not detach yourselves from distinctions of male and female, these remain ordinary things, not Buddha work. Even though we speak in connection with people's original Mind, there is no Buddha work at all, and no ordinary things. If you still do not know the original Mind, then we speak of ordinary things. Being able to clarify the original Mind is what we call "Buddha work."

When you are able to understand the original Mind, there are no signs of origination, no signs of extinction. How much less are there deluded people and awakened! When you are able to experience it in this way, the four great elements and five aggregates do not exist. How can the three realms and six destinies be established?[163] Therefore, there is no home to leave, no body to be lodged someplace. This is why it is called "home departure." Because there is nothing that can be lived in, the home is destroyed and the person perishes. Therefore, samsara and nirvana are exhausted spontaneously without any need to be swept away, and bodhi and defilement are originally gone without any need to be abandoned.

It is not like this just today, but from eon to eon you are not disturbed during the four eons of origination, abiding, change, and emptiness;[164] nor are you bound by the four signs of origination, abiding, change, and destruction. It is just like the sky being without inside or outside in its vastness, like water having no inside or outside. The original Mind of all beings is like this. Thus, one should not be afraid of being a layperson, nor should one be proud of making one's home departure. Just stop looking externally and discern it within.

People, try for a moment to look carefully without scattering your mind all over the place or directing your gaze in front or behind. At such a time, what can you call "self"? What can you call "other"? Since there are no signs of self and other, then what do you mean by "good" and "bad"? If you are thus, then the original Mind has been revealed from the beginning, as bright as the sun and moon. There is no dark place it does not illuminate.

Verse

Again, I have some humble words I want you to hear in order to make an analogy about this story.

> The original realm is ordinary, without an inch of grass;
> Where is there room here for the ways of Zen?

Prajnatara

Case

The twenty-seventh patriarch was the Venerable Prajnatara. Once the twenty-sixth patriarch asked, "Do you remember the past?" The master replied, "I remember being with the master eons ago. The Master propounded the great wisdom [*maha-prajna*] and I recited the profound sutra. The present event [of our meeting] probably is connected with that ancient cause."

Circumstances

The master was from eastern India. Punyamitra arrived in eastern India. The king there was Dridha. He was a non-Buddhist with an ascetic named Dirghanakha as a teacher. As the Venerable [Punyamitra] was about to arrive, the king and the ascetic saw a white vapor that pervaded heaven and earth. The king asked, "What is this omen?" The ascetic already knew of the Venerable [Punyamitra's] arrival in the kingdom and, fearing loss of the king's favor, said, "It is an omen of the arrival of a demon. It is not at all a good omen." Then he called together his followers and discussed this with them, saying, "Punyamitra is about to enter the city. Who can discourage him?" A disciple said, "We have various spells. With them we can move heaven and earth or enter fire and water. What is there to be concerned about?"

The Venerable [Punyamitra] arrived and first saw a black vapor on the palace walls, and he said, "Just a slight difficulty." Then he went directly to the king, who asked him, "Why does the master come here?" The Venerable [Punyamitra] replied, "To liberate sentient beings." The king asked,

"What method will you use to liberate them?" The Venerable [Punyamitra] answered, "I liberate each in accordance with his type." When the ascetic heard this, he could hardly control his anger, and, with arts of illusion, he became a mountain on top of the Venerable [Punyamitra's] head. The Venerable [Punyamitra] pointed to the mountain and suddenly it was on top of the heads of the followers [of Dirghanakha]. The followers were frightened and turned to the Venerable [Punyamitra]. The Venerable [Punyamitra] pitied their ignorance and delusion, and, pointing [to the mountain] again, the mountain disappeared. Then he preached the essentials of the Dharma to the king and made him turn to the true teaching.

He also said to the king, "There is a wise man in this kingdom who will succeed me." At the time, there was a Brahmin youth about twenty years old. He had lost both parents in his youth and did not know what his name was. He called himself Keyura, so people called him "the young man Keyura." He passed time wandering about in country villages begging for food. He was like the [Bodhisattva] Sadaparibhuta ["Never Slighting Others"]. When people asked him, "Why do you walk so fast?" he answered, "Why do you walk so slow?"' Or, if they asked his family name, he answered, "The same as yours." No one knew the reason for this.

Later, the king and the Venerable [Punyamitra] arrived in the same cart. Seeing the young man Keyura bowing his head respectfully, the Venerable [Punyamitra] asked him, "Do you remember the past?" and so on. Finally [the youth said], "This present event is probably connected with that ancient cause."' The Venerable [Punyamitra] also told the king, "This young man is none other than the Bodhisattva Mahasthamaprapta.[165] Following this wise man, there will be two men—one who will teach in southern India, and one who will find conditions [for teaching] in China. In four or five years I want to return to this place." Finally, as a result of past causes, he named [the young man] Prajnatara.

Teisho

With regard to the patriarchal teachers who transmitted the Mind Seal of the Buddha and the sages who clarified the realm of Mind, being either arhats or bodhisattvas because they were not ignorant of the original Way, they were also eternally perfect Tathagatas. Though they seemed like beginners or veterans, if for one moment they reversed [the movement of] their minds and unveiled their original merits, not even a hair was lacking. They were the same as the Tathagata and one with the Venerable Ones. Even though it was not one appearing and one disappearing, they did not all extend a single hand together, nor were there numerous kinds or special divisions. To see today is to see eternity; if you look back at eternity, you observe today. They are born with you, and they abide with me, and there is not a hair of separation. Nor can it be said that we are not companions for even a second. When you can reach this realm, it is not past, present, or future; nor is it a matter of sense faculties, objects, and consciousness. Therefore, it is said that Dharma succession transcends the three times, and realization and experience pervade past and present. Because it is thus, a golden needle and a splendid thread are connected intimately. When you look carefully, what is "other"? What is "self"? Neither slender thread nor sharp point appears. At this point, you get a seat and surely share together.

In this story also, "The master preached *maha-prajna* and I recited the most profound sutra." If form [or any other of the aggregates] is pure, then inherent perfect wisdom is also pure; there is no difference or distinction. Sentient beings are Buddha nature; Buddha nature is sentient beings. The one does not enter things from outside, and the other does not convey the Dharma from inside. Though the two are distinguished in this way, ultimately there is no difference in the multiplicity. [The master] was named "He Who Brought Across *Prajna*" [i.e., from another life], in the same manner that the earlier Basiasita [was so named because of causes in the past life].[166] Past and present cannot be separated, so how can emptiness and existence be different? An ancient said, "If you thoroughly comprehend this and become [a person] without problems, what do you care if substance and function are distinguished or not distinguished?"[167]

If you see emptiness as the substance of the myriad things, not a thread or gossamer hair stands before you. If you see the myriad things as the function of emptiness, there is not a thread's worth or gossamer hair's worth of difference in their journey. At this point, the way of master and disciple is transmitted. Even to understand that the seal of approval of the Buddha patriarchs takes many forms,[168] you still seem to make distinctions. Even understanding that [master and disciple] are not two different people, you are like someone carrying a plank on your shoulder [and able to see only one side of it]. If you carefully examine and deliberate, a white heron standing in snow is not the same color, and bright moonlight and [white] reed flowers are not similar. Sauntering about in this way, you manage to heap snow in a silver bowl and hide a heron in bright moonlight.[169]

Verse

In order to clarify this story, I have a few humble words. Would the great assembly like to hear them?

> Moonlight reflected in the bottom of the pond is bright in the sky;
>> The water reaching to the sky is totally clear and pure.
>> Though you scoop it up repeatedly and try to know it,
>> Vast, clarifying all, it remains unknown.

BODHIDHARMA

Case

The twenty-eighth patriarch was the Venerable Bodhidharma. Once, the twenty-seventh patriarch, the Venerable Prajnatara, asked, "What among all things is formless?"[170] The master replied, "Non-arising is formless." The Patriarch asked, "What among all things is the greatest?" The master replied, "The [true] nature of things is the greatest."[171]

Circumstances

The master was a member of the warrior-ruler class and his name was originally Bodhitara. He was the third son of the king of Koshi in southern India.[172] The king's respect for the Buddhadharma was above the ordinary. Once, he gave Prajnatara a precious jewel as alms. The king had three sons: Chandravimalatara, Punyatara, and Bodhitara. The Venerable [Prajnatara] wanted to test the wisdom of the princes. He showed them the jewel he had been given, and asked, "Does anything compare with this jewel?" The first two sons said, "This jewel is the most precious of the seven treasures, and truly nothing can surpass it. No one without the Venerable [Prajnatara's] power of the Way could receive it." The third son, Bodhitara, said, "This is a worldly treasure and still does not qualify as the best. I consider the treasure of the Dharma to be the best of treasures. The light [of this jewel] is a worldly light and still does not qualify as the best. I consider the light of wisdom to be the best of lights. This is worldly brightness and still does not qualify as the best. I consider the brightness of Mind to be the best of all brightnesses. The bright light of this jewel cannot illuminate itself but needs the light of wisdom

in order for it to be discerned. Once you thoroughly discern it, you know it
is a jewel; once you know it is a jewel, then you clarify the fact that it is precious. When you clarify the fact that it is precious, its preciousness is not itself
precious. When you discern the jewel, the jewel is not itself a jewel. The
jewel's not being a jewel is because it is necessary to use the jewel of wisdom
in order to discern the worldly jewel. The preciousness not being itself precious is because it is necessary to use the treasure of wisdom to clarify the
treasure of the Dharma. Because the master's Way is the treasure of wisdom,
you now experience this worldly treasure. Thus, when the master has the
Way, this treasure appears, and when beings have the Way, this treasure
appears. When beings have the Way, the treasure of Mind also appears."

When the Venerable [Prajnatara] heard this explanation, he knew a sage
had been born. He discerned that [Bodhitara] would be a Dharma successor,
but the time had not come yet, so he remained silent and let [Bodhitara]
remain with the others. Then he asked, "What among all things is formless?"
The master replied, "Non-arising is formless." The Venerable [Prajnatara]
asked, "What among all things is the most exalted?" The master answered,
"The human self is the most exalted." The Venerable [Prajnatara] asked,
"What among all things is the greatest?" The master replied, "The [true]
nature of things is the greatest." Even though they questioned and answered
in this way, and the minds of master and disciple merged, [Prajnatara] waited
awhile for the complete maturing [of conditions].

Later, [Bodhitara's] father, the king, died. While people were grieving,
Bodhitara alone entered samadhi in front of the bier. After seven days, he
came out of samadhi, went to Prajnatara, and asked to make his home departure. Prajnatara knew that the time had come and had Bodhitara make his
home departure and receive the full precepts. Afterward, [Bodhitara] did
zazen for seven more days in Prajnatara's room, and Prajnatara instructed
him extensively in the wonderful principles of zazen. The master listened
and aroused the supreme wisdom. Then Prajnatara said, "You have now
acquired everything there is to know about all things. 'Dharma' means
'greatness of comprehension' so you should be named 'Dharma.'" Thus, he
changed his name to Bodhidharma.

Having made his home departure and having received the Dharma, the
master knelt and asked, "Since I have obtained the Dharma, to what land

should I go to do Buddha work?" Prajnatara said, "Though you have received the Dharma, you should stay awhile in southern India and wait until sixty-seven years after my death. Then go to China and contact those with a large capacity [for the Dharma]." The master asked, "Will they be able to become great vessels of the Dharma there? Will difficulties arise after a long time?" Prajnatara said, "Those who will acquire awakening in that land are beyond count. Some slight difficulties may arise, but you will be able to handle them yourself. When you arrive there, do not stay in the South. They only value conditioned [mundane] work there and do not see the [true] principles of the Buddhas." Then, he said in verse:

> You will journey across the water and encounter a sheep.
> Alone, you will cross a river secretly in the dark.
> There, under the sun, a pitiable pair acting like horses.
> Two small young cinnamon trees will flourish forever.

"You will find someone in your assembly of monks who will acquire the fruits of the Way." Then he said in verse:

> Though China is broad, there is no other path.
> Your activities must rely on your descendants.
> The golden pheasant can take up a single millet seed
> And offer it to all the arhats in the ten directions.[173]

In this way, Bodhidharma carefully received the seal and prediction, and served at [Prajnatara's] side for forty years.

After Prajnatara's death, a fellow student, Bodhisena, having received the seal of approval from Prajnatara, taught beside the Patriarch [Bodhidharma]. [Another student,] Bodhishanta separated the followers into six schools. The master taught the six schools, and his reputation was respected everywhere. When sixty-one years had passed, he knew that conditions were ripe in China. He went to the king[174] and said, "I must honor the Three Treasures and promote benefit [for all]. When conditions are ripe in China and I have finished my work, I will return." The king wept with grief and asked, "What is bad about this country? What is so auspicious about that land? In any event, when your work in China is finished, please return here at once. Do not forget the land of your parents." They went together to the port and the king personally saw him off. The master spent three years crossing the sea and arrived in south China on the twenty-first day of the ninth month in the year 527. The first thing he did was to have an audience with Emperor Wu of Liang and so on [as in the well-known story]. This is [what Prajnatara was referring to] when he said, "Do not stay in the South."

For this reason, he went [north] to [the Chinese kingdom of] Wei. It is said that he sailed [across the Yangtze River] on a reed. Now, usually, people think that it was [literally] a reed. But, it is a mistake [to think] that he rode on a single reed. The so-called reed was a small boat for crossing, not a reed. Its shape resembles a reed. "Meet a sheep" refers to the Liang emperor, Wu, and "you will cross a river in the dark"' refers to the Yangtze River. Thus, he soon arrived at Shaolin Monastery on Mount Song and stayed in the East Hall there. No one could figure him out. He just did zazen all day long. They called him the "wall-contemplating Brahmin." He did not speak boisterously or lightly [about the Dharma] for nine years.

Nine years later, after conferring his skin, flesh, bones, and marrow to Daofu, Daoyu, Zongchi, and Huike, he knew that the potential had matured. At the time, there were two nonbelievers named Bodhiruci and Vinaya Master Guandong.[175] Seeing the master's merits spread through the land and people turning to him and respecting him, they could not help being indignant. They not only hurled stones and knocked out his front teeth, they also tried five times to poison him. On the sixth attempt, he put the poison on a big rock and the rock shattered. [He thought,] "Conditions for teaching have ended." He thought, "I received the seal and prediction from my teacher, witnessed great conditions in China, and realized for sure that there was a capacity for the Dharma of the Great Vehicle. But after meeting Emperor Wu of Liang, the potential was not fulfilled, and I did not find anyone. While sitting alone in idleness, I found the Great Being Shengong and transmitted to him all of the Way I had acquired. The work is finished and the conditions have ended, so I should leave." So saying, he sat upright and died. He was buried on Bear's Ear Peak. Although it has been said that he later met Songyun in the Onion Range [of mountains in Turkestan], really, he was buried on Bear's Ear Peak, and that is the truth.

Teisho

There is no doubt that Bodhidharma was the First Patriarch in China, due to the prediction and instruction of the twenty-seventh patriarch. At the beginning, when [Bodhidharma] was a prince, the Venerable [Prajnatara] asked, with reference to the discussion of the jewel, "What among all things is formless?" The master said, "Non-arising is formless." Now, even if you say "nothingness," really, that is not formless. You can understand [this realm] as inaccessible like a ten-thousand-fathom-high precipice, or as brightly illuminating the distinctions of the many things. You can think of all things as being nothing other [than that], and that they remain just what they are, changeless, along with oneself,[176] but these are not at all non-arising. Therefore, they are not formless. Prior to the separation of heaven and earth, how can you distinguish holy and ordinary? In this realm, not a single thing can sprout, not a speck of dust can defile. However, it is not [the realm of] the original nonexistence of anything. Right now, it is empty and intelligent, alert and undazzled. Nothing can be compared to this realm, nor does anything else accompany it. It is, therefore, the greatest of the great, and it is said that "the great is called inconceivable." It is also said that "the inconceivable is called Dharma nature." Not even a priceless jewel can compare with it; not even the clear light of the Mind can represent it. [Bodhidharma] said, "This is a worldly light and does not qualify as the highest. I consider the light of wisdom to be the highest." Though this is the way he understood it and what he said was truly natural wisdom, he did zazen again for seven days. When he heard [the twenty-seventh patriarch] express the wonderful principles of zazen, he aroused the unsurpassed wisdom of the Way.

Thus, you must understand that this example of Bodhidharma shows that by reaching such a realm through careful discernment, you will understand right away that [awakening] which the Buddha patriarchs verified, and clarify what former Buddhas have already verified, and become descendants of the Buddha patriarchs. Even though he seemed to have natural wisdom, he again aroused the supreme wisdom of the Way. Later, he was careful in his attention to guard and protect [the Dharma] in the future. He served at the side [of his teacher] and investigated thoroughly and in detail. He spent sixty years without forgetting the prediction about the future. Then he spent three years crossing the ocean. At last he arrived in an unknown land. During his nine years of zazen, he acquired a [successor with a] great capacity for the Dharma and for the first time spread the Tathagata's True Dharma [in China], thus requiting the vast debt to his master. His hardships were the greatest; his austerities, the most austere.

However, students these days still hope that it will be easy, despite the degeneracy of the times and the weakness of capacities. I am afraid that people like these, who say they have understood what they have not, are proud, arrogant fellows who should retire [like the five hundred arhats in the *Lotus Sutra*]. People, if you thoroughly penetrate the foregoing story, understand its loftiness more and more, smash the mind and abandon the body and intimately discern the Way, you will get secret help from the Buddhas and directly share what the Buddha patriarchs have proven. Do not think that a morsel of knowledge or half an understanding is sufficient.

Verse

Again, I have some humble words. Would you like to hear them?

> *There is no distinction or location, no edge or outside.*
> *How could anything be larger than an autumn hair?*[177]

Dazu Huike

Case

The twenty-ninth patriarch, [China's Second Patriarch,] Great Master Dazu [Huike] studied with the twenty-eighth patriarch and served him. One day, he said to the Patriarch, "I have already put an end to all conditions." The Patriarch asked, "Doesn't that result in death?" The master replied, "It does not result in death." "What is your proof?" asked the Patriarch. "I am always clearly aware. Therefore, words are inadequate," said the master. The Patriarch said, "This is the Mind substance realized by all Buddhas. Have no doubt."

Circumstances

The master was from Wulao and his family name was Ji. His father was dead. Before [his father] had children, he would think, "Our family has always revered the good, so why can't we have children?" He prayed a long time. One night he saw a strange light illuminating the room, and [Huike's] mother became pregnant. When [Huike] grew, he was named Kuang ["Light"] because of the omen of the illuminated room. From childhood, his determination was unusual. He lived a long time in the region of the Yi and Luo [Rivers] and read extensively. He was not interested in the family property but enjoyed wandering the mountains and rivers. He would lament, "The teaching of Confucius and Laozi are nothing but rules for decorum and the [abstruse] arts. The *Zhuangzi* and *Yi Jing* do not get to the bottom of subtle principles."

He made his home departure and received the precepts from Zen Master Baojing of Mount Xiang, in Longmen. He traveled around to discussions [of Buddhist teachings] and extensively studied the doctrines of the Great and Small Vehicles. One day, he saw [the teaching of] prajna in some Buddhist books and acquired it spontaneously in a flash. After that, he sat peacefully in zazen day and night for eight years, and in the silence [of meditation], a spirit appeared. It said, "If you want to acquire results, why be stuck here? The great Way is not far—go south.'" Realizing that the light was spiritual help, he changed his name to Shenguang ["Spiritual Light"]. The next day, his head hurt, as if he had been stabbed. While his master was trying to cure it, a voice from the sky said, "It is your bones changing, not an ordinary illness." Kuang finally told the master about seeing the spirit. The master inspected his head and found five lumps like mountain peaks. He said, "These signs are auspicious; you will become awakened. The south that the spirit directed you to must refer to the Great Being Bodhidharma at Shaolin Monastery. He should be your teacher."

Receiving this instruction, Kuang went to Shaolin Monastery on Mount Song. It was the ninth day of the twelfth month of the year 528. The Great Master [Bodhidharma] would not allow him to enter the room and so the master [Shenguang] stood outside the window. That night it snowed hard, but he remained standing in the snow, waiting for dawn. Deepening snow buried him to the waist, and the cold pierced his bones. His falling tears froze drop by drop, making him even colder. He thought to himself, "When the ancients sought the Way, they pounded their bones and extracted the marrow, drew blood to relieve thirst, spread their hair to cover mud, and threw themselves off cliffs to feed tigers. If the ancients were like this, what kind of man am I?" So thinking, he strengthened his resolve and remained standing, unmoving and unflinching.

When dawn came, the Great Master [Bodhidharma] saw that he had stood all night in the snow. He asked in pity, "You have stood a long time in the snow. What do you want?" The master answered, "I beg you, O priest, open the door of ambrosia in your compassion and deliver us common beings everywhere." The Great Master replied, "The supreme, wonderful Way of the Buddhas takes eons of diligently practicing what is hard to practice and enduring what is difficult to endure. How can you struggle in vain and hope to obtain the true vehicle with such slight merits, deficient understanding, thoughtlessness, and pride?" And so saying, he ignored [Shenguang]. When the master heard this compassionate instruction, he wept even more. His determination to seek the Way grew firmer and firmer.

He at once picked up a sharp sword and cut off his left arm. The Great Master realized that [Shenguang] was a receptacle for the Dharma and said, "When Buddhas seek the Dharma in the very beginning, they forget their bodies for the sake of the Dharma. You have now cut off your arm in front of me. You have the potential to seek [the Dharma]." The master subsequently changed his name to Huike ["Potential for the Dharma"] and was permitted to enter the room.

He served [Bodhidharma] for eight years. One time, the master asked Bodhidharma, "Can the seal of the Buddhadharma be had by hearing?" The Great Master replied, "The seal of the Buddhadharma cannot be acquired through hearing." Once [Bodhidharma] said, "When you still all conditions externally and there is no more gasping by the mind internally, and the mind becomes like a wall—then you will enter the Way." Even though the master [Huike] often spoke about Mind and essential nature, he did not become one with the truth. The Great Master just checked his errors without speaking of the substance of Mind that is no-thought.

The *Profound Functioning within the Room*[178] says, "Once [Huike] was attending Bodhidharma while they were climbing a great peak. Bodhidharma asked him, 'Which way does the path go?' The master answered, 'Please go straight ahead; that's it.' Bodhidharma said, 'If you try to continue straight ahead, you will not be able to move a step.' When the master heard this, he was awakened." Once, he said to the Great Master, "I have already put an end to all external conditions," and so on, and the Great Master said, "Have no doubt." Finally, [Bodhidharma] conferred the robe and bowl on him, saying, "Within, the seal of the Dharma is transmitted, thus confirming the enlightened Mind. Externally, the robe and bowl are conferred, thus establishing the [correct] teaching." Consequently, after the Great Master died, the master succeeded him and established the usages of the tradition.

When he conferred the Dharma on [his own successor,] Sengcan, he said, "I still have some karma from former lives and now I have to pay for it." Conferring [the Dharma on Sengcan], he preached the Dharma in the capitol of Ye as circumstances allowed, and the four groups [of female and male laity and monastics] took refuge in him. He spent thirty years doing this, concealing the light and obliterating all traces [of his status], mixing with ordinary people—sometimes entering wine shops, sometimes engaging in street talk, sometimes joining workers who empty the privies. People would ask him, "The master is a man of the Way; why do you do these things?" He would reply, "I am training my own mind; why should that concern you?" Later, he expounded the essentials of the Dharma beneath the gates of Kuangjiao Monastery in Guancheng District, and the four groups gathered in hordes. At the time, there was a person named Dharma Master Bianhe who lectured on the *Nirvana Sutra* at the monastery. When people heard the master's Dharma talks, they were gradually attracted to him. Bianhe could not help becoming angry, and he slandered the master to a local official named Di Zhongkan. Deluded by this wicked talk, Zhongkan accused the master of [preaching] false doctrine. The master submitted peacefully [to execution] on the sixteenth day of the third month of [the year] 593.

Teisho

To begin with, though there is neither superiority nor inferiority in the merits of the Patriarchs, the master is the honored of the honored and venerable of the venerable. The reason is that even though Bodhidharma came from India, if the master had not transmitted and spread [the Dharma], the teaching would not have come down to the present. His sufferings were greater than anyone's; his aspiration, beyond that of others. The First Patriarch [Bodhidharma] did not speak for a long time while he waited for a true man and did not give any special teachings to the Second Patriarch. He just said, "When you put an end to all external conditions and there is no grasping of the mind internally, and the mind becomes like a wall, then you will enter the Way." Truly, if you stop thoughts this way, you will reveal the substance of Mind. Hearing such words, you will try to become mindless like a wall. This is not the intimate experience of the Mind. [Huike] said, "I am always clearly aware." If you can become like this, then this is what the Buddhas have realized.

Therefore, if you put an end to conditions externally, the many thoughts will no longer exist internally. Without becoming darkened, you will be alert, clear and originally bright. You will not distinguish past and present, nor will you distinguish self and others. Because there is not a hair's tip of difference between what the Buddhas validated and the Mind that has been transmitted by the patriarchs, being completely harmonized and identical, this has been transmitted in India and China and unites China and Japan. It has been so in the past and it remains so now, so do not just yearn for the past. You must practice without finding fault with the present. Do not think that it has been a long time since we left the sage [Shakyamuni]. Do not give up on yourself [as worthless]; just clarify this.

Verse

As usual, I have some humble words. Would you like to hear them?

In the realm that is empty and bright, conditions and thought are exhausted;
It is clear, alert, and always bright.

JIANZHI SENGCAN

Case

The thirtieth patriarch, [China's Third Patriarch,] was Great Master Jianzhi [Sengcan]. He visited the twenty-ninth patriarch and said, "My body is infected with leprosy. I beg you, O priest, to cleanse me of my wrong doing." The Patriarch said, "Bring me your wrongdoing and I will cleanse you." The master paused awhile and then said, "When I look for my wrong-doing, I cannot find it." The Patriarch replied, "I have already cleansed you of your wrongdoing. You must rely on the Buddha, Dharma, and Community of believers."

Circumstances

It is not known where the master was from. He was a layman when he first called on the Second [Chinese] Patriarch. He was over forty and did not mention his family name. He just arrived suddenly, made prostrations, and said, "My body is infected with leprosy," and so on. [The Patriarch said], "You must rely on the Buddha, Dharma, and Community of believers." The master said, "Seeing you, I already know what a monk is, but I still do not know what you mean by Dharma and Community." The Patriarch said, "Mind is Buddha, Mind is Dharma. The Dharma and the Buddha are not two, and the treasure of the Community is the same." The master said, "Today, for the first time, I know that the nature of wrongdoing is neither inside nor outside, nor in-between. Mind is the same, and Buddha and Dharma are not two either." The Patriarch was deeply impressed with his capacity for the Dharma. So, he had his head shaved and told him, "You are my treasure.

You will be called, 'Jewel of the Community' [i.e., Sengcan]." He gave him the precepts at Guangfu Monastery on the eighteenth day of the third month of that year, and [Sengcan's] illness gradually went away.

He spent two years serving [the Second Patriarch], and the Patriarch said to him, "Great Master Bodhidharma came here from India and conferred both the robe and Dharma on me. I am also conferring them on you." He also said, "Though you have already acquired the Dharma, you must go into the deep mountains and not teach. There will be problems in the kingdom [for Buddhists]." The master said, "Since the master knows beforehand, please instruct me." The Patriarch replied, "I do not know. When Bodhi dharma passed on the prediction he got from Prajnatara, he said, 'Although [receiving the Dharma] is good luck in the mind, it is bad luck outside.' This [difficulty] is what he meant. When I calculate the years [he mentioned], they refer to you beyond doubt. You must think clearly about these words and not get involved in these secular difficulties." After that, [Sengcan] hid himself on Mount Huangong for over ten years. This was the time of the per-secution of the Buddhadharma by Emperor Wu of the [Northern] Zhou Dynasty. Consequently, he remained at Mount Sikong [and other places] without any permanent dwelling. He also altered his appearance.

While doing this, he met the monk Daoxin [and taught him]. Later, he told him, "After my former master transmitted [the Dharma] to me, he went to the capitol of Ye and spent thirty years there. Now that I have found you, why should I remain here?" He went to Mount Luofu and later returned to his former abode. People congregated in great numbers and supported him generously. When the master finished expounding the essentials of Mind for the four groups [of male and female monastics and laity] he joined his hands together beneath a large tree at the Dharma meeting and died [while stand-ing]. His words are recorded in *Inscriptions on Trusting Mind,* and the work exists today. Later, he was given the posthumous name of Jianzhi ["Mirror-like Wisdom"].

Teisho

When he first met [Huike] and said that he was ill, he had leprosy. How-ever, the story of karmic illness suddenly clearing up is not unusual. Under-standing that the nature of wrongdoing is ungraspable, he was enlightened to the fact the Mind is originally pure. As a result, he learned that Buddha and Dharma are not two and that Mind is the same. When you thoroughly understand the original Mind, there is no difference between dying here and being born there, so how could there be any difference between wrong doing and the roots of good? Consequently, the four great elements and the five aggregates ultimately do not exist; the skin, flesh, bones, and marrow are intrinsically liberated. Therefore, the leprosy was cured and the Original Mind appeared. Finally, he ranked as the Third Patriarch.

In extensively preaching the essentials of the Dharma, he said [in *Inscriptions on Trusting Mind*], "The Supreme Way is not difficult; it is just avoiding picking and choosing." At the end of the poem, he says, "Words are terminated and it is not past, present, or future." There is no inside or outside [here], nor between, so what is there to choose or reject? You cannot take, nor can you reject. Once there is neither hate nor love, you are bright and clear. There is nothing lacking with regard to time, nothing left over with regard to things. However, though this is how it is, by carefully investigating you will find the place of the ungraspable and arrive at the limit of the inconceivable. If you do not become an annihilationist and do not become like wood or stone—if you strike the sky and make an echo, bind together the clouds and make forms, carefully observe the place where all traces are gone and still not hide there—you will be fine. If you become thus, then even though [the supreme Way] is not something you can observe or something reachable by eyes or ears, you will be able to see it without a hair of hindrance and be able to understand it without a speck of error.

Verse

Now, how can I say something of a discerning nature about this story?

> *Empty of essential nature, without inside or outside,*
> *Good and bad leave no traces.*
> *Mind and Buddha are fundamentally the same,*
> *And Dharma and Community can be understood in the same way.*

DAYI DAOXIN

Case

The thirty-first patriarch [China's Fourth Patriarch], Zen Master Dayi [Daoxin], bowed to the Great Master Jianzhi and said, "I beg the priest in his great compassion to give me the teaching of liberation." The Patriarch replied, "Who is binding you?" The master said, "No one is binding me." The Patriarch answered, "Then why are you seeking liberation?" With these words, the master was greatly awakened.

Circumstances

The master's name was Daoxin. His family name was Sima. The family had lived for generations in Henei. Later, they moved to Guangji District in Shanzhou. From birth, he was highly remarkable. From youth, he was fond of the teaching of liberation of the schools that taught emptiness, as if he had known them from former lives. He went to see the Great Master, the Third Patriarch, at the age of thirteen. [Some time later][179] he asked him, "I beg the priest in his compassion," and so on. Hearing these words, he was greatly awakened. He served [the Third Patriarch] for nine years. Later he received the precepts at Shanzhou, guarded them, and was very conscientious about them. The Patriarch repeatedly tested him on the deep subtleties, and when he knew the time was ripe, he conferred the robe and bowl.

Succeeding the Patriarch, the master was mindful [at all times] and did not sleep in a prone position for nearly sixty years. In 617, he went to Shanzhou with some followers. A band of robbers had surrounded the city for seventy days and the many inhabitants were terrified. The master pitied them and taught them to recite the *Maha-prajna [paramita Sutra]*. When the robbers looked at the walls of the city, it looked as if there were an army of spirits, and they said, "There must be a remarkable person in the city. We had better not attack." So, they went away. In 624, the master returned to Shanzhou and stayed that spring on Mount Potou [i.e., Potou Shan, "Broken Top"]. Students came in droves. One day, on the road to Huangmei, he became deeply acquainted with Hongren [his successor], and also [met Farong and] produced a branch of his line on Mount Niutou.[180]

In 643, Emperor Taizong took an interest in the master's teachings and wanted a taste for himself, so he summoned him to the capitol. The master humbly refused three times and finally refused because of illness. On the fourth attempt, the emperor ordered his emissary, "If he does not come, cut off his head." The emissary went to the monastery and explained the royal edict. The master stretched out his neck for the sword, composed in mind and body. The emissary thought that this was remarkable and relayed the master's attitude to the emperor. The emperor respected the master even more and expressed his admiration with a gift of precious cloth.

On the fourth day of the ninth month in 651, he suddenly said to his followers, "All things are completely liberated. You must each keep this in mind and pass it on to posterity." When he finished speaking, he sat peacefully in meditation and expired. He was seventy-one years old. He was entombed there on the mountain. The next year, on the eighth day of the fourth month, the door of the tomb opened by itself. He looked just as he had in life. After that, his disciples did not dare to shut the door again. Later, he was given the posthumous name of Dayi ["Great Physician"].

Teisho

Even though there is neither superiority nor inferiority in the conduct of the patriarchs, he was inclined toward the teaching of emptiness from his youth, almost as if it were a habit from a former life. Throughout his life, he never associated with rulers or their officials. Studying and training, he never retrogressed in his determination. In the beginning, he expounded the teaching of liberation. In addition, when he died, he opened the Dharma gates of liberation, teaching people in the end that they are not bound by life and death. He was a truly remarkable person, one encountered but once in a thousand years. The practice [of the doctrine] of emptiness has been called the teaching of liberation right from the beginning. If neither beings nor Buddha bind you, how can you be concerned with life and death? Thus, it is not to be pondered as body or mind, neither is it to be discriminated as delusion or enlightenment. Though you may speak of Mind or the objective world, and though you may speak of defilement or awakening, these are all just names for one's [true] Self. Therefore, mountains and rivers are not apart from it, nor is it different from you and your external environment. When it is cold, you become totally cold; when it is hot, you become totally hot.[181]

Once this barrier [of liberation] is crossed, this principle [of liberation] no longer exists [either]. That is to say, there is no bondage, no liberation, no that, no this. Therefore, none of these names is established, none of the shapes of things is distinguished. You penetrate the results [of practice], so how can you be concerned with relative and absolute.[182] There are no distinctions in this place, nor should you get stuck in any direction. If you can see in this way, you will not use the word "liberation," so how can you hate bondage?

You truly have a light, and this is called "seeing the three worlds." Your tongue has an abundance of the sense of taste. This is called "blending the six tastes." You emanate the light everywhere and blend delicacies at all times. Taste and taste though you may, there is something delicious where there is nothing delicious. Look and look though you may, there is a true form where there are no forms. Therefore, there are no rulers or officials to associate with, nor a body-mind that sits or lies down. If you can reach this realm, then the Fourth Patriarch, the Great Master, will be you, and you will surely be the Fourth Patriarch. Isn't this [Daoxin's] "All things are liberated"? Isn't this his "Pass it on to posterity"? The door of the seamless tomb opens by itself, and the everyday features are revealed peaceful and mild.

Verse

I also have some humble words today, and I would like to express the meaning of this story. Would you like to hear them?

> Mind is empty, and pure knowing contains no right or wrong.
> In this, what is there to be bound or liberated?
> Even though it becomes the four great elements and five skandhas,
> In the end, seeing, hearing, forms, and sounds are nothing else [than Mind].

DAMAN HONGREN

Case

The thirty-second patriarch, [China's Fifth Patriarch,] Zen Master Daman, met the thirty-first patriarch on the road to Huangmei. The Patriarch asked him, "What is your family name [Ch. *xing*]?" The master replied, "I have a nature [Ch. *xing*] but it is not an ordinary name [Ch. *xing*]." The Patriarch asked, "What is its name?" Replied the master, "It is Buddha nature [Ch. *fo xing*]." The Patriarch asked, "Have you no name?" The master answered, "Because [Buddha] nature is empty, I have none." The Patriarch thought to himself that he was a vessel of the Dharma and transmitted the Dharma and robe to him.

Circumstances

The master was from Huangmei Province in Shanzhou. Previously [in his former life] he had been a pine-planting pilgrim on Mount Potou. He once asked the Fourth Patriarch, "May I hear the Buddhadharma?" The Patriarch replied, "You are old. Even if you hear it, would you be able to teach it very long? If you come again [in the next life], I will wait for you." [The pilgrim] left and went to a river, where he saw a young girl washing clothes. He bowed and asked her, 'May I have lodging for the night?" [i.e., "May I temporarily borrow your womb?"]. The girl replied, "I will have to ask my parents." He said, "If they consent, I will go [and do it]." She assented, and finally she returned to her village.

The girl was the youngest daughter of a family named Zhou. When she returned home, she was pregnant. Her parents detested her and drove her out of the house. She had no place to turn to, so she worked in the village as a spinner by day and stayed at an inn by night. Finally, she had a child and, thinking that he was unlucky, left him in the river. However, he was not swept away by the current, and he was not even wet. Spirits protected and cared for him for seven days. These spirits were two birds who covered him with their wings during the day, and two dogs who guarded him at night by crouching over him. He remained fresh in body and mind with no loss of faculties. When she saw this, his mother thought it was remarkable and began to feed him. He begged for food with his mother while he was growing up. People called him the "nameless child." A wise man said, "The child has all but seven of the marks of a Tathagata."

Later, he met the Fourth Patriarch on a walk on Mount Huangmei. The Fourth Patriarch thought that his bone structure was unusual and quite unlike that of an ordinary boy. So he asked him, "What is your name?" and so on, and silently recognized him as a vessel of the Dharma. [The Patriarch] asked [the master's] mother if [the master] could be his attendant. [The Patriarch] had him make his home departure. At this time, [the master] was seven years old. After he made his home departure, he received ordination, the robes [of a monk], and the Dharma. There wasn't an hour out of the whole day when he did not do zazen. Though he did not neglect his other tasks, this is how much he did zazen. At the end, in 675, he said to his followers, "My work is finished, so I will depart." Saying, "I am going to die," he died sitting.

Teisho

There is a name [xing] that is not received from one's father or ancestors, and that is not inherited from the Buddhas or Patriarchs. It is called "Buddha nature." Now, fundamentally, practicing Zen and learning the Way is for the sake of reaching the fundamental, and clarifying the nature of Mind. If you do not reach the fundamental, you are born and die in vain, deluded about self and others. As for so-called intrinsic nature, you people die and die and are born again and again. Even though face after face and body after body is different, never for a moment are you lacking in completely clear knowing. This is clear from the present story.

From the time in the past when the pilgrim requested the Way of the Dharma to the present when [Hongren] received the robe and Dharma as a seven-year-old boy, the Mind had not changed because of the life, nor had its nature altered as the body changed. In Zen Master Hongzhi's eulogy to the true portrait of Great Master Hongren, he said, "Previous and later lives, two bodies; past and present, one Mind." Even though the two bodies were different, there was not a different Mind in past and present, so, you must realize that for incalculable eons, it has been just like this. If you can attain this original nature, this nature cannot be understood in terms of the four [Hindu] social classes, of course. Since the four classes all have the same nature, and since this is the way original nature is, then when any of the four classes make their home departure, all [individuals] are called "Shakya'" to show that there are no distinctions of class [in Buddhism].

Truly, [this nature] is not separated into "me" and "you." It merely bears the faces of self and other, and we discriminate it like the previous and later bodies [of Hongren]. By not being able to clarify the Mind, we ignorantly become fascinated with what we see in front of us and divide it into this body and that body. Consequently, we become attached to each thing and are often deluded. However, once you are able to clarify this realm, even though you change forms and move from life to life, how can that hinder the Self or alter the Mind?

You should understand this through [the story of] the pilgrim and the boy. Since he was born without a father, you should realize that people are not necessarily born from the blood lines of father and mother. Thus, even though according to popular views, the body, hair, and skin are inherited from one's father and mother, you must understand that this body is not the five aggregates. If you understand the body like this, there is nothing at all besides the Self, and there is not an instant when you are different from the Self. Therefore, an ancient said, "All sentient beings have eternally been immersed in the samadhi of ultimate reality."[183] If you can experience it in this way and practice it in this way, you will speedily meet the Fourth Patriarch and stand shoulder to shoulder with the Fifth Patriarch. There is no separation between Japanese and Chinese, no distinction of past and present.

Verse

How can I comment appropriately?

> Moon bright, water pure, the autumn sky clear,
> How can a speck of cloud mark this immense purity?

Dajian Huineng

Case

The thirty-third patriarch, [China's Sixth Patriarch,] was Zen Master Dajian [Huineng]. He worked in the rice-hulling shed at Huangmei. Once, Zen Master Daman [Hongren] entered the shed and asked, "Is the rice white yet?" The master answered, "It's white, but it hasn't been sifted yet." Daman struck the mortar three times with his staff. The master shook the sifting basket three times and entered the Patriarch's room.

Circumstances

The master's family name was Lu. His ancestors were from Fanyang. His father was named Xingtao. In the first quarter of the seventh century, [Xingtao] was demoted and sent to Xinzhou in the far south, where he finally settled. [Huineng's] father died and his mother took care of him. While he was growing, the family was very poor and the master earned a living chopping and selling wood. One day he went to the city with a bundle of kindling and he heard a customer reciting the *Diamond-cutter Sutra* [*Vajracchedika-prajnaparamita Sutra*]. When the customer reached the place where it said, "You should raise an unsupported thought," [Huineng] was awakened. He asked the customer, "What scripture is this? From whom did you get it?" The customer replied, "This is the *Diamond-cutter Sutra* and I got it from the Great Master Hongren, at Huangmei."

The master spoke to his mother at once about looking for a teacher so he could find the Dharma. He went directly to Shaozhou and visited a lofty-minded man named Liu Zhiliu and they became friends. The nun Wujin

Cang was Zhiliu's mother-in-law and she was always reciting the *Nirvana Sutra*. The master listened to her for a while and then told her what it meant. The nun picked up a scroll and asked about some words. The master said, "I can't read." The nun marveled at this and said to the village elders, "Huineng has the Way. We ought to invite him [to stay] and support him." So, the people competed to greet him and pay their respects.

There was an old temple nearby by the name of Baolin. The people all got together, rebuilt it, and invited the master to stay there. The four groups [of male and female monastics and lay people] gathered in droves. It quickly became a place where the Dharma flourished. One day, the master suddenly thought, "I am seeking the great Dharma. Why stop halfway?" He left the next day and went to the caves of the western part of Zhangluo Province. There he met Zen Master Zhiyuan, whom he asked for help. The master said, "When I look at you, I see an expression that is quite superior, not at all like that of ordinary people. I hear that the Indian Bodhidharma has transmitted the Mind Seal to [Hongren] Huangmei. You should go there to see him and become certain."

The master thanked him and left, going directly to Huangmei, where he visited Zen Master Daman. The Patriarch asked him, "Where are you from?" The master replied, "I come from Lingnan." The Patriarch asked, "What are you looking for?" The master answered, "I just want to become a Buddha." The Patriarch said, "People from Lingnan have no Buddha nature. How can you expect to become a Buddha?" The master answered, "Among people there are northerners and southerners, but can that be true of Buddha nature?" The Patriarch realized that he was an unusual person and sent him to the rice-hulling shed. Huineng bowed and left. He went to the rice-hulling shed where he toiled at the mortar day and night without letup for eight months. The Patriarch, realizing that the time had come for passing on [the Dharma], told the monks, "The True Dharma is hard to understand. Don't just pointlessly remember what I say and make that your responsibility. I want each of you to compose a verse that shows what you understand. If the words display the truth, I will confer the robe and the Dharma."

At the time, Shenxiu, senior monk among more than seven hundred monks, was conversant with both Buddhist and non-Buddhist learning and was admired by everyone. They praised him, saying, "If not the honorable

Xiu, then who?" Shenxiu caught wind of this and thought no more. When he finished composing his verse, he went several times to the master's room to present it, but he felt unsure and broke out in sweat. He could not present it. He tried fourteen times in three days but could not present the verse. Then he thought, "It would be better if I write it on the wall. If Hongren sees it and says it is good, I will appear and say it is mine. If he says it is unsatis-factory, I will go into the mountains and spend my time there. What kind of path can I practice just accepting the homage of others?" That night around midnight, when no one could see him, he took a lamp and wrote a verse on the wall of the South Hall, presenting his understanding. Here is the verse:

> The body is the tree of enlightenment;
> The mind is like a bright mirror-stand.
> Wipe it clean over and over,
> And do not let the dust gather.

The Patriarch was walking around and saw the verse. He knew it was Shenxiu's verse and praised it, saying, "If later generations practice in accor-dance with it, they will get excellent results." He made everyone memorize it. The master was pounding rice and heard someone reciting the verse. He asked another monk, "What are these phrases?" The other monk said, "Don't you know? The master is looking for an heir and everyone has to compose a verse about Mind. These sentences were composed by the sen-ior monk Shenxiu. The master praised them highly. He will surely pass on the Dharma and robe [to Shenxiu]." The master asked, "How does the verse go?" The other student recited it for him. The master was silent for a while and then said, "It's really excellent, all right, but it's not quite perfect." The other monk shouted at him, "What does a simpleton like you know? Don't talk crazy!" The master replied, "Don't you believe me? Then I'll add a verse to it." The student just looked at him and laughed. That night, the master took a young servant boy with him and went to the hall. The master held a lamp and had the servant add a verse next to Shenxiu's. It said,

> Enlightenment is essentially not a tree;
> The bright mirror is not a stand.

From the beginning, not a single thing exists;
Where can the dust collect?

When they saw the verse, everyone in the monastery said, "This is the verse of a living bodhisattva." Everyone praised it loudly. The Patriarch knew it was Huineng's verse and said, "Whoever wrote this has not yet seen his [original] face," and erased it. Consequently, the other monks totally ignored it. During the night, the Patriarch secretly went to the rice-hulling shed and asked, "Is the rice white?" The master answered, "It's white, but it hasn't been sifted yet." The Patriarch then struck the mortar three times with his staff and the master shook the sifting basket three times and entered the [Patriarch's] room.

The Patriarch said, "Buddhas appear in the world for the sake of the one great matter and guide people according to their faculties. Finally, such things as the ten stages, three vehicles, and sudden and gradual [enlightenment] become teachings. Moreover, [the Buddha] conferred the unsurpassed, extremely subtle, intimate, perfectly marvelous true Treasury of the Eye of the True Dharma on his senior disciple, the Venerable Mahakashyapa. It has been transmitted successively from patriarch to patriarch up to Bodhidharma in the twenty-eighth generation. When he came here, he found Great Master Huike, and it was [eventually] passed on to me. Now, I pass on the Dharma treasure and robe that have been transmitted. You must guard them well and not allow [the Dharma] to perish."

The master knelt and received the robe and Dharma and asked, "I have now received the Dharma, but on whom should I confer the robe [later]?" The Patriarch replied, "Long ago, when Bodhidharma first arrived, people lacked faith, so he transmitted the robe to show that one had obtained the Dharma. Faith has matured now, but the robe will become a point of contention, so let it stop with you and not be passed on. You had better go away and hide. Wait for the right time before you teach. It is said that the life of a person who has received the robe hangs by a thread." The master asked, "Where should I hide?" The Patriarch said, "Stop when you get to Huai; hide a while when you reach Hui." The master prostrated himself before the Patriarch, took the robe and left. There was a ferry at the foot of Mount Huangmei and the Patriarch personally escorted him there. The master bowed and said, "You should go back. Since I have found the Way, I should cross over myself." The Patriarch answered, "Though you have already found the Way, I still have to cross over." So saying, he took the pole and crossed over to the other shore. The Patriarch returned alone to the monastery without anyone finding out.

After that, the Fifth Patriarch no longer entered the hall [to give Dharma talks]. If monks came and questioned him, he said, "My Way is gone." They would ask, "Who has received the robe and Dharma?" and the Patriarch would answer, "An able [neng] one has acquired it." The monks reasoned, "The workman Lu's name is neng [able]," but when they called on him, he was missing. They realized that he had acquired [the robe and Dharma] and set out after him.

At that time, there was [a monk] named Huiming who had aroused the thought of enlightenment after having been in the army, and he became their leader. He followed the master and overtook him in the Dayu Range [of mountains]. The master said, "This robe symbolizes faith. It is not something to compete for with force." He placed the robe and bowl on a rock and hid in some grass.

When Huiming arrived and tried to lift them, he could not do it, try as he may. He said, trembling greatly, "I came for the Dharma, not the robe." Huineng emerged and sat on the rock. Huiming bowed and said, "Please, workman, explain the essentials of the Dharma for me." The master said, "Not thinking of good, not thinking of evil, at the very moment, what is your original face?" Hearing these words, Huiming was greatly awakened. Then, he asked, "Is there a secret meaning beyond the secret words you have spoken just now?" The master answered, "What I have said to you is not secret. If you reflect inwardly, the secret is there within."' Huiming said, "Although I dwell at Huangmei, I have not yet looked within and discovered my own face. Now, I have received your teaching and I am like someone who drinks water and knows for sure whether it is warm or cold. You are now my master." The master said, "If it is as you say, we both have Huangmei [Hongren] for a master." Huiming bowed gratefully and withdrew.

Later, when [Huiming] was an abbot, he changed his name from Hui ming to Daoming, to avoid using the first part of the master's name [out of respect]. When someone came there to practice, he always sent him to practice with the master.

After receiving the robe and Dharma, the master hid himself among hunters in Xixian. After ten years, on the eighth day of the first month of 676, he moved to the far south where he encountered Dharma Master Yinzong lecturing on the *Nirvana Sutra* at Fa Xing Temple. He lodged in the hallway. The wind was blowing a banner and he heard two monks arguing, one saying it was the banner that was moving, and the other saying that it was the wind moving. They talked back and forth but did not hit on the truth. The master said, "If a lowly layman may interrupt your lofty discussion, it is neither the banner nor the wind that is moving; it is your minds that are moving."[184] When Yinzong heard about this discussion, he was astonished and thought it was quite remarkable. The next day, he summoned the master to his room and asked about the meaning of the banner and wind. The master explained the principle fully and Yinzong arose involuntarily, saying, "You are definitely not an ordinary person. Who are you?" The master then told him of the circumstances of receiving the Dharma, concealing nothing. Thereupon, Yinzong made the bow of a student and asked for the essentials of Zen. He told his own followers, "I am a thoroughly ordinary man, but I have just met a living bodhisattva." He then pointed to the layman Lu in the group and said, "There he is." Then he asked that the robes of faith that had been transmitted be brought out so that everyone could pay homage to them.

On the fifteenth of the same month, all the well-known monks were called together so that [Huineng] could have his head shaved. On the eighth day of the second month, he received the complete precepts from Precept Master Zhiguang of Faxing Temple. The platform used for giving the precepts had been established earlier in the Sung Dynasty by Tripitaka Master Gunabhadra.[185] He had predicted, "Later there will be a living bodhisattva who will receive the precepts on this platform." Also, near the end of the Liang Dynasty, Tripitaka Master Paramartha had planted two *bodhi* trees beside the platform with his own hands, telling the monks, "A hundred and twenty years from now a greatly awakened man will appear and expound the unexcelled Way beneath these trees and liberate innumerable beings."[186] After taking the precepts, the master taught the Dharma teaching of the Eastern Mountain, just as had been foretold so long ago.

The next year, on the eighth day of the second month, the master suddenly said to the monks, "I do not want to stay here anymore; I am going to return to my former dwelling." Accordingly, Yinzong and more than a thousand monks and lay people escorted him back to Baolin Monastery. Weiju, the governor of Guangzhou, invited him to turn the wheel of the Dharma at Dafan Temple and also received the formless precepts of Mind. Huineng's followers recorded his talks, calling them the "Platform Scripture," which is well known. Then he returned to Caoxi Monastery and showered down the rain of the great Dharma. His students numbered over a thousand. At the age of seventy-five, he died sitting in dignity in zazen.

Teisho

When the transmission took place, like water passed from one container to another without a drop being spilled, [Hongren] asked, "Is the rice white yet?" These grains of rice are surely the marvelous sprouts that will become a King of Dharma, the life-roots of both sages and ordinary people. Once planted in wild fields, they grow even without weeding. Husked and polished, they take on no impurity. However, though this is how they are, they are still unsifted. If they are sifted, they pervade inside and outside, and move up and down. When the mortar was struck three times, the rice grains were scooped out of the mortar spontaneously and the functioning of Mind was suddenly bared. When the rice was sifted three times, the [spirit of the] Patriarch was transmitted. Since then, the night when the mortar was struck has not brightened, the day of transmission has not darkened.

It seems that the master was a wood cutter from Lingnan and was the workman Lu in the rice-hulling shed. In old times, he wandered in the mountains earning a living with an ax. Even though he had not studied the ancient [Buddhist] teachings and illuminated his mind, still, just by hearing one sentence from the scriptures about raising an unsupported thought, he finally ended up in the rice-hulling mill with a mortar and pestle. Although he never practiced Zen, raised Dharma questions, or experienced awakening [in the usual manner], by working diligently for eight months, he illumined the mind as a bright mirror that is not a stand. In the middle of the night, the transmission took place and the lifeblood of successive patriarchs was transmitted. Though it was not necessarily the result of many years effort, it is clear that for just a brief period he put forth the utmost effort. The achievement of the Way by all Buddhas cannot essentially be measured in terms of long and short time periods. How can you grasp the transmission of the Way by patriarchal teachers through such distinctions as past and present?

Moreover, for ninety days this summer [during the *ango*, training period],[187] I have spoken of this and that, commenting on the past and present, and explaining the lives of the Buddha patriarchs with wild and gentle words. I have gone into the subtle and fine [which words cannot describe] and treated you all like sons and grandsons, and more, besmirching the Zen tradition and displaying our shame. Consequently, you may think that you have penetrated the truth and acquired power, but you do not seem to have accorded intimately with the intentions of the patriarchs. Your behavior is not at all like that of our wise predecessors. Because of causes in past lives and good luck, we have been able to meet. If you single-mindedly make an effort in the Way, you will achieve the Way, but many of you have not yet reached the other shore. You have still not peeked into the profound heart of the matter. It has been a long time since the Buddha went away. You have not completed your work in the Way, and life is slipping away, so why wait until tomorrow? Summer is over and fall begins. You will be taking off in all directions, scattering here and there as always. How can you recklessly memorize a word or half a sentence and call that my Dharma or my Way, or hang onto a piece of knowledge or half an understanding and think that this is the Way of the Mahayana? Even if you have acquired power sufficiently, the shame of our family is still exposed. How much less should you preach the Dharma pretending to be something you are not and spouting nonsense! If you really want to reach this realm, do not vainly waste time day or night or recklessly misuse your minds and bodies.

Verse

Striking the mortar—the sound was loud, echoing beyond time and space;
Sifting the clouds—the silver moon appeared, and the night was deep and clear.

QINGYUAN XINGSI

Case

The thirty-fourth patriarch was Great Master Hongji [Qingyuan Xingsi]. He practiced in the community of Caoxi [the Sixth Patriarch]. He asked [the Patriarch], "What should I do so as not to land in some class or stage?" The Patriarch asked, "What have you done so far?" The master replied, "I have not even tried the [four] holy truths." The Patriarch asked, "Into what stage will you end up?" The master said, "If I still have not tried the holy truths, what stage can there be?" The Patriarch was greatly impressed with his potential.

Circumstances

The master was from the Liu family of An city in Jizhou. He made his home departure while still young. Whenever he was in a group discussing the Way, he remained silent. Later, he heard about the Dharma talks at Caoxi and went there to pay his respects. He asked, "What should I do so as not to land in some class or stage?" and so on. The Patriarch was greatly impressed with his potential.

Though there were many monks in that community, the master was foremost. It was like the Second Patriarch remaining silent and Bodhidharma saying, "You have acquired my marrow." One day, the Patriarchal Teacher [Huineng] said, "Formerly, the robe and bowl were both passed on from master to disciple. The robe represents faith; the Dharma seals the Mind. Now I have found you, so why should I worry about being believed? Since receiving the robe, I have run into much trouble. There will certainly be more contention in later generations. The [transmission of the] robe will end and thus bring peace to the monastery. You should teach elsewhere and not allow [the teaching] to be extinguished."

Having acquired the Dharma, the master lived in the Jingju Monastery on Mount Qingyuan in Jizhou, sharing the teaching with Caoxi [Huineng]. Eventually, after he found Shitou, many others came to follow in his footsteps after joining Caoxi's group. He was Dajian [Huineng]'s bright light. On the thirteenth day of the twelfth month in 740, he appeared in the [Dharma] hall, spoke to the monks, sat in cross-legged meditation, and expired. Later, he was given the posthumous title of Great Master Hongji.

Teisho

He never discussed Buddhism with the crowd, his silence an especially unusual continuous practice. With such power of attention to making a strenuous effort, while he was with Caoxi he asked what he should do so as not to land in some class or stage. Truly, he experienced [the Way] fully and ended by not having any inclination to go further. The Patriarch promptly tried to get him to present his realization, asking, "What have you done so far?" Finally, the point was exposed and not shut up in the needle case. He said, "I have not even tried the holy truths." Hearing this is hard to hear and meeting this is hard to meet. Even though you cease continuing, there is still an attachment to the self, and, if this is so, you make the mistake of falling into the deep pit of liberation. In the past and present, this situation is called "Dharma attachment." Yunmen called this the "two sicknesses of the Dharma body."[188] In truth, this results from not passing completely through this situation. However, [Qingyuan] not only just acknowledged his original nature, he penetrated this barrier. The Patriarch asked, "Into what stage will you end up?" In this deep, secluded place, there is no inside or outside after all. In this deep, final realm, not even a knife or ax can separate it. Therefore, he asked, "What stage can there be?" Unclouded, he penetrated this realm totally. He said, "If I have still not even tried the holy truths, what stage can there be?"

Even if you try to establish a class or stage, there are no boundaries in the sky right from the start. Where can you build stairs? Those who understand this realm [of emptiness] literally have, since ancient times, fallen into a view that all things are empty and arrive at an understanding that the myriad things are nonexistent. Since [Qingyuan] cried out, "I have not even tried the holy truths," how could he remain in the emptiness of things? Look carefully—this bright, empty realm is brighter than the rising sun. Even though this vast, marvelous, true nature is not an object of discrimination, it possesses complete, perfect, clear understanding. Though it is not bound by bones and marrow, it has a bright body that is not covered or hidden. This body cannot be discerned through motion or stillness, nor can its knowing be discerned through ordinary awareness and understanding. Since ordinary knowing is also this wisdom, motion and stillness are also nothing else [than this].

Even bodhisattvas who reach the tenth stage by stages still do not see Buddha nature really clearly. Why? The Buddha said, "Because they postulate an essence of things and establish practices [apart from ordinary activities], they do not see Buddha nature clearly. Because for Buddhas there are ultimately no practices and no realm of essence, they see Buddha nature thoroughly." In the eighth book of the *Great Nirvana Scripture* in the chapter "Awakening of the Tathagata Nature," it says, "Although innumerable bodhisattvas are endowed with all the perfections and practice the ten stages, they still are unable to see their own Buddha nature. The Buddha has consequently said that their views are deficient. Thus, good sons, the bodhisattva on the tenth stage still does not clearly know or see Buddha nature, so how much less are disciples or self-enlightened people able to see it?" With no reliance on seeing and hearing, and with no reliance on an external world or use of the thinking mind, just try to look beneath them. There will surely be an unexpected realization of an alert knowing not gotten from someone else.

Verse

Now, can you add some word to this story? Reaching this realm, if you can add a word to this story, you will make the Tongueless One speak. If you can hear this principle, you will make the Deaf One hear at once, and make That Person nod, speak, and laugh.

> *When a bird flies, it comes and goes, but there are no traces.*
> *How can you look for stages on the dark path?*

SHITOU XIQIAN

Case

The thirty-fifth patriarch, Great Master Wuji [Shitou Xiqian], visited Qingyuan. Qingyuan asked, "Where are you from?" The master replied, "I come from Caoxi." Qingyuan then raised his *hossu*[189] and asked, "Does this exist at Caoxi?" The master answered, "It's not only nonexistent at Caoxi, but it doesn't exist in India either." Qingyuan asked him, "You haven't been to India yet, have you?" The master said, "If I went, it would exist." Qingyuan said, "That's not good enough; say more." The master replied, "Master, you should say half of it and not depend completely on me." Qingyuan said, "I don't refuse to speak to you, but I am afraid that after this, no one will be deeply awakened." The master said, "It's not that it will not exist, it's just that no one will be able to express it." Qingyuan hit him with the *hossu* and the master was greatly awakened.

Circumstances

The master's name was Xiqian and he was from the Chen family of Gaoan in Duanzhou. After his mother became pregnant, she took no pleasure in strong-smelling vegetables or food that was meat-like. Even as an infant, he did not trouble his nurse. Even when he was young, he had a lot of self-confidence. Hunters in his native place were afraid of demons and spirits, and many offered sacrifices [to appease the spirits]. It was their practice to slaughter oxen and offer wine libations. The master went there once, demolished their shrine, and freed the oxen. This occurred more than ten times a year, and the village elders could not make him stop.

When he was thirteen, he paid a visit to Caoxi and became a [novice] monk, but he did not receive the complete precepts. The Sixth Patriarch was about to die, and the master asked him, "After you die, if I am still uncertain, on whom should I rely?" The Patriarch answered [something that sounded like] "Go and think about it." When the Patriarch died, the master would sit in meditation in a quiet place, so still it seemed as if he were dead. The senior monk Nanyue Huairang asked him, "Your master has died; why are you sitting for no reason?" The master replied, "I received his final instructions, so I am investigating." Huairang told him, "You have an elder Dharma brother named Xingsi, who now lives at [Mount] Qingyuan. That is where you have an affinity. The Patriarch's words were extremely unambiguous; you just deluded yourself [by thinking that he had said 'go and think (si)' while he really said, 'go to Si,' meaning Xingsi]."

So, the master paid reverence at the shrine for the Sixth Patriarch and left at once for [Mount] Qingyuan. [The Patriarch] Qingyuan said, "There are people who say that something is happening in Lingnan." The master replied, "There are people who do not say that something is happening in Lingnan." Qingyuan said, "If that is so, where did the teachings of the Mahayana and Hinayana come from?" The master answered, "They are wholly from *here*." Qingyuan affirmed this as correct and after that they often engaged in question and answer discussions.

Teisho

Once, Qingyuan raised his *hossu* and asked, "Does this exist at Caoxi?" The master replied, "It's not only nonexistent at Caoxi, but it doesn't exist in India either." In past and present, they have raised the *hossu* to demonstrate some principle, to instigate action, to make people depart from the crooked path, or to make people point directly [to true reality] without delay. Qingyuan also raised the *hossu* as a test. However, the master did not yet understand what "this" is. Still fixing his gaze on the raised *hossu*, he said, "Not only is it non-existent at Caoxi, but it doesn't exist in India either." When this *hossu* is raised, how can you say that there is either a Caoxi or an India? Yet, this view is still only a verbal understanding of something external. Therefore, Qingyuan pressed him, asking, "You haven't been to India yet, have you?" But [Shitou] still did not understand these words. Unable to forget himself, he said, "If I went, it would exist." Even though he could say this, if he didn't know that it exists, he would not be the [right] person. Qingyuan spoke again, saying, "Not good enough, say more." He was being kindly and compassionate, dripping mud and water, and thus he spoke fully in this way.

Here [Shitou] had no chance to speak appropriately. He said, "Master, you should say half of it and not depend completely on me." Meeting in this way and speaking in this way, if each just communicates a half, how can the whole thing be expressed? Even if heaven and earth collapsed and the entirety was revealed alone, this would still be going halfway. This place is still reached by oneself, not by borrowing someone else's resources. How much less can you inform someone else by continuing to go halfway when you are trying to communicate intimate words and absolutely not depend on someone else? On the contrary, you can only experience the fundamental [True Self] alone. Therefore, [Qingyuan] said, "I don't refuse to speak to you, but I am afraid that after this, no one will be deeply awakened." Even if someone speaks of pain or speaks of bitterness, if that person doesn't experience pain deep in his bones or experience bitterness ripping apart his tongue, he ultimately cannot understand the reality of it. You cannot get it through words.

Because this is the way it is, spiritual teachers do not use words indiscriminately or do things pointlessly, thus protecting [the principle of self-effort]. However, still thinking that "true reality" was not the same as the *hossu*, and not knowing deep inside that there was a passageway, [Shitou] did not see it fully. He said, "It's not that no one will be deeply awakened, but no one will be able to express it." I am afraid that this is what Shitou said, but when a person reaches this realm, how can he not have something to express? If he reaches this realm, what can he have? [Shitou] sought externally and separated himself from inner realization for no reason. In order to make him realize at once the existence of such a thing, and in order to make him realize at once the existence of his original head, [Qingyuan] struck him with the *hossu*, whacking the grass and scaring away the snakes. Consequently, the master was greatly awakened.

Through this story, you must experience carefully the whole of understanding and true realization. See it minutely and reach it close up. When [Shitou] said, "It is not only nonexistent at Caoxi, but it doesn't exist in India either," although he could demolish heaven and earth and expose the whole body standing alone, he still suffered the misfortune of recognizing a self. This is why he could speak so grandly. However, in the end he realized that the whole thing was exposed when the *hossu* was raised. He knew it existed when he was struck. Lately, Zen people get lost in sounds and sights, and search in seeing and hearing. Even though they intone the Buddha's words, get mired in words on the road to liberation, and say that, "It does not exist in either Caoxi or in India," they still do not understand. If this is how they are, then even though they shave their heads and wear the robes, thus resembling Buddhas, they cannot finally escape the bondage of imprisonment in the triple world. How will they ever stop going and coming in the six paths? Alas, people like this vainly hang the patch robe on blocks of wood. The Buddha said, "They are not sons of the Buddha. There is no name for them. They are no different from blocks of wood." This is what I mean. Vainly squandering the donations of the faithful for a whole lifetime, when they end up miserable from drinking molten pellets [in hell], they will really have many regrets.

Thus, if you investigate fully and completely and reach that place Shitou reached in the beginning where the whole body is exposed alone, you will understand that there is nothing at Caoxi or in India. Where can you come and go? In this realm of vision, you will not wear the patch robe pointlessly. Even more will you understand that it exists, when struck by the *hossu* [like Shitou], and quickly forget the self and understand the [true] Self. You will be alive in the midst of death, and in the dark your eyes will be bright. This is the intimate reality beneath the patch robe.

Since he had already seen it in this way, the master eagerly went to the south monastery at Mount Heng in the early 740s. East of the monastery there was a stone terrace on which he build a hut. At that time he was called the "Stone Monk" [Shitou Heshang].

Once, he was reading the *Treatise of [Seng]zhao*.[190] When he came to where it said, "Is it only the wise person who understands the myriad things as himself?" he struck his desk and said, "For the sage there is no self, and there is nothing that is not his [true] Self. The Dharma body is formless; who can speak of self and other? The round mirror reflects clearly and the wonderful forms of the myriad things appear in it spontaneously. Knowledge and its objects are not one or two; who can say they come and go? How true these words [of the treatise] are!" He finally rolled up the scroll and fell asleep. In a dream, he and the Sixth Patriarch were riding on a turtle, swimming around in a deep lake. When he awoke, he thought about the dream carefully. He interpreted the marvelous turtle to be wisdom and the lake to be the ocean of [essential] nature. He and the Patriarchal Teacher were riding on marvelous wisdom, swimming on the ocean of [essential] nature. Later, he wrote the *Cantongqi* ["Identity of Relative and Absolute"], which is well known all over the world.

It happened like this because his marvelous wisdom was equal to that of the Sixth Patriarch, and no different from that of Qingyuan. Not only that, but once he entered the hall and said, "My teaching was received from the patriarchs of the past—to arrive at the knowledge and perception of a Buddha, without recourse to meditation and effort. 'This body is Buddha,' 'Mind,' 'Buddha,' 'beings,' '*bodhi*,' 'defilement'—the words are different but the substance is the same. You must realize that the substance of your own mind is beyond annihilation and eternity, and its nature is beyond purity and impurity. Deep and complete, it is the same in sages and ordinary people. It responds freely and differs from ordinary mind in its various functions. The triple world and the six paths[191] appear spontaneously as nothing but Mind. How can the reflection of the moon in water or the shapes reflected in a mirror originate or cease to be? If you can understand this, there is nothing you lack." If he had not demolished heaven and earth and seen himself as independent, this talk would never have occurred. As a result of attaining realization when he was struck and experiencing clearly [original Mind], he became the thirty-fifth patriarch.

How can your own marvelous nature be distinct from his? How can the realm of Mind not be common to all? It is only due to arousing determination or not arousing it, meeting an enlightened teacher or not meeting one, that one rises or sinks, and not all are miserable or happy alike.

Verse

How can I examine this story? Would you like to hear?

> With one raising of the hossu, he held up the totality of the Way;
> Never by so much as a hair did Shitou ever deviate from it.

YAOSHAN WEIYAN

Case

The thirty-sixth patriarch, Great Master Hongdao [Yaoshan Weiyan], visited Shitou and asked him, "I understand the twelve-part teachings of the three vehicles for the most part, but I hear that in the south they directly point to the human mind, see their natures, and become Buddhas. This is still not clear to me. I humbly ask you in your compassion to explain it." The Patriarch said, "This way won't do and not this way won't do, and both this way and not this way won't do. How about you?" The master was speechless. The Patriarch said, "Your conditions [for understanding] are not here. You should go to Great Master Ma." Accordingly, the master went and paid his respects to Mazu and asked the same question. The Patriarch said, "Sometimes I make Him raise his eyebrows and blink, sometimes I do not make Him raise his eyebrows and blink. Sometimes raising the eyebrows and blinking is all right, sometimes raising the eyebrows and blinking is not all right. How about you?" With these words, the master was greatly awakened and he bowed. The Patriarch asked, "What truth have you seen that makes you bow?" The master replied, "When I was with Shitou, it was like a mosquito mounting an iron ox." The Patriarch said, "Since you are so, you must guard it well, but still, your master is Shitou."

Circumstances

The master's name was Weiyan. He was the son of the Han family in Taozhou. He made his home departure when he was sixteen, under Zen Master Huizhao in the western mountains in Luoyang. He took the precepts from Precepts Master Xicao of Mount Heng. He was widely acquainted with the sutras and treatises and observed the precepts scrupulously. One day, he lamented to himself, "A true man ought to purify himself apart from the laws. Who would believe that it is simply a matter of being scrupulous about trifling actions?" Right away, he went to Shitou's room and asked, "I understand the twelve-part teachings of the three vehicles for the most part," and so on. [Mazu] said, "You must guard it well."

He was Mazu's attendant for three years. One day, the Patriarch asked, "How do you see things these days?" The master replied, "I have 'shed my skin' totally and there is only the one reality." The Patriarch said, "What you have acquired is said to agree with Mind essence and pervades all your activities. This being so, you should gird your loins with three strips of bamboo sheathing and go live on a mountain somewhere [and teach]." The master said, "How could I dare say I will go live on a mountain [and teach]?" The Patriarch said, "If otherwise, you will always be going when you are staying and staying when you are going. Even if you want to benefit [others], you will have no one to benefit. Even if you want to carry out practice, there will be nothing to practice. You should make a boat [to ferry others across] and not stay here very long." So, the master left the Patriarch and returned to Shitou.

One day, while he was doing zazen, Shitou asked him, "What are you doing here?" The master answered, "I'm not doing anything at all." The Patriarch said, "In that case, you are sitting idly." The master replied, "If I was sitting idly, I would be doing something." Shitou asked, "You say you are not doing anything; what are you not doing?" The master replied, "Not even the ten thousand sages know." Shitou praised him with this verse:

> Though we have been together from the beginning, I do not know His name.
> We go about together like this, leaving all to destiny.
> Even the great sages of antiquity do not know Him.
> How can ordinary people understand?

Later Shitou said, "Both speech and activity are unrelated to it." The master answered, "Not being speech and activity are also unrelated to it." Shitou said, "With me, not even a needle point can enter." The master said, "With me, it's like planting flowers on top of stones." Shitou confirmed this. Later, [the master] lived on Mount Yao in Lizhou and monks gathered there in hordes.

Teisho

You can clearly understand through this story that the Zen schools of Qingyuan and Nanyue are not different.[192] Truly, these [two] were Caoxi's [Huineng's] two horns. They were white oxen standing alone on open ground. [Yaoshan] studied with Shitou and was enlightened through Mazu. He understood one and succeeded the other. There wasn't the slightest difference [between the two schools]. Therefore, in the beginning, [Yaoshan] said, "I understand the twelve-part teaching for the most part, but what is the meaning of 'directly pointing to the human mind, seeing one's nature, and becoming a Buddha'?" Speaking accurately of this realm, [Shitou] said, "This, way won't do, and not this way won't do, and both this way and not this way won't do at all." At this point, there was no chance to protect himself, and the other could not be doubted. This is why [Shitou] spoke in this way. However, at this stage, [Yaoshan] was attached to the ungraspable, so, hearing these words, he did not know what they were about. He stood there for a while and thought.

Then [Shitou] sent him to Jiangxi [Mazu] so that Mazu could explain in his place. Jiangxi, knowing his mind, said on behalf of Shitou, "I make Him raise his eyebrows and blink; I do not make Him raise his eyebrows and blink. Sometimes it's all right and sometimes it's not all right." He showed how it differs according to circumstances. [Yaoshan] was awakened to this realm and realized its existence in everything from raising the eyebrows and blinking to such activities as seeing, hearing, and understanding. He bowed. The Patriarch asked, "What truth have you seen that makes you bow?" The master replied, "When I was with Shitou, it was like a mosquito mounting an iron ox." He couldn't get a bite, and his views and attitudes all vanished. Even though he wasn't aware of it, he was a true man.

Later, the Patriarch [Mazu] asked him, "How do you see things these days?" Knowing there is not a speck of dust here or a spot of blemish, [Yaoshan] said, "I have shed my skin totally, and there is only the one reality." It is very difficult to reach this realm through penetrating study. For this reason [Mazu] praised him highly, saying, "What you have acquired is said to agree with mind essence and pervades all your activities." There was no place it did not go and nothing it did not pervade. Finally, he realized he could say that in all the activities he had experienced up to then, he was not doing anything; it was like planting flowers on a rock. Truly, he sought the direct pointing to the human mind which he had questioned earlier. Being shown that which raises the eyebrows and blinks, he was greatly awakened. When he taught the Dharma to monks [later], he said, "Right now, I am speaking these words to reveal to you He who is wordless. That One is fundamentally lacking in eyes and ears." Because he was skillful in the beginning [with Shitou] and [in the] middle [with Mazu] he was skillful in the end and acted for the sake of others by showing the truth.

Thus, all students should study like Yaoshan. Though none of the patriarchal teachers was superior or inferior in virtue, Yaoshan was particularly lofty in his relationship with students. He lived a very simple life. As a consequence, he is said to have never had more than twenty students. The small number of students was a result of the simplicity of his life. It happened in this way because people could not tolerate hunger and cold. However, there were many enlightened monks and laymen there, including Yunyan, Daowu, Chuanzi, the novice Kao, the workman Kan, and the layman Li'ao.[193] Therefore, the students considered thorough study to be the most important thing and did not take notice of the abundance or scarcity of worldly things. For this reason, Yunyan, Daowu, and Chuanzi were alike in their resolve and never lay down prone [to sleep] for forty years. There are no patch-robe sons like these if it is not a community of enlightened people. Zen students, you should vow to become brothers of Yunyan and Daowu, and try to reach [the realm of] Mazu and Shitou.

Don't you see? Making the eyebrows rise and the eye blink is all right and not all right. That realm is beyond doubt. Everyone is already endowed with it. When you try to understand that place, it has no features such as ears and eyes. You cannot discern it through seeing and hearing; nothing at all is done. However, although you are both together from the beginning, and finally it is something the name of which you do not know, it is something magnificent. Not only that, but that which gives you life and makes you die, makes you do such things as come and go, and makes you understand through seeing and hearing, is surely *This*. Do not seek the True Dharma apart from it. How can you expect to see it some other time? Even the twelve-part teachings point to this truth, and all sentient beings are inseparable from its functioning. How could you seek elsewhere for proof? Can you understand? Aren't you raising your eyebrows and blinking right now? If you just thoroughly see that which understands through seeing and hearing, you will never doubt what all the old masters said.

Verse

Now, how can I add a little to this truth?

> *That One whose whole life is extremely active and lively*
> *We call the One who raises the eyebrows and blinks.*

YUNYAN TANSHENG

Case

The thirty-seventh patriarch was Great Master Yunyan Wuzhu [Yunyan Tansheng]. He studied at first with Baizhang[194] for twenty years, and, afterward, he studied with Yaoshan. Yaoshan asked him, "What Dharma does Baizhang teach?" The master said, "Once he entered the hall [to speak] and all the monks were standing in rows. He suddenly scattered them with his staff. Then, he called out 'O monks!' When they turned around, Baizhang asked, 'What is it?'" Yaoshan said, "Why didn't you say that before? Today, thanks to you, I have been able to meet brother [Huai]hai." With these words, the master was greatly awakened.

Circumstances

The master was from the Wang family of Jianchong in Zhongling. He made his home departure at Shimen while he was still young. He studied with Baizhang [Huai]hai for twenty years without success. After that, he paid a visit to Yaoshan. Yaoshan asked him, "Where are you from?" The master said, "I come from Baizhang." Yaoshan asked, "What does Baizhang say to the monks?" The master replied, "He usually says, 'I have an expression that contains one hundred flavors.'" Yaoshan said, "Salt tastes salty and bland tastes bland. What is neither salty nor bland is the right flavor. What is the expression that has one hundred flavors?" The master could not answer. Yaoshan asked, "What do you intend to do about the birth and death right in front of you?" The master answered, "There is no birth and death in front of me." Yaoshan asked, "How long were you with Baizhang?" "Twenty years," said the master. Yaoshan said, "You were with Baizhang for twenty years and still have not got rid of your commonness."

Another time, [Yunyan] was standing beside [Yaoshan] in attendance. Yaoshan asked him, "What Dharma does Baizhang teach?" The master said, "Sometimes he says, 'Look beyond the three statements; understand beyond the six propositions.'" Yaoshan said, "That doesn't have the remotest connection with it." He asked again, "What Dharma does he teach?" The master replied, "Once he entered the hall..." and so on [as in the main case]. Hearing these words [of Yaoshan], he was greatly awakened.

Teisho

The basic point of studying Zen and learning the Way is to clarify Mind and awaken to the essential. So, even though the monk Yunyan practiced with Baizhang for twenty years, the conditions were not right. Later he studied with Yaoshan. Thus, you must not think that lengthy cultivation, practice, and study are necessarily good. The only basic thing is to clarify Mind. Meeting with the right conditions has nothing to do with whether you are a beginner or someone who has practiced for a long time. It is conditions from past lives that make good conditions. It isn't that Baizhang was not the right man, but simply that conditions were not right [for Yunyan].

Being a spiritual teacher is not a matter of pointlessly gathering together a community of monks and teaching them. It is nothing but getting them to penetrate directly to the source and be deeply awakened at once. The ancients always asked, "Where are you from?" Extensive travel [by monks] was done to test spiritual teachers, so the teacher tried to find out where they were from. They would also ask, "Why are you here?" This clarified the depth or shallowness of determination and whether conditions [for awakening] were near or remote. Therefore, here [in this story, Yaoshan] asked [Yunyan] where he was from. In order to show that he had not just wandered here and there, studying with this one or that one, he said that he came from Baizhang. Yaoshan and Baizhang appeared at the same time as representatives of the Qingyuan and Nanyue [lines].[195] This is why [Yaoshan] asked "What Dharma does Baizhang teach the monks?"

At this point, if Yunyan had experienced the truth, he would have presented what he had heard [and understood], but he merely repeated what he had heard. He said, "He usually says, 'I have an expression that contains one hundred flavors.'" This one expression contains [all] and is filled completely [with countless virtues]. Nevertheless, can people hear that expression or not? In order to get him to see it thoroughly, [Yaoshan] said, "Salt tastes salty and bland tastes bland. What is not salty or bland is the right flavor. What is the expression that contains one hundred flavors?" [The expression] was something that Yunyan had not heard thoroughly. As a result of using his ordinary ears and hearing [what might well have been] the croaking of a bullfrog, he was dazed and had no answer.[196]

That is why Yaoshan asked him, "What do you intend to do about the birth and death right in front of you?" Both the beginner and the veteran have to consider this the one great matter. Impermanence is swift, and the matter of birth and death is grave. Even if one who has aroused an aspiration travels around and looks like a monk, if he does not clarify the matter of birth and death and reach the path of liberation, he does not understand the secret beneath the patch robe. Therefore, he does not escape the bondage of the triple world. It is hard to get out of the rut of birth and death. He resembles someone who wears the patch robe pointlessly, like someone who carries the eating bowls aimlessly. Ancients [like Yaoshan] questioned people [like Yunyan] like this so that they would not fritter away the time for strenuous practice but maintain energetic activity. But Yunyan spoke carelessly, saying, "There is no birth and death in front of me." If you just reach the realm of tranquillity and joy, and carefully attain the original purpose of your wanderings and practice, then such a viewpoint will be unnecessary.

Yaoshan asked, "How long were you with Baizhang?" He was asking how many years he had been cultivating the Way since he began wandering around as a monk. [Yunyan] said, "Twenty years." Though this ancient did not waste any time in training for the Way, it seemed as if he had spent the time in vain. Therefore, [Yaoshan] said, "You were with Baizhang for twenty years and you still have not got rid of your commonness." Even if [Yunyan] understood that there is no birth and death and saw that there is no self and other, he was still unaware of his own original head with this view. He had no chance to release his grip on the cliff [and jump]. If one does not quickly turn back to emptiness, one has still not got rid of one's commonness. Neither has one destroyed discrimination and attitudes, nor destroyed one's prison. Isn't that pitiful? [Yaoshan] questioned him repeatedly in an attempt to get him to touch [his True Self], but he did not notice it. Even if he was awakened beyond the six propositions, still, [it was not real, just as] an iron hammer without a socket does not create a standard. Even if he had cut off the myriad distinctions, still, the fundamental clarity of the [true] Self was obscured. [Yaoshan] said, "That doesn't have the remotest connection." He pointed out again that coming to see him seemed useless.

At this point, although [Yunyan] repeated Baizhang's words when the monks were leaving the hall ["What is it?"], he still clung to what someone had said and did not arrive at his own realization. However, by mentioning it, he immediately mentioned what is the most authentic Zen Way by far. Therefore, [Yaoshan] said, "Why didn't you say that earlier? Thanks to you, today I have been able to meet brother [Huai]hai."

The meaning of the monks standing in rows and being suddenly scattered by the staff is that they were liberated and free. He did not have to trouble himself to test them again but, if he had stopped there, it seems that they would not have got it in a million eons. Consequently, in order to startle them, he shouted, "O monks," in a loud voice. If you strike a blow in the south, there is movement in the north. They turned their heads unconsciously. Since awakening is ultimately unconnected with thought, they nodded in this way. For that reason, he asked, "What is it?" Unfortunately, not a single person in Baizhang's community understood, but though no one here answered, far away Yaoshan said, "Thanks to you, I have been able to meet brother Hai."

When one of the ancients expressed a phrase from this realm, [others] said that they had met. This is like the same wind blowing for a thousand miles, like not being separated by so much as a hair. [Yunyan] studied with Baizhang at first and [later] was able to climb Mount Yao. In the end, there was no gap between master and disciple, and he reached the Great Dharma. If you awaken to this realm, you will not only stop doubting your eternal Self, you will be able to see through all the Buddhas of the three times, successive generations of patriarchs, and thoroughly ordinary patch-robe monks with one glance. You will cut through them with a single blow, meet Yaoshan and Baizhang at once, and directly see eye to eye with Yunyan and Daowu.[197]

Verse

How can I concisely express this principle? Would you like to hear?

A solitary boat proceeds unaided in the bright moonlight;
If you turn around and look, the reeds on the ancient shore do not sway.

DONGSHAN LIANGJIE

Case

The thirty-eighth patriarch was Great Master Dongshan Wuben [Dongshan Liangjie]. He visited Yunyan and asked, "Who can hear the non-sentient preach the Dharma?" Yunyan answered, "The non-sentient can hear the non-sentient preach the Dharma." The master asked, "Do you hear it?" Yunyan replied, "If I could hear it, you would not be able to hear me preach the Dharma." The master said, "In that case, Liangjie does not hear you preach the Dharma." Yunyan said, "If you still don't hear me preach the Dharma, how much less [can you hear] the non-sentient preach the Dharma?" The master was greatly awakened at this point and he spoke this verse:

Wonderful! Wonderful!
The preaching of the Dharma by the non-sentient is inconceivable.
If you try to hear with your ears, it is hard to understand;
When you listen with your mind's eye, then you know it.

Yunyan approved.

Circumstances

The master's name was Liangjie. He was from Huiji and his family name was Yu. While still young, he read the Heart Sutra with a teacher. When he reached the place where it said, "There is no eye, ear, nose, tongue, body, or mind, he suddenly felt his face with his hand. He asked his teacher, "I have eyes, ears, nose, tongue, and the rest. Why does the scripture say that they do not exist? His teacher was amazed and, realizing that he was unusual, said, "I am not your teacher," and sent him to Zen Master Limo on Mount Wuxie, where he had his head shaved.[198] When he was twenty, he went to Mount Song, where he took the complete precepts. He was his mother's favorite child, since his elder brother had died, his younger brother was poor, and his father was dead. But once he yearned for the teaching of emptiness, he left his old mother for good, vowing, "I will not return to my native place and pay respects to my mother before I acquire the Dharma." With this vow, he left his native place.

Eventually, he completed his study and later went to live on Mount Dong. Since his mother was alone and had no one else to depend on, she looked for him every day, finally wandering around with some beggars. When she heard that her son was on Mount Dong, she yearned to go and see him, but Dongshan avoided her, barring the [entrance to the] room so she could not enter because he didn't want to meet her. Consequently, his mother died of grief outside his room. After she died, Dongshan went personally and took the small amount of rice she had collected as a beggar and mixed it with the community's morning rice gruel. By offering it to the whole community of monks, he made a funerary offering to assist her on her journey [to future enlightenment]. Not long after, she told Dongshan [in a dream], "Because you firmly maintained your resolve and did not meet me, I severed the delusive feelings of love and attachment. As a result of the power of these good roots, I was reborn in the Realm of the Satisfied Celestials."[199]

Teisho

Though none of the patriarchal teachers was superior or inferior in virtue, Dongshan, the ancient Patriarch of our school, especially promoted Soto Zen in this way. It was the power of leaving parents and strongly maintaining his resolve. When he began his study, he studied in Nanquan's community at first, [200] and was involved in the anniversary of Mazu's death. While they were preparing offerings, Nanquan asked the monks, "Tomorrow we are going to provide offerings to Mazu, but do you think that he will come?" The monks were silent. The master stepped forward and said, "If he has a companion, he will come." Nanquan said, "Though he is young, he is extremely suitable for cutting and polishing." The master said, "Don't turn the good [liang] into something shameful."

Next, he studied with Guishan.[201] He asked him, "Lately, I hear that National Teacher [Hui] zhong of Nanyang[202] has a saying about the non-sentient preaching the Dharma, but I still don't grasp its subtleties." Guishan asked, "Do you remember it?" The master said, "Yes, I remember." Guishan said, "Well, then, give it a try." The master said, "A monk asked, 'What is the Mind of the ancient Buddhas?' The National Teacher said, 'Fences, walls, roof tiles, and pebbles.' The monk asked, 'Aren't these all nonsentient?' The National Teacher said, 'They are.' The monk asked, 'Will you explain how they preach the Dharma?' The National Teacher said, 'They constantly preach, vigorously, without ceasing.' The monk asked, 'Why can't I hear it?' The National Teacher replied, 'You don't hear it, but that doesn't stop others from hearing it.' The monk asked, 'I wonder if anyone else can hear it?' The National Teacher said, 'The holy ones can hear it.' The monk asked, 'Can you hear it?' The National Teacher replied, 'I can't hear it.' The monk asked, 'If you can't hear it, how do you know that the nonsentient preach the Dharma?' The National Teacher answered, 'Fortunately, I can't hear it. If I did hear it, I would be the same as the holy ones and then you would not be able to hear me preach the Dharma.' The monk asked, 'Then, do sentient beings have no part in it?' The National Teacher said, 'I preach it for the sake of sentient beings, not for holy people.' The monk asked, 'After sentient beings hear it, then what?' The National Teacher said, 'Then they are no longer sentient beings.' The monk asked, 'What is the scriptural basis for the preaching of the Dharma by the nonsentient?' The National Teacher replied, 'Clearly, words that do not accord with scripture are not discussed among gentlemen. Don't you know that the *Avatamsaka Sutra* says, "Worlds preach, sentient beings preach, and all things of the past, present, and future preach."'"

When the master finished, Guishan said, "I have it too, but I have had no chance to meet an awakened person." The master said, "It is still not clear to me. I beg you to instruct me." Guishan raised his *hossu*[203] and asked, "Do you understand?" The master replied, "No, I don't. Please explain." Guishan said, "I can't explain it to you in words." The master asked, "Is there someone else who sought the Way when you did?" Guishan said, "If you go to the stone caves in Liling in Youxian, you will find someone named Yunyan. If

you stir up the grass and gaze into the wind, you will certainly be welcome."
The master asked, "What is he like?" Guishan said, "Once he asked me,
'What should a student do when he wants to serve the master?' and I said,
'He can do it for the first time when he puts an end to delusion quickly.' He
asked, 'Would he still be able to not violate the master's teaching?' I
answered, 'The main thing is that you should not say I am here.'"

The master ended by leaving Guishan and going straight to Yunyan.
When he finished telling the above story, he asked, "Who can hear the nonsentient preach the Dharma?" Yunyan said, "The nonsentient can hear it."
The master asked, "Can you hear it?" Yunyan replied, "If I heard it, you could
not hear me preach the Dharma." The master asked, "Why can't I hear it?"
Yunyan raised his *hossu* and asked, "Do you hear it?" The master said, "No,
I don't hear it." Yunyan said, "If you still don't hear me preach the Dharma,
how much less can you hear the nonsentient preach the Dharma?" The master asked, "What is the scriptural basis for preaching by the nonsentient?"
Yunyan replied, "Don't you know that the Amida Sutra [204] says, 'Streams,
birds, and trees all praise the Buddha and praise the Dharma'?" Hearing this,
[Dongshan] was awakened.

This situation started in the community of the National Teacher and
finally came to an end at Yunyan's place. That is, he uttered the verse, "Wonderful! Wonderful!" and so on. When he heard with his mind's eye, he understood at once. The master told Yunyan, "I still have some habits that are not
yet exhausted." Yunyan asked, "What have you done so far?" The master
said, "I haven't even done the [four] holy truths." Yunyan asked, "Are you
happy or not?" The master said, "I'm happy. It's like finding a bright pearl in
a trash heap." He asked Yunyan, "What should I do when I want to meet [my
original Self]?" [Yunyan] said, "Ask the interpreter." The master said, "I'm
asking right now." [Yunyan] asked, "What is he telling you?"

When the master was leaving Yunyan, he asked, "After you die, if someone asks me, 'What was the master's truth?' what should I say?" Yunyan
paused and then said, "Just this, this." The master was silent for a while. Yunyan said, "You must be extremely careful and thorough in realizing this
thing." The master still had some doubts. Later, he was crossing a stream and
saw his reflection. As a result, he was greatly awakened to the prior instruction. He said in a verse:

Avoid seeking Him in someone else
Or you will be far apart from the Self.
Solitary now am I, and independent,
But I meet Him everywhere.
He now is surely me,
But I am not Him.
Understanding it in this way,
You will directly be one with thusness.

Dongshan's life work was completed and he was at once freed from doubt. This story is how it happened.

As for this story about the nonsentient preaching the Dharma, the workman Zhangfen of Nanyang asked the National Teacher [Huizhong], "I humbly confess that when you speak of the nonsentient preaching the Dharma, I do not understand. I entreat you to instruct me." The National Teacher said, "If you ask about the nonsentient preaching the Dharma, you will understand 'nonsentience' and then you will be able to understand my preaching. You just asked about the nonsentient preaching the Dharma." Zhangfen said, "Please explain what nonsentience is right now so that a sentient being can understand it." The National Teacher said, "Right now, within everyone, when [ideas] about the two classes of ordinary and holy do not arise or cease in the least way, there is a subtle consciousness that is unrelated to being and nonbeing, keenly aware, but without attachments. This is why the Sixth Patriarch [Huineng] said, 'The six senses discriminating their external objects is not [subtle] consciousness.'"

This is how Nanyang [Huizhong] discussed the preaching of the Dharma by the nonsentient. He said, "Within everyone, when the two classes of ordinary and holy do not arise or cease in the least way, there is a subtle consciousness that is unrelated to being and nonbeing, and is keenly aware." However, people usually think that the nonsentient must be fences, walls, roof tiles, pebbles, lamps, and pillars. But that is not what the National Teacher says here. The views of ordinary and holy are not discriminated, and attachment to delusion and awakening do not appear. Even less is it the scheming of passionate thought and discrimination, or the motions and forms of life and death. There is a subtle consciousness, and, truly, this subtle consciousness is keenly aware and is not the attachment of passionate consciousness. Dongshan also said that you must understand it in this way. Then you will be able to accord with this true reality.

If you know that wherever you go, you go alone, then there is never a moment when all things do not accord with this true reality. The ancients said, "There is no knowing outside of reality that is authenticated through reality; no reality outside of knowing that is cultivated through knowing. True reality is unmoving, clear and distinct, constant knowing." Therefore, it is said that it is perfectly clear knowing and unconnected with thought. Keen awareness is not attachment. Guishan said, "Ultimately, I cannot tell you in words." He also said, "If sentient beings could hear it, they would no longer be sentient beings." Because he received the instructions of several masters and understood true nonsentience, [Dongshan] promoted the Soto tradition extensively as our ancient ancestral Patriarch.

Thus, good people, by inspecting fully, you become keenly aware of this subtle consciousness; it is called "nonsentient." It is called "nonsentient" because there is no running off after sounds and forms, and no bondage to passionate consciousness. This principle must be preached carefully. Therefore, when you hear preaching about the nonsentient, do not think that this refers to fences and walls. It is simply that when you are not attached to emotion and thought, and your perceptions are not scattered, the subtle consciousness is clear and unobscured, clearly and distinctly bright. Even though you attempt to grasp this realm, it is not possible. Since it is not bound by form, it does not exist. Even though you attempt to get rid of it, you cannot leave it. Since it has accompanied you since time immemorial, it is not nonexistent. Still, it is not the working of consciousness, knowing, or thought, much less something connected to the four elements or five aggregates.

Hongzhi[205] said, "There is a knowing apart from passionate thought and discrimination; there is a body that is not the four elements and five aggregates." That is, it is the subtle consciousness. "Always preaching keenly" means that its manifestation at all times is "preaching." It makes one raise one's eyebrows and blink. It makes one walk, stand, sit, and lie down, be confused, get into trouble, die here and be born there, eat when hungry and sleep when tired—all these without exception are "preaching." Speech, work, movement, and cessation of movement are also "preaching." It is not just a verbal or nonverbal preaching; it is That One who appears magnifi-cently, is very bright, and never dark. Since it is revealed in everything, including the croaking of bullfrogs and the sounds of earthworms, it con-stantly preaches keenly without cessation. If you can see it fully, then some-day, like our eminent Patriarch Dongshan, you will be able to be an example for others.

Verse

How can I express this principle concisely?

> *Extremely fine subtle consciousness is not emotional attachment,*
> *It constantly makes that One preach keenly.*

YUNJU DAOYING

Case

The thirty-ninth patriarch was Great Master Yunju Hongjue [Yunju Daoying]. He studied with Dongshan. Dongshan asked him, "What is your name?" The master replied, "Daoying." Dongshan said, "Say it from beyond."[206] The master said, "If I speak from beyond, I cannot say that I am Daoying." Dongshan said, "That is the same answer I gave when I was with Yunyan."

Circumstances

The master was from Wangdian in Youzhou, and his family name was Wang. He made his home departure at Yanshou Temple in Fanyang while he was still young. He became a full monk when he was twenty-four. His teacher had him study the books of the Small Vehicle, but he did not like them, so he left them and went traveling. When he arrived at Cuiwei [Monastery] he asked about the Way [from Master Cuiwei]. It so happened that a monk arrived from Youzhang and vividly recounted Dongshan's teaching, and, in the end, the master went there. Dongshan asked him, "Where are you from?" The master answered, "I come from Cuiwei." Dongshan asked, "What does Cuiwei say to his followers?" The master said, "Cuiwei was making an offering to the arhats"[207] and I asked, 'You are making offerings to the arhats, but do you think that they will come [to accept the offerings]?' Cuiwei asked, 'What do you eat every day?'" Dongshan asked, "Did he really say that?" and the master said, "Yes." Dongshan said, "You didn't meet that adept in vain." Then he asked, "What is your name?" and so on, concluding, "My answer was the same."

The master was awakened when he saw the Dong River, and he discussed it with Dongshan. Dongshan said, "Thanks to you, my Way will spread endlessly." Not only that, but once, he asked the master, "I hear that the Great Priest Si[208] was born in Japan and became the emperor. Is that correct?" The master answered, "If you're talking about Great Priest Si, he wouldn't become a Buddha, let alone an emperor." Dongshan thought that this was correct.

One day, Dongshan asked, "Where have you been?" The master said, "Out walking in the mountains." Dongshan asked, "What mountain is fit to live on?" The master replied, "What mountain is not fit to live on?" "In that case," said Dongshan, "you've taken over the entire country." The master said, "No, I haven't." Dongshan said, "If that is so, have you found an entry path?" The master said, "There is no path." Dongshan said, "If there is no path, how could you meet me?" The master replied, "If there were a path, we would never have met." Dongshan said, "Hereafter, not one thousand, not even ten thousand people will be able to restrain him."

The master was accompanying Dongshan, and as they were crossing a stream, Dongshan asked, "Is the water deep or shallow?" and the master answered, "It's not wet." Dongshan said, "Coarse fellow." The master said, "How about you, master?" Dongshan said, "Not dry."' He told the master, "Nanquan[209] asked a monk what scripture he was reading and the monk answered that it was the *Sutra on Maitreya's Appearance in the World*.[210] Nanquan asked, 'When will Maitreya appear?' The monk answered, 'Right now he is in the celestial realm and he will appear in the future.' Nanquan said, 'There is no Maitreya either in the celestial realm or on earth.'" The master asked Dongshan, "If there is no Maitreya either in the celestial realm or on earth, what does the name mean?" Hearing this, Dongshan's seat quaked, and he said, "Daoying, once when I was with Yunyan, I asked a question and the hearth quaked. Today I was asked a question and my whole body is dripping with sweat." There was no difference in the questions and answers between master and disciple. In the whole community no one could stand shoulder to shoulder [as an equal with Yunju].

Later the master built a hut on Mount Sanfeng and did not come to the monastery for ten days. Dongshan asked him, "Why don't you [come here and] eat, these days?" The master answered, "Every day, a spirit brings offerings." Dongshan said, "I thought you were an enlightened man, but you still have these kinds of views. Come tonight [and visit me]." That night, [Yunju] went, and Dongshan called, "O Hermit Daoying!" The master replied. Dongshan said, "Without thinking of good, without thinking of evil, what is it?" The master returned to his hermitage and sat silently in zazen. After this, the spirit came but could not see him. After three days of this, the spirit left.

[Once,] Dongshan asked the master, "What are you doing?" The master said, "I'm making bean paste." Dongshan asked, "How much salt are you using?" The master said, "I added a little." Dongshan asked, "How does it taste?" The master said, "It will do." [Another time,] Dongshan asked him, "If someone without Buddha nature [211] commits the five unpardonable sins, how can he take care of his parents?" The master replied, "He observes filial piety for the first time [then]." After this, Dongshan gave him his approval and made him the head monk in the monastery. The master stayed at Sanfeng at first, but his teaching did not spread. Later, he established the Dharma at Mount Yunju, and the four groups [of male and female monastics and laypeople] gathered in droves.

Teisho

After the master met Cuiwei, he studied with Dongshan and was the elder [Dharma] brother of Caoshan. [212] Through the above questions and answers, the doubts of master and disciple were completely settled. Dongshan predicted, "Thanks to you, my Dharma will continue endlessly into the future." His words were not meaningless, for [his Dharma] has been passed on generation after generation down to today. Truly, the waters of Mount Dong have flowed onward and continue to bubble and sparkle today, passed on in the school that has preserved the purity [of Dongshan's teaching]. Its source has not dried up [even] now, and it remains cool and clear.

When [Yunju] asked the question, he put his great functioning into motion. As a consequence, not only did [Dongshan's] seat rock, his whole body dripped with sweat, something which is rare now or in the past. However, since [Yunju] lived in a hut on Sanfeng and received food offerings from a spirit, Dongshan said, "I thought you were an enlightened man, but you still have these kinds of views." That night, he summoned [Yunju] and called,

"O Hermit Daoying!" and [Yunju] answered. The one who answered was one who should not take food from a spirit. To settle it, [Dongshan] said, "Without thinking of good, without thinking of evil, what is it?" When you arrive in this realm fully and see it like this, spirits have no way to spread flowers, and demons and outsiders secretly seeking you cannot find you. On such an occasion, even the Buddhas and patriarchs are resentful. Even the eye of a Buddha cannot spy on you. When [Yunju] experienced it in this way, he made bean paste and added just enough salt—self-reliant, and sufficiently capable by himself. Therefore, he who lacks the Buddha nature kills his father, kills his mother, kills the Buddha, and kills patriarchs, committing the five unpardonable sins over and over. There is no thought at such a time of reverence toward parents. Trying to get [Yunju] to be intimately aware of this realm, [Dongshan] asked, "How can he care for his parents?" Yunju replied, "He cares for his parents for the first time [then]." Caoshan said the same thing.

When [Yunju] entered the [Patriarch's] room as the top candidate for the transmission and received the Dharma intact, Dongshan made a point of asking him "What is your name?" In a meeting between master and disciple, you don't proceed on the basis of former circumstances, so [Dongshan] asked him "What is your name?" You must realize that Dongshan knew the master's name, but he had a reason for asking like this. The master answered, "Daoying." Even if asked over and over in countless ways, it would still have to be "Daoying." He made no excuses. Even though [Dongshan] did not deny such a notion still, in order to get him to say whether or not he had the capacity to pass through barriers and escape limitations, he asked, "Say it from beyond." The master already lacked the six senses and seven forms of consciousness.[213] He was like someone whose face was missing, or like a straw dog, so he said, "If I say it from beyond, then I cannot say that I am Daoying." It is extremely difficult to reach this realm. If a student has not reached this realm, he lacks the power to proceed. He will still be confused by false views. Because [Yunju] guarded this realm carefully, the two of them had this dialogue about the person utterly lacking the Buddha nature. There was no violation [of Dongshan's teaching]. If you monks become fully aware [in awakening], you will be true patch-robed monks who have completely resolved the [one great] matter.

Verse

What can I say today so that you will fully understand this story?

(After a pause, he said:)

Never has it been bound to names and forms;
How can you speak of it as "beyond" or "relative"?

TONGAN DAOPI

Case

The fortieth patriarch was Zen Master Tongan Daopi. Once, Yunju said, "If you want to acquire such a thing, you must become such a person. Since you are such a person, why be anxious about such a thing?" Hearing this, the master was awakened.

Circumstances

No one knows where the master was from. He practiced with Yunju and spent years as his attendant. Once Yunju entered the hall and said, "When monks vomit out words, they should have a reason and not speak negligently. What do you think this abode is? How can it be easy? Whenever you are asked about this matter, you must be sufficiently aware of good and evil....[214] The primary thing is, do not cling. If you cling, [what you find] will be different.... If you are a person who thoroughly knows of its existence, you will naturally know how to guard and preserve it. In the end, you will not spread it around but only speak once out of every ten times you are asked. Why? Probably it would not do any good [to speak]. The thoroughly accomplished person is one whose mind is like a fan in winter and mold grows on his lips. This is not an effort on his part; it is natural. If you want to acquire such a thing...why be anxious about such a thing."

Hearing it said like this that such a matter is hard to acquire, the master understood. Finally, he took care of the [great] matter of his life. Later, he lived in Tongan Monastery on Mount Fenshi in Hongzhou. This was Zen Master Daopi. He expounded Yunju's tradition extensively.

Once, a student asked him, "How can I stop mistaking my reflection for my head?" The master asked him, "Who are you talking to?" The monk said, "What is the right thing to do?" The master replied, "If you seek from someone else, you will get farther and farther away from it." The monk asked, "What about when I don't seek it from someone else?" The master asked, "Where is your head?"' The monk asked, "What is your family style?" The master said:

> The golden fowl, embracing its young, returns to the Milky Way;
> The jade rabbit, pregnant, enters the purple sky.

The monk asked, "When you receive an unexpected guest, how do you welcome him?" The master replied:

> A monkey plucks the golden fruit early in the morning;
> A phoenix munches the jade flowers at night.

Having been able to know the true realm through what his former teacher had said, when he expressed the style of his tradition, he said:

> The golden fowl returns to the Milky Way;
> The jade rabbit enters the sky.

When he was welcoming people, he said:

> Golden fruit is picked daily;
> Jade flowers are munched every night.

Teisho

Although there is neither superiority nor inferiority in stories of Zen practice, you should study this story carefully. The reason is, if you want to acquire such a thing, you must become such a person. Even though you mistakenly look for your own head, this [looking, itself,] is your head. As the founder Eihei [Dogen] said, "Who am I? I am the one who asks 'who.'" When Abbot Liangcui visited Magu, Magu shut the door upon seeing him coming.

Liangcui knocked on the door, and Magu called out, "Who is it?" Liangcui said, "Liangcui." Just as he called out his name, he was suddenly awakened. He said, "Don't fool me [any longer], master. If I had not come and paid my respects to you, I would have really wasted my whole life on the sutras and treatises of the canon."[215] When he returned to lecture [on the scriptures], he dismissed the class and told his followers, "Whatever you know, I know; what I know, you do not."

The winds [of discrimination] cannot enter this place of knowing. Thus, people, when you penetrate it thoroughly and fully, [you will realize that] you have possessed it since time immemorial and that it has not been absent for a second. Even though you seek it through thought, that [itself] is the Self and nothing else. Even reflecting inwardly on yourself is not discrimination; it is Self and not something new. Using eyes, ears, and mouth, opening your hand and moving your feet—these are all Self. Fundamentally, it is not grasped with hands or seen by the eyes. Therefore, it cannot be discussed in terms of sounds and forms, and it is not approached with ears and eyes. When you see it fully, you will doubtlessly know that there is an "I" and that there is a Self. If you want to know this place, when you toss out right and wrong for the first time and do not depend on others or get involved with them, this Mind shines naturally with a brightness brighter than the sun and moon. Its purity is purer than frost and snow. Thus, it is not blind, unaware of right and wrong. This Self is spontaneously manifested pure and bright.

People, do not think that there is no one apart from speech, silence, movement, and stillness, or no one unconnected with skin, flesh, bones, and marrow. Also, do not stand alone, immobile, without a thought of self and others, without any mind at all, unconnected with things, like a stump, and think that having no mind is like grass or trees. How could the study of the Buddha Way resemble grass and trees? The view that fundamentally there is no self or other and that not a single thing exists is the same as the nihilism of non-Buddhists and the view of nothingness of the two vehicles.[216] How could the ultimate standard of the Great Vehicle be like that of the two vehicles or non-Buddhists? When you finally arrive and settle properly in the true reality, you will not be able to say that it exists, because it is empty and clear. You will not be able to say that it is nonexistent because it is bright and keenly aware. It cannot be discriminated with the body, mouth, or mind, nor can it be discerned with mind, conceptualization, or perception.

Verse

How can I convey this truth?

> Seeking it oneself with empty hands, you return with empty hands;
> In that place where fundamentally nothing is acquired, you really acquire it.

TONGAN GUANZHI

Case

The forty-first patriarch was Great Master Tongan the Latter. He studied with the former Tongan. He said, "The ancients said, 'What worldly people love, I love not.' I wonder what you love." Tongan [Daopi] said, "I have already been able to be like this." With these words, the master was greatly awakened.

Circumstances

The master's name was Guanzhi. His biography has not been recorded in detail. He studied with the Former Tongan and his realization was deep. When the Former Tongan was about to die, he entered the hall and said:

> *In front of the Shrine of Many Children, an ancestral child excelled;*
> *What about what occurred before Wulao Peak?*

He said this three times, but no one responded. Finally, the master stepped forward and said:

> *They stand in the bright night in orderly rows outside the curtain;*
> *Their singing is heard for ten thousand miles, expressing the Great Peace.*

Tongan [the Former] said, "This donkey will get it." After that, [the master] remained at Mount Tongan and was called "Tongan the Latter."

Teisho

"In front of the Shrine of Many Children an ancestral child excelled" means that the encounter between Shakyamuni Buddha and Mahakashyapa took place in front of the Shrine of Many Children.[217] Once they met, the robe and Dharma were transmitted. Later, [Mahakashyapa] practiced the twelve kinds of austerities. Later, he shared the Buddha's seat. Although he was not present at the death [of the Buddha], the entire community was entrusted to him. This is what is meant here by "an ancestral child excelled." Now, Tongan [Daopi] was the legitimate [spiritual] grandson of Dongshan, so the tradition of Qingyuan's family flowed back to here. In order to reveal his legitimate [spiritual] son when he was about to die, he asked, "What about what occurred before Wulao Peak?" He asked this way three times, but none of the monks understood, so no one answered.

Mount Sumeru stands out lofty among the other mountains; the orb of the sun shines bright before the many beings. Therefore, "They stand in the bright night in orderly rows outside the curtain." Truly, no one could compare with [Guanzhi]. Because he was liberated and independent, he had no second. There is not a speck of dust for ten thousand miles. Where, now, are the clever officials and fierce generals? Singing, singing, all is the Great Peace. This is the wonderful patch-robe monk. He who studies will find it for the first time when he reaches this realm.

This kind of practice of eradicating commonness and achieving excellence revealed his character right from the start. Therefore, he said, "What worldly people love, I love not. I wonder what you love, master." This "What the world loves" means people love themselves and others, and this love increases little by little. They love their environment and their own bodies, and this love gets deeper and deeper. They add iron shackles to iron shackles by loving the Buddhas and loving the patriarchs, and in this way the impurity of love grows filthier and filthier. Finally, the conditions for their karma continue endlessly, and they are born without freedom and die without freedom. These are the consequences of love. Therefore, this kind of love of beings, Buddhas, males, females, and the sentient and nonsentient must be banished at once.

When you no longer discern anything, whether rules or things, know nothing and are aware of nothing, this is love of the formless. Do not stop here. As for attachment to form, once you arouse the thought [of enlightenment], you may naturally end up [attached to formlessness]. If you become attached to the view of formlessness and end up in the realm of formlessness, even after ever so many eons have passed and your celestial life [in the formless realm] has ended, you will unfortunately fall into [the hell called] "Uninterrupted."[218] This is what is meant by no-mind as the annihilation of thought. Worldly people desire this form and formlessness repeatedly. Seeing self and others in forms, and forgetting self and others in formlessness, are totally wrong.

Thus, as eminent Zen monks, whether you are beginners or veterans, you are descendants of the Venerable Shakyamuni and use [the same robes and bowl] he used. How can you be attached in the same way worldly people are? First, you must free yourselves of all false views of such things as right and wrong, good and evil, male and female. Next, do not get stuck in the nihilism of nonaction, indifference, and formlessness. If you want to experience this realm personally, do not look for it in others or beyond yourselves. You must go back to the time when you had no body, before you were conceived, and have a close look. You will not find the slightest sign of the many distinctions. Do not be like a demon in a dark cave. This Mind is fundamentally wonderfully clear, bright, and undarkened. It illuminates perfectly and is open as the sky. Here, there is not a hair of connection with skin, flesh, bones, and marrow. How could there be anything such as the six senses, their objects, delusion, awakening, impurity, or purity?

The Buddha can do nothing for you and there is nothing to be had from a teacher. Not only is it not distinguished through sound and form but it has no ears and eyes. However, the Mind-moon shines round and bright; the eye-flower opens, and forms are fresh. You must arrive here fully and be worthy like [Tongan Guanzhi].

Verse

Zen worthies, how can we understand this principle? I will add a word. You must fix your eye on what was before you had a body.

The light of the Mind-moon and colors of the eye-flower are splendid;
Shining forth and blooming beyond time, who can appreciate them?

LIANGSHAN YUANGUAN

Case

The forty-second patriarch was Priest Liangshan. He studied with Tongan the Latter and served him. Tongan asked him, "What is the business beneath the patch robe?" The master had no answer. Tongan said, "Studying the Buddha [Way] and still not reaching this realm is the most painful thing. [Now,] you ask me." The master asked, "What is the business beneath the patch robe?" Tongan said, "Intimacy." The master was greatly awakened.

Circumstances

No one knows where the master was from. His name was Yuanguan. He studied with Tongan the Latter, and as his attendant, was responsible for [Tongan's] robe and bowl. Once, Tongan entered the hall and was supposed to wear his robe, so when it was time, the master brought the patch-work Dharma robe. As he took the robe, Tongan asked, "What is the business beneath the patch robe?" The master had no answer, [and at the conclusion of the dialogue] he was greatly awakened. He made full bows, and tears of gratitude wet his robe. Tongan said, "Now that you have had a great awakening, can you express it?" Yuanguan said he could. Tongan asked, "What is the business beneath the patch robe?" The master said, "Intimacy." Tongan said, "Intimacy, intimacy."

Teisho

Later, the master often spoke of intimacy in his teaching. After he settled [on Mount Liang] many students asked him about what was beneath the patch robe. Once, a student asked, "What is the business beneath the patch robe?" The master replied, "Not even all the holy ones reveal it." A student also asked, "What about when it is hard to protect the house against thieves?" The master replied, "If you are aware of them, they won't trouble you." [The monk] asked, "After you recognize them, what then?" The master said, "You can banish them to the land of no-birth." [The student] asked, "Isn't that the place where they live in peace?" The master said, "Stagnant water does not harbor dragons." [The student] asked, "What about when all the pools are emptied and the mountains are leveled?" The master got down from his seat, grabbed the student, and said, "Don't wet the corners of this old monk's robe." Also, [once,] someone asked, "What is the student's Self?" The master said, "Within the imperial walls, the emperor; beyond the frontier, the general." This is how he always exemplified intimacy to others.

In this story, [the Patriarch] says, "Studying the Buddha Way and still not reaching this realm is the most painful thing." How true these words are! Even if you demolish your meditation seat [from prolonged sitting], and persevere mindless of fatigue, and even if you are a person of lofty and spotless conduct—if you still have not reached this realm, it will be hard for you to escape the prison of the triple world.[219] Even if you possess the four kinds of eloquence and eight sounds, and even if your preaching covers everything like mist, your speech rolls like [the waves in] the sea, your Dharma preaching astounds heaven and earth, and you make flowers rain from the sky and make rocks move—if you still have not yet reached this realm, old Yama [Lord of the Dead] will not fear your eloquence. Even if you practice for an exceedingly long time and exterminate thoughts and calm your emotions, even if you make your body like a withered tree and your mind like dead ashes, mind never reacting to external things and never losing mindfulness when confronting events, even if you become liberated while sitting or die while standing and you seem to have acquired independence and freedom with regard to life and death—if you still have not reached this realm, all that is valueless in the house of the Buddha patriarchs. Thus, an ancient said, "Our predecessors all considered this business to be the one great matter."

Thus, our first patriarch [of the Soto lineage, Dongshan,] asked a monk, "What is the most painful thing in the world?" He answered, "Hell is the most painful thing." Dongshan said, "Not so. Wearing the robe but not clarifying the great matter is the most painful." His disciple, Yunju, revealed his horns and quoted him, saying, "My former teacher said, 'Hell is not the most painful thing; wearing the robe but not clarifying the great matter is the most painful thing.' If you put a little spirit into it, you will do fine and not give in to a life of peace and tranquillity or violate the [spirit of the] Zen community. The ancients said, 'If you wish to be able to take care of this matter, you must stand on top of the highest mountain and walk about on the floor of the deepest ocean. Then you will have a little life. If you have not yet figured out this great matter, then you must constantly tread the dark road.'"

Not only that, but the Buddha, Shakyamuni, and all other Buddhas throughout space and time say, in the "Skillful Means" chapter [of the *Lotus Sutra*], "All Buddhas appear in the world only for the sake of the one great matter." That is to say, to make [beings] reveal their Buddha wisdom and vision, awaken to it, and enter it. Clarifying this is the great matter. Do not take pleasure in simply looking like a disciple of the Buddha. If you do not clarify this matter, you are virtually no different from a worldly householder. This is because you are no different in seeing with your eyes and hearing with your ears. It is not just a matter of externals; inwardly you cannot forget about attachment to the externals. This is nothing but a change in appearance. Ultimately, you are like them. In the final analysis, when your breathing stops and your eyes close, your spirit will be attracted by objects and flow through the triple world. In the end, although there may be excellent results such as rebirth among humans or celestials, you will be like a wheel turning and turning endlessly [in the paths of rebirth].

What was the original intention in getting people to leave home and escape the passions? It was just to get them to arrive at Buddha wisdom and vision. Taking the trouble to establish Zen communities and gathering together the four groups [of female and male monastics and laypeople] was only for the purpose of clarifying this matter. Therefore, we speak of the meditation hall as the place for selecting Buddhas. Those who excel are called "guides." It is not simply in order to create an uproar by gathering together a community. It is only for the purpose of getting people to thoroughly clarify the self.

Even if you look like a monk and halfheartedly join in the Zen community, if you have not clarified this matter, you are just struggling pointlessly

without any results. Even less can either beginners or veterans in these corrupt times of the last days of the Dharma[220] study thoroughly if their spirits
waver, even if they try to model their mental states and physical deportment
after former enlightened ones. Monks these days are not stable in their conduct and do not thoroughly learn the major and minor forms of deportment
and the internal and external mental arts, so it looks as if there is no monastic deportment. Even if mental states and physical deportment are like those
of antiquity, if you have not clarified the realm of Mind, these are no more
than the defiled state of humans and celestials. How much more do people
who do not clarify the realm of Mind or control physical deportment receive
the offerings of the faithful in vain and fall into the hells!

Thus, a former worthy said, "The world has deteriorated and people are
lax. Even if one's mental states and physical deportment are not like those of
the ancient holy ones, if one is able to clarify the one great matter thoroughly
and intimately, perhaps one will not differ from all the Buddhas of the three
times. He will become a brother of all the patriarchs and ancient worthies in
history. From the beginning, there has been no triple world to escape, much
less six paths to be traveled." Therefore, investigate thoroughly and study
meticulously. Clarify the business beneath the patch robe. This one great
matter has nothing to do with the three periods of the Dharma[221] or differences between India, China, and Japan. Do not be sad about living in the
evil time of the last days of the Dharma or hate being a resident of a peripheral land far away [from India and China].

Of course, even if any number of Buddhas came and tried to offer you
this one great matter, even their power would not suffice in the end. Therefore, this is not a path you can pass on to your children or a path you can
receive from your father. You have to do it yourself, awaken to it yourself,
and acquire it yourself. Even though you practice for infinite eons, self-
authentication and self-awakening happen in an instant. Once you rouse
yourself, not so much as a hair in all of heaven and earth will get in the way.
Once you reach this realm, nothing is hidden in the whole of eternity. How
can there be anything to receive from Buddhas?

If you want to reach this realm completely, you must first abandon everything. You must not even seek the realm of Buddhas and patriarchs. Much
less can there be any love or loathing of self or others. Just look directly

within, without a hair of intellectualizing. There is without doubt something that has no skin or flesh. Its body is like space, without any specific form. It is like pure water, which is clear to the bottom. Completely clear and bright, you just have to know it thoroughly.

Verse

Now, how can I reveal this principle?

> *The water is clear to the very bottom;*
> *The pearl gleams naturally, without need of cutting and polishing.*[222]

DAYANG JINGXUAN

Case

The forty-third patriarch was Great Master Dayang Mingan [Dayang Jingxuan].
Once, he asked Priest Liangshan, "What is the formless site of enlightenment?"[223] Liangshan pointed to a picture of [the Bodhisattva] Guanyin and
said, "This was painted by the scholar Wu." The master was about to speak,
when Liangshan suddenly grabbed him and said, "This is what has form; what
is it that has no form?" With these words, the master comprehended.

Circumstances

The master's initiatory name was Jingxuan. In the *Transmission of the
Lamp*[224] and elsewhere, he is called Jingyan because of the [taboo on the]
name of the [then] current emperor.[225] However, his real name was Jing
xuan. He was from the Chang family in Jiangxia. He made his home departure with Zen Master Zhitong. When he was eighteen, he became a full
monk. He heard [lectures on the] ultimate meaning in the Scripture on
Perfect Awakening[226] and no one could equal him in classes. He went traveling. When he first visited Liangshan, he asked, "What is the formless site
of enlightenment?" [and] finally he comprehended.

   Then, he bowed and stood in place. Liangshan asked, "Why don't you
just say something?" The master answered, "I am not avoiding speaking, I
just worry that it will end up in writing." Liangshan smiled and said,
"Those words will end up on a stone tablet." The master presented a verse,
saying:

> Long ago, as a beginner, I studied the Way in error,
> Seeking knowledge over thousands of rivers and mountains.
> Clarifying the present, discerning the past, in the end I could not understand.
> They spoke directly of no-mind, but my doubt remained.
> My teacher showed me the mirror of Qin,[227]
> And it reflected what I was before my parents bore me.
> Having understood thoroughly now, what did I obtain?
> If you release a black bird at night, it flies clothed in snow.

Liangshan said, "Dongshan's tradition will flourish because of you."

[Dayang's] reputation grew all at once. When Liangshan died, [Dayang] left the city and went to Mount Dayang and called on Zen Master Jian. Jian resigned his position and made him the head of the community. From then on, he made Dongshan's tradition flourish and people got wind of it. The master's appearance was unusual and dignified. From the time he was a child, he ate only one meal a day. Because he put a great deal of importance on what he had inherited from his predecessors, he never left the monastery. He never lay down to sleep, and he did this until he was eighty-one. Finally, he gave up his position, bade farewell to the community, and died.

Teisho

The most essential thing in the study [of Zen] is this "formless site of enlightenment." It is not bound by form and has no name. Although it is therefore unrelated to words, it definitely turns out to be something clear. It is the meaning of "your face before you were born." Therefore, when he tried to indicate this realm, [Liangshan] pointed to a painting of Guanyin that had been painted by the scholar Wu, as if he were pointing to a mirror. This is what is meant by having eyes but not seeing, having ears but not hearing, having hands but not holding, having a mind but not discriminating, having a nose but not smelling, having a tongue but not tasting, and having feet but not walking. It is as if none of the six faculties was being used and the entire body became useless furniture. One is like a wooden figure or an iron man; at such a time, seeing forms and hearing sounds quickly disappear. When [Dayang] started to speak at this point, [Liangshan,] in order to prevent him from saying something delusory, suddenly grabbed him and asked, "This is what has form; what is it that has no form?" He got Dayang to understand the faceless by means of something that has no function. It was like knowing who he was by looking into a clear mirror. (There was a mirror long ago in the time of Emperor Jin. By looking into it, it seemed that all the body's internal organs, eighty-four thousand pores, and three hundred sixty bones could be seen.) Even though you have ears and eyes, when you do not use them, you see what is not bound by a body or mind. Not only do you break through the thousand mountains and ten thousand rivers of form, you quickly break through the darkness of no-mind and nondiscrimination, heaven and earth are no longer separated, none of the myriad forms sprouts, and everything is perfectly complete. It was not only [Dayang] who made Dongshan's tradition flourish all at once in this way; all the patriarchs saw it the same way.

After he was made to grasp this point, while he was at Dayang, a monk asked him, "What is the style of your tradition?" The master said, "The brimming container is turned upside down but is not emptied, and there are no famished people in all the world." Truly, though you tip this realm over, it does not empty; though you push on it, you cannot open it. Though you try to lift it, you cannot pick it up. Though you touch it, there is nothing there. You cannot get it with your ears and eyes, and, although it is accompanied by speech and silence, movement and stillness, it is not at all hindered by movement and stillness. It is not just Zen masters who possess this thing. There is not a single person in the whole world who does not have it. Therefore, [Dayang] said, "There are no famished people."

Zen worthies, you have fortunately become descendants in Dongshan's family and have encountered the family style of enlightened predecessors If you practice precisely and carefully and are personally awakened to the time prior to birth and the arising of form and emptiness, reach the realm where there is not a fragment of form, experience the realm where there is not the least atom of external stuff, you will not find the four great elements and five aggregates in countless eons. If you can clarify that which is never missing even for a second, then you are really a descendent of Dongshan's family and one of Qingyuan's offshoots.

Verse

Now, how can I convey this principle? Would you like to hear?

> The mind mirror hangs high and reflects everything clearly;
> The vermilion boat is so beautiful that no painting can do it justice.

TOUZI YIQING

Case

The forty-fourth patriarch was Priest Touzi. He studied with [Fushan] Yuanjian [Fushan Fayuan]. Yuanjian had him inspect the [story of the] non-Buddhist asking the Buddha, "Aside from speech, aside from silence." After three years, one day [Yuanjian] asked him, "Do you remember the case? Try to present it." The master was about to speak when Yuanjian put his hand over his mouth. The master was thoroughly enlightened.

Circumstances

The master's initiatory name was Yiqing. He was of the Li family in Qingshe. At the age of six, being unusually bright, he left home and lived at the Miao-xiang Monastery. He examined the scriptures and when he was fourteen he became a monk. He studied the *Treatise on the Hundred Dharmas*[228] but pretty soon he lamented, "Three incalculable eons [required for complete enlightenment] is a long road to travel; even if I take the trouble, what is the value in it?" So, he went to Luoyang and listened to [lectures on] the *Avatamsaka Sutra*, the meaning of which explained everything. [Once] he was reading verses of the bodhisattvas named Lin.[229] When he came to where it speaks of the "self-essence of Mind,"[230] he seriously reflected, "The Dharma is separate from words and letters, so how can it be conveyed in lectures?" So he gave it up and went traveling to hear talks by [Zen masters of] our tradition. At that time, Zen Master Yuanjian was at Huisheng Peak. One night, he dreamed he was raising a green hawk. He thought that this was auspicious. The next day, the master arrived. Yuanjian welcomed him courteously and had him inspect the story of the non-Buddhist questioning the Buddha [and so on]. The master was thoroughly awakened and made bows.

Yuanjian asked, "Have you been wonderfully awakened to the subtle functioning?" The master said, "Even if I have it, I should vomit it out." At that time, an attendant off to the side said, "Today, Yiqing is like a sick man who is able to sweat." The master turned to him and said, "Stop your yapping. If you keep prattling on like this, I'll vomit." Three years later, Yuanjian brought out the essential teachings of the Caodong line and revealed them [to Touzi]. [Touzi] was in complete accord with them. [Yuanjian] entrusted him with Dayang's portrait, leather shoes, and robe, and ordered, "Continue the teaching of the tradition in place of me. Don't remain here long and take good care of it." Then, he composed a verse and presented it to Touzi:

> Mount Sumeru stands in the great sky,
> The sun and moon encircle it.
> One after another, a host of mountains lean on it,
> And the white clouds change from time to time.
> The style of Shaolin [Monastery] rises and flourishes;
> The screen that obscured Caoxi and Dongshan is rolled up.
> A golden phoenix lodges in a dragon's nest;
> How can the moss in the imperial compound be crushed by carts?

Teisho

The Tathagata's teaching of the True Dharma was intimately conveyed from East to West,[231] and the five schools flourished vigorously. Methods diverged and the styles of the schools were somewhat different. There were phoenixes and dragons. They were not the same, but none was inferior. Yiqing Huayan [Touzi Yiqing] accorded with Dayang in word and deed. He must really be called a descendent of the Caodong line. Master Yuanjian inherited the teaching from Shexian. This is in a Linji line of transmission.[232] A phoenix must not be put in a dragon's nest; therefore, Yuanjian sent him to Zen Master Yuandong Faxiu. When he arrived there, he did not make inquiries but just slept a lot. An official at the monastery informed Yuantong, "There is a monk in the hall who just sleeps all day. You should enforce the rules." Yuantong asked,

"Who is he?" The official said, "The senior, Yiqing." Yuantong said, "That won't do. Let me test him." He took his staff and proceeded to the hall, where he saw the master actually sleeping. He struck the floor and scolded [Touzi], "We have no spare food here to waste just so you can eat and sleep." The master asked, "What do you want me to do?" Yuantong said, "Why don't you make inquiries and do zazen?" The master said, "Exquisite food does not tempt someone whose stomach is full." Yuantong asked, "What do you think about the fact that I don't very much acknowledge that." The master replied, "What's the point of waiting for acknowledgment?" Yuantong asked, "Who have you visited so far?" The master replied, "Fushan [Yuanjian]." Yuantong said, "I wondered about such obstinate laziness." Then, they clasped hands and laughed together and went to [Yuandong's] quarters. From then on, his reputation in the Buddhist community spread far and wide. First, he resided at [Mount] Baiyun. Later he moved to [Mount] Touzi. All this is recorded in the *Compendium of the Five Lamps*.[233]

Also, the *Continued Record of the Sayings of Ancient Elders*[234] says that the master received the Dharma from Zen Master Yuanjian. Yuanjian had first studied with Great Master Dayang Mingan. He was in complete accord with [Dayang's] words and actions. In the end, [Dayang] wanted to transmit the teachings of the tradition to him, along with the robe and leather shoes, but Yuanjian refused them, saying that he had already received the Dharma [from someone else]. Mingan lamented, "There is no one to whom I can transmit my branch." Yuanjian said, "The tradition of Dongshan is exhausted and will be difficult to revive. If you have no one to transmit it to, then I will certainly hold the robe of faith [for you] and pass it on later to someone else." Mingan agreed, saying, "I will compose a verse and leave it with you as proof." He wrote:

> *The grass of Mount Yangguang*
> *Depends on you for its value to grow.*
> *When different sprouts grow in profusion,*
> *Deep and hidden, splendid roots are strong.*

He said, at last, "Whoever receives the Dharma should remain hidden for ten years and then bring it out into the open."

Later, the master and Yuanjian met. [Yuanjian] entrusted him with the essential teaching of Caodong, the portrait of Dayang, and the robe, saying, "You inherit Dayang's line through me." Later, as expected, he appeared after ten years as the inheritor of [the Dharma of] Dayang. The "Mount Yang-kuang" of the poem is Mount Dayang. The "different sprouts" refers to the present master, Yijing. "Growing value" refers to Yuanjian.

As foretold by the prediction, [Touzi] made his formal appearance. He offered incense, saying, "Do you know, O monks, where this stick of incense comes from? It was not produced by heaven and earth, nor was it created by *yin* and *yang*. It has existed since before the first Buddha,[235] and does not fit into categories [such as sacred and secular]. Since Dipamkara Buddha, it has been transmitted by seven Buddhas,[236] directly reached Caoxi [Huineng], and it's stream divided in China. In the beginning of 1064, this mountain monk was given the teaching and a verse by Zen Master Fushan Yuanjian in person, and I was certainly confirmed. He said, in his compassionate instruction, 'Continue Dayang's teaching in place of me.' Although this mountain monk did not know Dayang, his teaching was inherited and passed on like this through the recognition of a person [capable of preserving it]. I am determined not to turn my back on the kindness bestowed on me through Priest Fushan's bequest of the Dharma. I respectfully [offer this incense] for Great Priest Mingan of Mount Dayang in Yingzhou. Why? Mother and father are not parents of Buddhas; the Dharma is their parent." After that, he expounded Dayang's teaching and found Zen Master Furong [Daokai] and made him his heir.

Zen Master Yuanjian of Mount Fushan was in the seventh generation of Priest Linji and a successor to Priest Shexian Guixing.[237] Earlier, he had made his home departure with Priest Sanjiao Zhisong,[238] becoming a novice monk while still young. A monk came to [Sanjiao's] quarters and asked about the story of Zhaozhou's oak tree.[239] Watching from the side as Zhisong pushed the monk, [Yuanjian] was awakened. He visited various teachers and was in accord with all of them. He had audiences with Fenyang and Shexian, receiving the seal of approval from both. Finally, he became Shexian's Dharma heir. He also visited Dayang, and there was a meeting of minds. However, when [Dayang] tried to transmit the teaching to him, he rejected it, saying that he had already acquired it elsewhere [from Shexian]. Although he did not accept it himself, because Dayang had no one else [to whom he could transmit it], Yuanjian consequently accepted it [temporarily] so it did not die out. Later, Yuanjian found the potential [in Touzi] and intimately passed it on. At this point, you should realize that [the two lines of] Qingyuan and Nanyue are fundamentally not separate.[240]

Because he was sad that Dayang's tradition might fall apart, Yuanjian became his surrogate and transmitted Dayang's essential teachings. However, followers of our own tradition say that Nanyue's line is inferior, and that Qingyuan's teaching is superior. Linji people also say that Dongshan's teaching died out [with Dayang] and was helped by Linji followers. Both sides appear to be ignorant of the teaching. Whether our school or theirs, if they are true men, neither can be doubted. Why? Qingyuan and Nanyue were both followers of Caoxi [Huineng], like two horns on a bull's head. Therefore, Yaoshan was enlightened with Mazu but then became Shitou's heir. Danxia [Zhitong][241] also was enlightened with Mazu and succeeded Shitou. There is truly neither superiority nor inferiority in the flesh and bones of brothers. However, we say that only our patriarchal teachers are [true] heirs, while others are offshoots. You must realize that Linji followers are excellent and our own followers are excellent. If something were lacking in Linji [Zen] or if it were inferior, Yuanjian would have succeeded Dayang. If there were something inferior about Dayang or something wrong, how could Yuanjian transmit [the Dharma] to Touzi? Thus, O monks, do not quarrel about the five houses and seven traditions,[242] just clarify Mind. This is the true Dharma of all the Buddhas. How can you disagree concerning self and other? You must not discriminate superior and inferior.

However, [Hui]hong Jiaofan says, in his *Records of Shimen and Linjian*[243] "The Keeper of the Old Tower [Zen Master Cheng'gu][244] lived, roughly, a hundred years after Yunmen, but he called himself his heir.[245] Yiqing Huayan never knew Dayang, but he never doubted that he was Dayang's heir, as a result of [Dayang's] transmission words. Those two old fellows did it because of the transmission words and were content with that. They took themselves very seriously but took the Dharma very lightly. Those who took the Dharma seriously were Yongjia and Huangbo.[246] Yongjia was awakened to the tradition of the Buddha Mind when he heard the *Vimalakirtti Sutra*. Yet, he went to the Sixth Patriarch and said, 'I want to be certain about the essential of the teaching.' Huangbo awakened to Mazu's meaning, yet he succeeded Baizhang."

As I reflect on this explanation, Huihong Jiaofan seems to have still mis-understood something. Why? Dayang's Buddhadharma was entrusted to Yuanjian. That is beyond doubt, especially since he left proof when he found someone [in Yuanjian]. There is no question that ten years after he died, [Touzi] fulfilled the prophecy. If [Huihong] doubts that [the Dharma] was bequeathed to Yuanjian, then Dayang's transmission would also be in doubt. The reliable instructions of patriarchal teachers cannot be compared with confused ordinary events. Even ordinary people consider the words of a real person proof. How much more did Yuanjian, a man who knew the Dharma, have Dayang's face-to-face transmission and accord with him in word and spirit. Jiaofan criticized Touzi for not doubting Yuanjian's words. Yuanjian, being the heir to Shexian, was a true descendent of Linji. The ancients did not doubt this. How could Buddha patriarchs make false claims? As the recipient of generations of patriarchs' approval and prediction, [Yuanjian] was hon-ored and respected, so why should Touzi doubt it was as if Dayang were still living?

The life of the Buddha patriarchs continues without beginning or end. It transcends past, present, and future; master and disciple do not differ. They become one, like gourd vines encircling a gourd. You can say they are one. Everyone from Fayang to Yuanjian and Touzi came to be the one Dayang. In the end, Shakyamuni continues [through India, China, and Japan] down to the present. Such being the innermost reality of the Buddha patriarchs, how can Yuanjian be doubted? If you doubt Yuanjian, why didn't Kashyapa doubt Shakyamuni? Why didn't the Second [Chinese] Patriarch doubt Bodhi-dharma? Buddha patriarchs cannot be deceived. They esteem selflessness in the Buddhadharma, and in this way, it is inherited and continued. Dayang depended on Yuanjian. Touzi respected Yuanjian, not doubting what he was told to do and considering the Dharma primary. These three masters did not let the teaching of their predecessors end. They continued Dongshan's tra-dition down through many subsequent generations. Truly, this is something fine in our tradition and a great treasure in the Buddhadharma.

Now, too, when a suitable vessel [for the Dharma] cannot be found, it can be [temporarily] entrusted to a well-informed person. Jiaofan was careless and compared Touzi Yiqing to the Keeper of the Old Tower, but this was quite a mistake. Cheng'gu, of Qianfu [Monastery] was called the "Keeper of the Old Tower." He lived in front of Zen Master Yunzhu Hongjiao's memorial tower, about a hundred years after Yunmen. He understood Yunmen's words somewhat, so he said, "Huangbo's insight was not perfect. How can you separate past and present? Even though he understood Mazu's words, he didn't succeed Mazu. Since I understand Yunmen's words, I should succeed Yunmen." In the end, he claimed that he was Yunmen's successor. All the records list him as Yunmen's heir. This is a mistake by the recorders and is really laughable. Xiangyan[247] was awakened when he heard bamboo being struck, so why didn't he become a successor to bamboo? Lingyun[248] was awakened by peach blossoms, so why didn't he become the successor to peach blossoms? It is a pity that Cheng'gu did not realize that succession takes place in the quarters of Buddhist patriarchs. If Jiaofan also doubted Priest Yiqing, it seems that he did not know of the mutual recognition there in the room. It can be said that you [Jiaofan] belittle yourself and do not reach the Dharma. Therefore, the *Record of Linjian* is undependable.

In the earlier story, the non-Buddhist asked the Buddha, "Aside from speech, aside from silence [what is it]?" Since it is a path that simply does not fall into [the extremes of] speech and silence, the World-honored One was silent for a while. It is not hidden or revealed, not self or other, not within or without, not relative or absolute. When it was revealed as like space or like the water of the ocean, the non-Buddhist suddenly understood. He bowed, saying, "The World-honored One in his great compassion has lifted the cloud of my delusion and made me enter [the truth]." Having said that, he left.

He was able to become like the great purity of the sky when not a fragment of cloud remains, like the stillness of the great ocean when the winds die down. However, Ananda did not understand and he respectfully asked the Buddha, "What did the non-Buddhist attain so that he could speak of entering?" The Buddha replied, "He is like an excellent horse who goes when he sees the shadow of the whip." This is the means employed by Buddha patriarchs. In personally making the treasury [of each individual] open, thorough awakening appears and total clarity arrives without a single device being used or a single word being spoken. It is like seeing the shadow of the whip and reaching the true road.

Thus, do not get stuck in the realm of no thought, but continue to use your eyes. Do not get attached to speechlessness, but continue to clarify Mind. Many people misunderstand this silence [of the Buddha]. They say, "When a single thought does not occur, the whole [Mind] is revealed. When one goes beyond the forms of names, it is bared spontaneously, just as a mountain is exposed when all the clouds are gone. One is resolutely independent of all things, exactly like this." If you compare this with one's former intellectual understanding and galloping about seeking for it externally, there seems to be a little rest; but one still has not forgotten skin and flesh, nor has [ordinary] perception departed. If you want to be fit for this realm, try to end your panting and sever the life force. When you see what is exposed, how can you say it is non-thought? Since you cannot say it is anything, how can you [even] say it is silence? It is not just the cessation of panting and the eyes closing; look at that place where the hundred bones are scattered and not a remnant of skin and flesh remains. There is something that is neither light nor darkness and is neither male nor female.

Verse

How can I communicate this principle?

The outline of a peak so high that birds can hardly cross;
Sword blades and thin ice—who can walk on them?

FURONG DAOKAI

Case

The forty-fifth patriarch was Zen Master Daokai of Mount Furong. He studied with Priest Touzi Yiqing. He asked him, "The words of the Buddha patriarchs are like ordinary rice and tea, but is there anything else apart from these to help people?" Yiqing replied, "Tell me, does the emperor's mandate in his kingdom depend on [the ancient emperors] Yao, Shun, Yu, and Tang?" The master was about to answer when Yiqing struck him in the mouth with his *hossu*[249] and said, "When you gave way to thought, you immediately deserved thirty blows." The master was awakened.

Circumstances

The master's name was Daokai. Even as a youth, he enjoyed peace and quiet, secluding himself on Mount Yiyang. Later he traveled to the capitol and registered at Taishu Monastery, where he examined the *Lotus Sutra* and became a monk. He called on Touzi at Haihui [Monastery]. He asked, "The words of the Buddha patriarchs are like ordinary rice and tea, but is there anything else apart from these to help people?" and he was awakened. He bowed several times and started to go. Touzi said, "Come here a minute, sir," but Daokai did not turn around. Touzi asked, "Did you arrive at the realm of no doubt?" The master covered his ears with his hands.

Later he became head cook. Touzi said, "Taking care of the kitchen isn't easy." The master replied, "Not at all." Touzi asked, "Do you boil the gruel and steam the rice?" The master answered, "Assistants sort the rice and light the fire; workers boil the gruel and steam the rice." Touzi asked, "What do you do?" The master said, "The Master, in his compassion has let Him go."

One day, while he was attending Touzi, they walked around in the veg-etable garden. Touzi handed him his staff and he took it and followed. Touzi said, "This is how it should be." The master said, "I don't consider it improper to carry your shoes or staff." Touzi said, "There is Another walk-ing with us." The master said, "That Person doesn't take orders." Touzi left to rest. That evening, he said to the master, "We still haven't finished our ear-lier talk." The master said, "Please, Master, say something." Touzi said, "The sun comes up in the morning; the moon rises in the evening." The master then lit a lamp. Touzi said, "Your actions are not futile." The master replied, "If I am with you, this is how it should be." Touzi said, "In whose house are there no servants?" The master replied, "The master is getting old; it won't do to be without them." Touzi said, "You are so obliging." The master said, "It is my duty to repay kindness."

Teisho

In this way, he thoroughly and meticulously clarified the great matter. The meaning of his question "The words of the Buddha patriarchs are like ordi-nary rice and tea, but is there anything else apart from these to help peo-ple?" is, "Do Buddha patriarchs teach anything else apart from their everyday lives?" It sounds very much as if he were presenting his understanding. How-ever, Touzi asked, "Tell me, does the emperor's mandate in the kingdom depend on Yao, Shun, Yu, and Tang?" Really, issuing orders now ultimately does not rely on the ancient emperors Yao and Shun. It's just that when one person is blessed, the whole citizenry is naturally blessed. In the same way, even though old Master Shakyamuni appeared in the world [today] and Great Master Bodhidharma still lived, yet people should not rely on their power. When you just affirm and authenticate it yourselves, you will become it completely. Therefore, if you try to add some flavor when you explain the truth, you end up seeing it as another and do not escape plotting and scheming. That is why [Touzi] struck the master in the mouth with his *hossu* when he started to speak. In order to show him that he was perfect right from the beginning with nothing lacking, he said, "When you gave way to thought, you immediately deserved thirty blows." This is not confirma-tion [of understanding but rather chastisement].

Once you give way to thought, trying to decide what "Mind" is or what "Buddha" is, you deny yourself and look elsewhere. Even though you can say, "The entirety is revealed," or "It is naturally bright," or you speak of "Mind," "Nature," "Zen," or "the Way," you have not at all escaped plotting and scheming. If there is plotting and scheming, then immediately there are clouds for ten thousand miles and you will be deluded about Self for a long time. Even if I were to give you not just thirty blows but strike you in life after life for ten thousand eons, it would be hard for you to escape your offenses.

[Daokai] was awakened at the words [of Touzi]. He made bows and left without even turning around [when called]. When asked, "Have you reached the realm of no doubt?" [if you ask], "What is the need to reach the realm of no doubt?" then you are separated from it by ten thousand miles of obstructing mountains. When we hear the words of the Buddha patriarchs with our ears, they defile our ears at once. Though we cleanse our ears for a thousand lives over ten thousand eons, we cannot get them clean. Therefore, [Daokai] covered his ears not letting in one word. Because he had experienced this realm fully, when he was the head cook, he said, "The Master has set Him free." "He" is not the one who steams rice nor the one who gathers vegetables. Therefore, carrying firewood and water is something for workers and laborers to do, not the head cook. Though "He" never seems to stop rolling up his sleeves and scrubbing pots throughout the twenty-four hours, ultimately, "He" never does anything, nor does "He" come in contact with things. Therefore, [Daokai] spoke of setting "Him" free.

Although he had experienced it like this, when they went to the vegetable garden, Touzi tried to get him to mature [his insight]. He handed him his staff, and the master took it and followed along. Touzi said, "This is the way it should be." He showed the master that [the staff] was not something a priest ought to carry himself, that there was someone who does not carry things, and [Daokai's] insight was ripened. Therefore, he said, "I don't consider it improper to carry your shoes and staff." Even though he knew what moved its toes in the priest's shoes and carried the staff, he still retained a little doubt in understanding that extending one's hands and moving one's feet was not improper. So [Touzi] tested him, saying, "There is Another walking with us." Not only do you not know His name, even though you have lived with Him from the beginning, he is the Old Fellow whose face is also unknown. He is "Another walking with us." [The master] had experienced this a long time before, so he said, "That Person doesn't take orders."

However, there was still something he had not achieved. Why? Even though he knew that there was someone who does not join you when you extend your hand and who is not affected when you move your feet, if this was the extent of his understanding, there was still some doubt. Therefore, Touzi went to take some rest without getting to the bottom of the truth. That night he told the master, "We still haven't finished our discussion." At the time, the master knew of its existence and that it was beyond doubt. Feeling that there was nothing he had not reached, he said, "Please, Master, say something." Then, Touzi said, "The sun comes up in the morning; the moon rises in the evening." Surely, the night deepens, stars move, and the moon is darkened; white clouds spread across the many mountains so that they are hidden. However, there is a sun that rises that is not one of them. The sun sinks behind the western hills and the many forms are unseen. Although no one comes and goes, and the road cannot be discerned, there is also something that is not emptied out. Therefore, the moon comes out. Although in this realm everything is the same and unalloyed with anything else, and nothing else is seen [or heard], it is something naturally clear and bright. It illuminates the darkness at once. Therefore, the master lit a lamp. This showed that he had really arrived there and seen it fully. Touzi said, "Your actions are not futile." When [Daokai] became familiar with this realm, there was no time during the day and night for being lax in his concentrated efforts. He said, "If I am beside you, this is how it should be."

Although he had seen it fully, he seemed to understand it as the wonderful functioning [of the Self]. Therefore, [Touzi] tested him again, saying, "In whose house are there no servants?" Who has no servants to use? The master said, "You are getting old; it won't do to be without them." There is Someone who is venerable and eminent who does not mingle with the dust of the world. That body is wonderfully bright and ultimately not separate [from oneself]. The master said, "You are getting old; it won't do to be without them." Coming to see it like this, he cannot be said to have not reached it exactly. So [Touzi] said, "You are so obliging."

For eons and eons, He has supported us and never left us. We have received His kindness for a long time. If you try to compare His kindness, even Mount Sumeru is not as large. If you try to compare His virtue, not even the four oceans and nine continents can equal it. The reason is that Mount Sumeru, the sun and moon, the great ocean and the rivers all move [and change] with time, but the kindness of this "Old Priest" never takes on form or ceases to exist. There is never a time when we do not receive His kindness. If we are born in vain and die in vain without once paying our respects to that venerable face, then as unfilial people, we will flounder in the ocean of birth and death for a long time. If you are thorough and see Him sufficiently, you will utterly repay the vast kindness of a thousand lives and ten thousand eons. Therefore, [Daokai] said, "I must repay kindness."

Having seen this so precisely in such a way, when he took up residence [as a teacher] and a monk said, "A Tartar flute does not use the five tones [of classical Chinese music], but its sound fills the dark night. Please, Master, play it," the master said, "A wooden rooster crows at midnight; an iron phoenix cries at dawn." [The monk said,] "In that case, then, a single note includes a thousand ancient songs. All the monks in the hall know the sound." The master said, "Even a tongueless youth can continue it."

Maturing like this, no green hills blocked his eyes, no clear stream washed his ears. Fame and fortune were like dust in his eyes. Seeing forms and hearing sounds were like planting flowers on a stone. Finally, he never left the monastery, nor did he attend feasts. He did not care if people came or if they went. His community was never fixed in size, sometimes being large and other times being small. They ate [only] one bowl of gruel a day. If there was not enough, they had it thinned with hot water. The essential teachings of Caodong flourished at this time.

He had an intimate view [of the Dharma] and made no errors in guarding it. Therefore, he never forgot what former masters had entrusted him with. Even though he heeded the counsel of the enlightened ones of antiquity like this, he still said, "You cannot use this mountain monk's conduct as an example. I am ashamed to be the master of this monastery. How can I be here wasting the communal goods [of the community] and so quickly forget what former masters entrusted me with. Now, every time I try to emulate the former abbots...and every time this mountain monk speaks of the doings of the sages of old, I am aware that I have no hiding place.[250] I am ashamed of how soft and weak their successors have become."

Now, [I, Keizan] as a Dharma descendent in the ninth generation [after Daokai] am prematurely preaching the teaching of our tradition. My daily activities are poor examples for my successors. My attention to the four kinds of deportment[251] wanders completely. How can I face three or four monks and give a talk of a phrase or half a phrase? It is shameful, terrible! [There is no place to hide from] the glances of our ancient patriarchs or the penetrating looks of former sages. Although this is how it is, you should be grateful to be distant descendants of Zen Master Furong Daokai and to be in the family of the school of Eihei [Dogen]. You should clearly discern the realm of Mind and thoroughly take care of it. Without a hair of interest in fame and fortune and without an atom of pride and conceit, settle your minds and govern your physical actions. Reach what you should reach, penetrate what should be penetrated, and settle the business of your life practice. Do not forget what you have inherited from former patriarchs. Follow in the footsteps of former sages. Meet the former awakened ones eye to eye and despite the decadence of these final days [of the Dharma], you will be able to see a tiger in the market place or perhaps find gold under your hat. This is my greatest prayer, my earnest hope.

Verse

Now, tell me, how can I concisely explain this story?

Even without cosmetics, no ugliness shows;
We naturally admire the ornaments of lustrous jade bones.[252]

Danxia Zichun

Case

The forty-sixth patriarch was Zen Master Danxia. He asked Furong, "What is the single phrase that all the sages have transmitted from ancient times?" Furong replied, "If you call it a phrase, you really bury the Caodong tradition." With these words, the master was greatly awakened.

Circumstances

The master's name was Zichun. He was from the Jia family of Jianzhou. At the age of nineteen he made his home departure and he was greatly awakened with Furong. At first he stayed at [Mount] Xuefeng, later at [Mount] Danxia.

Teisho

His first question was, "What is the single phrase that all the sages have transmitted from ancient times?" Even though Buddha after Buddha and patriarch after patriarch has changed in appearance, there is without doubt something that has been transmitted that is without front and back, without up and down, without inside or outside, without self or other. It is called "nonempty emptiness."[253] It is the true place to which all must return. There is none that does not possess it fully.

However, many students mistakenly think that it is original nonbeing that cannot be expressed or conceived. The ancients called such people "non-Buddhists who fall into nothingness." Even after the lapse of eons as numerous as the sands of the Ganges River, they will never be liberated. Even if you are thorough and meticulous and by all means put an end to all things and make them utterly empty, there is still something that cannot be emptied. Investigating carefully, if you once get a peek at it, you will surely be able to get hold of a phrase to express it. Therefore, it is called the "single phrase that has been transmitted."

At that time, Furong said, "If you call it a phrase, you will really bury the Caodong tradition." Truly, this realm cannot be referred to as a phrase. Using words incorrectly is like bird tracks in the snow. It is therefore said, "There are no traces where you conceal your body." When bodily awareness utterly ceases, and skin, flesh, bones, and marrow are all gone, what traces can remain? If you leave not even a hair [of traces], sure enough, it will appear. This is not something others know about. It is not something that is passed on [publicly]. However, when this realm is understood, it is said to be transmitted from Mind to Mind. This occasion is referred to as the "oneness of lord and retainer," the "oneness²⁵⁴ of absolute and relative."

Verse

Now, tell me briefly, what do you think the form of this realm is?

> The pure wind circles the earth and shakes it time after time,
> But who can pluck it up and show it to you?

Zhenxie Qingliao

Case

The forty-seventh patriarch was Zen Master Wukong [Zhenxie Qingliao]. He studied with Danxia. Danxia asked him, "What is the Self prior to the empty eon?"[255] The master started to speak and Danxia said, "You're noisy; go away for a while." One day, [Qingliao] climbed Boyu Peak and was suddenly awakened.

Circumstances

The master's initiatory name was Qingliao and his Buddhist name was Zhenxie. Wukong was his title as a Zen master. When his mother went to a temple hugging him to her bosom in his baby clothes, he saw [an image of] the Buddha and raised his eyebrows and blinked in delight. Everyone thought this was unusual. When he was seventeen, he lectured on the *Lotus Sutra*. He became a monk and went to Daci Temple in Chengdu [in Szechwan]. There he learned the scriptures and treatises and grasped their great meaning. He left Szechwan to go to [the area of the] Jiang, Mian, and Han [Rivers], and knocked on Danxia's door. Danxia asked him, "What is the Self prior to the empty eon?" [Later] he was suddenly awakened. He returned at once [from Boyu Peak] and stood before Danxia. Danxia slapped him, saying, "I think that you know it exists." The master joyfully bowed.

The next day, Danxia entered the hall and said:

> *The sun illuminating the solitary peaks is green;*
> *The moonlight falling on the valley streams is cold.*

The deep, subtle secret of master and disciple
Must not be lodged in a one-inch heart.

Then he left his seat. The master immediately came and stood before him. He said, "Your talk from the high seat today cannot deceive me." Danxia said, "Try to present [the meaning of] what I said from the high seat." The master was silent for a while. Danxia said, "I think that you got a glimpse of that realm."

The master then left [Danxia]. Later, he traveled to Mount Wutai, went to the capitol, crossed the Bian [River], and arrived at Mount Changlu, where he had an audience with Zuzhao. Once they talked, they were in complete agreement. [Zuzhao] had him be his attendant. A year later, they shared teaching. Pretty soon, Zuzhao retired, saying that he was ill. He asked the master to carry on the talks. At the end of 1130, he traveled to [Mount] Ximing and [later] was the head of monasteries at Mount Putuo, Mount Tianfeng in Taizhou, and Mount Xue Peak in Minzhou. Then he was abbot at Ayuwang Monastery as a result of imperial decree. He subsequently moved to Longxiang Monastery in Wenzhou, and then to a monastery at Mount Jing in Hangzhou. [Later,] he founded Chongxian Monastery in Gaoning prefecture by decree of the emperor's mother, Cining.

Teisho

From the time his mother held him wrapped in baby clothes, he was not one of the herd but rather stood out. Moreover, when he made up his mind to practice Zen, he made a concentrated effort. Therefore, when he was asked about the Self prior to the empty eon, he tried to give an answer. Danxia did not approve, but sent him away for a while. One day, he climbed to the top of Boyu Peak. [He saw] the ten directions unobstructed and the four cardinal points gateless. When the ten directions appeared right in front of him, he was awakened. He returned and stood before Danxia without saying a word. Danxia realized that he knew it existed, and said, "I think that you know it exists." Then [Jingliao] joyfully bowed. Danxia finally entered the hall [the next day] and acknowledged [the awakening]. Later when he appeared [as a teacher] the master said, "When I was slapped by my former teacher, my cleverness disappeared, and when I tried to open my mouth, I couldn't. Is there anyone here who has not completely experienced such joy? If you [are lucky and] do not have a bit in your mouths or a saddle on your backs, you must each apply yourselves to the means [of awakening]."

When patriarchal teachers see eye to eye, they walk [in this realm] prior to the empty eon and immediately illuminate the scenery of this fundamental realm. If you cannot see this realm yet, then even if you sit [in zazen] speechless for a thousand, or ten thousand years, immobile as a withered tree, like dead ashes, what's the use? However, when people hear of "prior to the empty eon," they mistakenly think that "there is no self, no other, no before or after, no origination or extinction, no beings or Buddhas. It cannot be called one or two, it cannot be discerned as identical, nor can it be called different." Scheming and plotting like this, thinking that if one utters a single word one distances oneself from it, or that if a single thought arises one turns one's back on it, they are like corpses harboring ghosts as dead as withered trees. Or else, they think that anything they do is all right. They may think that you can speak of "mountains," "rivers," "self," and "other." Or, they think, "You can say it is a mountain but it is not a mountain," "You can call it a river but it is not a river," "Only this is a mountain," "Only that is a river." What is the use of saying such things? They all end up on the wrong path. They either become attached to form or else they fall into the views of nihilists.

How can you locate this realm in either being or nonbeing? There is no chance to poke in your tongue, no chance to spin your thoughts. It does not depend on heaven a bit, nor on earth, and it does not depend on before and after. Notice where there is no place to take a step right beneath you, and you may have some slight awareness of it. Some say that it transcends models, some say it is beyond calculation. All this is scheming and turning away from the Self, even more so if you say it is "moon," "clouds," "water," or "wind." All these people unfortunately have cataracts in their eyes, seeing flowers in the sky [where there are none]. What do they mean by "mountains"? Ultimately, they do not see a single thing. What can be felt as cold or warm? Ultimately, not a single thing is imparted to them. Therefore, they cling to trees and grass [like ghosts]. If they sweep away the way of the world and the Buddhadharma at the same time, then, if they look, they will not doubt.

Do not look within; do not look outside. Do not try to quiet thought; do not try to calm your bodies. Just know intimately and understand intimately. Cut off [discrimination] at once and try to do zazen a little. Even though it is said that there is no place in the four directions to take a step, and no place in heaven and earth to place your body, in reality, you will not need to get power from elsewhere. When you see it like this, no skin, flesh, bones, and marrow are distributed to you. The coming and going of birth and death do not change you. When you have totally shed your skin, there is only the single reality [remaining]. It lights up past and present and transcends time and space. How can it be called simply "prior to the empty eon"?

This realm is not something that can be said to be before or after. The reason is that this realm is not affected by [the four eons of] formation, existence, destruction, and nothingness.[256] Can self and others be considered causeless? When you forget the external world and rid yourself of conditioning notions in your head, still, "the sky receives a blow" and you become utterly stripped and exposed. If you see it carefully, being like the sky, it is mysterious; being empty, it is subtle. If you are not thorough, you will ultimately not reach this place. Clearing up [that which has persisted through] countless eons occurs in the snap of your fingers. Though it is momentary and brief, without any feeling of indecision, not showing any sign of intellection,[257] try to suddenly cast your eyes on its face and you will become independent, liberated and free.

However, students, by turning your thoughts [in the wrong direction], you have already started in the wrong direction. Though you think that this is an extremely minute deviation, you should realize that if you do this, you will not find rest for a thousand lives and ten thousand eons. Try to think about this carefully and reach [this realm]. Without relying on anything else, completely clear, you will be like the sky when you are awakened.

Verse

Tell me briefly, how can you communicate this realm even a little?

The icy spring of the valley stream—no one peeks into it.
It does not allow travelers to penetrate its depth.

TIANTONG ZONGJUE

Case

The forty-eighth patriarch was Zen Master Tiantong Zongjue. He was Wukong's attendant for a long time. One day, Wukong asked him, "How do you see it these days?" The master said, "Suppose I say that I am like this." Wukong said, "That's not enough; say some more." The master said, "Why isn't it enough?" Wukong said, "I didn't say it was not enough, but you aren't familiar with that which is beyond." The master said, "I expressed that which is beyond." Wukong asked, "What is that which is beyond?" The master said, "Even supposing that I can express that which is beyond, I cannot put it into words for you, master." Wukong said, "You can't really express it." The master said, "I beg you to say it." Wukong said, "Ask me, and I'll say it." The master asked, "What is that which is beyond?" Wukong replied, "Suppose I say that I am not like this." The master was awakened when he heard this, and Wukong gave his approval.

Circumstances

The master's initiatory name was Zongjue. He was Wukong's attendant for a long time. He practiced unceasingly day and night in every possible way, so he seemed to be constantly ready. Wukong asked, "How do you see it these days?" The master replied, "Suppose I say that I am like this." Wukong said, "That's not enough; say more" [and so on].

Teisho

When [Zongjue] says, "like this," there is still something lacking. Even though he understands the so-called comes in this way, he did not know that there is one who "does not come in this way." The entirety being exposed and nothing concealed, he wondered what could be lacking. He asked, "What is lacking?" Those who understand it like this, and can be like green mountains lofty and solitary when the white clouds disperse, still do not realize that there is another mountain taller than the other. Wukong therefore said, "I didn't say that what you said wasn't enough, but you are not familiar with that which is beyond." Although practicing like this is itself "that which is beyond," still, [Zongjue] made the mistake of not knowing its existence. [Wukong] said, "You can't really express it."

What is more, when you utter a single word, spin thoughts, and say "like this," you fall into the secondary and tertiary [and miss the primary]. [Thinking that] there was not a single point he had missed, he said, "Even supposing I can express that which is beyond, I cannot put it into words for you." He did not know the Self and was still concerned with distinctions. For that reason, Wukong said, "You can't really express it." At that point, [Zongjue's] breath stopped. He lost his power and asked, "What is that which is beyond?" Wukong replied, "Suppose I say that I also am not like this." This expression and the former one [by Zongjue] are as far apart as heaven and earth, as different as fire and water. Zongjue thought that everything was exposed, but Wukong said that it was not so. Saying "like this," [Zongjue] was merely the solitary moon clear and bright, but when he perceived his error, he received approval.

Later, he appeared [as a teacher] and preached the Dharma to others. A monk asked him, "What is the Way?" The master replied, "Stop standing at the crossroads gazing into the distance." Once, he entered the hall and said, "Walk [in the time] prior to the beginning of time; stretch out beyond the world. Wonderful realization cannot be accomplished with thought; true realization cannot be communicated with words. When you get it at once, stillness suppresses the mist, and white clouds are barred from the chilly peak. A glorious light rends the darkness, and the bright moon accompanies the boat in the night. Right at that moment, how do you embody it? Relative and absolute never leave the fundamental state. How can this situation have anything to do with words?"

Emptiness and stillness have no boundaries. Even if you cannot put it into words, you are not apart from it. This is how you must be if you want to be aware of what is beyond. Still, talking about "Mind" or "essential nature" is not at all that which is beyond. Also, just saying "mountains are mountains and water is water" and thinking that this is "beyond" is, without doubt, a mistake. Dongshan said, "When you experience that which is beyond Buddha, then you can express it somewhat." A monk asked him, "What are the words?" Dongshan replied, "If I say them, you won't hear them." Also, Panshan said, "The single path beyond was not transmitted by any of the sages."[258] Truly, it is not a matter of "rambling freely as one pleases" as people like to say. Also, a monk asked Zen Master Wukong, "What is that which is beyond?" Wukong replied, "That marvel exists prior to [the appearance of] a bubble [of your body]. How can it submit to the eyes of a thousand sages?" "Bubble" means after your body has appeared [in the womb]. When it has not yet appeared, it is called "that which is beyond."

Zen Master Kumu Facheng,[259] a true spiritual son of Furong Daokai, said to the monks, "When you realize that there is something beyond the Buddha patriarchs, you will be able to express it. O Zen worthies, tell me, what is that beyond the Buddha patriarchs? He is someone who lacks the six senses and whose seventh consciousness is incomplete.[260] He is the great *icchantika,* [a being] who has no Buddha nature. When he meets a Buddha, he slays the Buddha; when he meets a patriarch, he slays the patriarch. He cannot be confined in heaven, nor can hell hold him. O monks, do you know that person?" He paused for a moment, then said, "When you meet him, you are dull and full of sleep and your drowsy words spill out."

As for that which is beyond, even if a Buddha were to appear, he would lose his life; even if a patriarch appears, his whole body is reduced to powder. If [he] tries to enter the celestial mansion, the mansion is demolished; if he goes to hell, hell shatters at once. What do you think celestial mansions are? Where is hell? What do you mean by "the myriad forms"? From the beginning, there are no traces. It is just like when you are asleep. You are not aware of yourself, let alone others. There is no reason. It just clearly is the way of nonawakening. These are truly the words of our eminent patriarchs. If you know that which is beyond, and open your eyes, you will at this time have a chance to become it.

Verse

Now tell me, what is this principle?

> *It is like trying to drive a wedge between two planks;*
> *You can't drive in the wedge or pry them apart.*

XUEDOU ZHIJIAN

Case

The forty-ninth patriarch was Zen Master Xuedou Zhijian. When Zongjue was at [Mount] Tiantong, one day he entered the hall and said, "The World-honored One spoke with a hidden meaning, but it was not concealed to Kashyapa." When the master heard this, he was suddenly awakened to its profound meaning. Standing there in the ranks with the others, his tears fell. He unconsciously burst out, "Why haven't I heard this before?" Zongjue finished his talk and summoned the master. He asked, "Why were you weeping?" The master replied, "The World-honored One spoke with a hidden meaning, but it was not concealed to Kashyapa." Zongjue gave his approval, saying, "You must be the one that Yunju predicted."

Circumstances

The master's initiatory name was Zhijian. He was from the Wu family of Chuzhou. When he was a boy, his mother washed a sore on his hand and asked him what it was. He replied, "My hand is like a Buddha's hand." When he grew older, his parents died. He went to see Zhenxie [Changlu] in Changlu.[261] At that time, Zongjue was the senior monk and he thought the master was a vessel [of the Dharma]. Later, [the master] secluded himself on Mount Xiang and the wild animals would not trouble him. Late one night, he was enlightened. He sought confirmation from Yanshou,[262] but he went back to practice with Priest Zongjue. At that time, Zongjue was the abbot at [Mount] Tiantong. He appointed the master to the important position of clerk. One day, he brought up the above situation [in the case].

This situation occurs in the *Nirvana Sutra* [scroll five, in the chapter on "Tathagata Nature"]. Once, Kashyapa Bodhisattva said to the Buddha, "O World-honored One, according to what the Buddha has said, all Buddhas, World-honored Ones, speak with a hidden meaning. But this is not what he means. Why? All Buddhas, World-honored Ones, have a hidden meaning, not a hidden body of teaching. It is like a magician's mechanical man. Even though people see it lean over, stretch, and look up and down, they do not realize that there is something inside it that makes it the way it is. The Buddhadharma is not like that but instead allows people to understand completely. How could it be said that Buddhas, World-honored Ones, have a secret body of teachings?" The Buddha praised Kashyapa: "Very good, very good, good son. As you say, the Tathagata truly has no secret body of teachings. Why? Just as the full moon in autumn is clear and exposed in the sky, pure and unobscured and seen by everybody, so are the Tathagata's words. He utters them clear and exposed, pure and unobscured. Deluded people say that it is a secret body of teachings, but the wise understand completely and do not call it a secret body of teaching." Since then, this expression has been used for a long time by followers of the patriarchal teachers. Therefore, when it was brought up here, Zhijian was awakened. It was truly not concealed.

Teisho

When you hear words, you must know their inner meaning and not get trapped by the words. Saying "fire" is not fire, and saying "water"' is not water. Therefore, you do not burn your mouth when you say "fire," nor is your mouth wet when you say "water." You must realize that fire and water are not words. Priest Shitou[263] said, "When you hear words, you should understand their meaning and not set up any rules of your own." Also, Yaoshan[264] said, "You have to look yourself. You cannot eliminate language. I am saying these words right now and they reveal what is unspoken. Who is That One who lacks ears, eyes, and so on, right from the beginning?"

Also, Zhangqing[265] said, "The twenty-eight generations [of Indian patriarchs] spoke of transmitting Mind, not of transmitting words." Great Master Yunmen said, "If this matter existed beyond words, wouldn't the twelve-part canon of the three vehicles be wordless? Why do we speak of a 'special transmission outside the scriptures'? If you proceed by using intellectual understanding like the saints of the ten stages, then even though your preaching of the Dharma is like clouds and rain [in its abundance], you will be criticized for seeing essential nature as if through thin silk. You should realize as a result of this that all discriminating minds [are as apart from it] as heaven and earth." Though this is how it is, if you are a thoroughly accomplished person, you won't burn your mouth when you say "fire." You can talk all day and nothing will cling to your lips and teeth. You won't utter a word.

Monks, you should know that there is Someone who is not only speechless but also mouthless. Not only is He mouthless but He also has no eyes. From the beginning, He has not possessed a hair's worth of the four elements and six senses. Though it is like this, it is not emptiness, nor is it nothingness. Even though you say you see things and hear sounds, it is not your eyes seeing or your ear hearing; it is this Faceless Fellow doing it. Your mind and body were provided by this Fellow. Therefore, the mind and body are not at all created things. If you haven't reached this point, then you may think that your body was created as a result of your parents, and that your body is a result of karma. Thus, you may think that your body resulted from the union of sperm and egg, or that your body is covered with skin and flesh. This is because you have not thoroughly clarified Self.

In order to get you to know this realm, spiritual teachers use unlimited means to get you to put an end to the six senses and stop everything. At such a time, there is something that cannot be destroyed, something that cannot be crushed. When you become aware of it, it surely cannot be reduced to emptiness or existence, nor is it bright or dark. Therefore, it is hard to talk about whether you are deluded or enlightened. For this reason, this realm is not called "Buddha," "Dharma," "Mind," or "essential nature." It is nothing but bright light existing brilliantly. Therefore, it is not the light of fire or the light of water; it is just boundless clarity and brightness. You cannot see it, though you try; nor can you acquire it, though you try. It is just alertness. When the three disasters of water, fire, and wind occur, and the world is destroyed,[266] it is not destroyed. When the triple world and its six paths arise [again][267] and the myriad things sprout profusely, this thing does not change. Even Buddhas do not know what to make of it; even patriarchs do not know what to make of it. O monks, if you want to reach this realm in person, you must close your eyes for a while, regulate your breathing, forget your body, have no place to lodge your body, have no need for any relationship with things, become like a cloudless blue sky, and become like the great ocean without waves. Then you will have some experience of It.

At this time, even though Buddha patriarchs cannot figure you out, there is a bright light. It is not like the moon in the dark sky, or like the sun. The whole sky becomes the moon, and there is nothing else [remaining] to be illuminated. The whole universe becomes sun, and there is nowhere to shine. You must experience this completely. If you do not experience this realm, not only will you be deluded about monk and layperson, male and female, but you will transmigrate through the triple world and six paths of rebirth. While as disciples of the Buddha you look like monks, you will still end up in the hands of old Yama [judge of the Dead]. Won't you be mortified!

There is no place in all the many worlds where the Buddhadharma of Shakyamuni does not exist fully. How can you fail to reach it if you seek it? It is not easy to acquire a human body. You received it as a result of [good] roots in the past. If you once reach this realm, you will be completely liberated. It is not male or female, divinity or devil, worldling or sage, monk or lay. If you can reach this realm, though you are a monk, you are not a monk; though you are a layperson, you are not a layperson. You will not be deluded by your six senses, nor will you be at the mercy of the six kinds of consciousness. If you fail to reach it, you will be completely deluded and enslaved by those things. Wouldn't that be too bad? It exists with you from the beginning but, if you still want to reach it, you must use your power. Though no one is without it, people are deluded by their eyes [and other senses]. How much more pitiful it is that they transmigrate ever so long.

Just look carefully, forgetting the senses and their objects. Have no recourse to mind or consciousness, and you will surely reach it. You do not have to reach it gradually [by stages]. Once you arouse your determination with all your power, you will experience it. Even though it is brief, just immediately become aware of the source, without giving rise to partial understanding, and you will reach it. Once you reach it, just as if you were standing on four feet, you will not be moved by the eight winds.[268] The ancients said, "Learning the Way is like making fire by rubbing two sticks together. Do not stop a second when you see smoke." Once you exert all your power, you will get fire. What is "smoke"? When you encounter the skill of a spiritual teacher and not a single thought arises, this is when you see smoke. If you stop here and rest, it is like stopping at warmth; but if you continue on, you will see fire. This means knowing the One who does not give rise to a single thought.

If you are not thoroughly aware of the Self, then even though it seems that you have found some rest now and in so doing you are like a withered tree, you are nothing but a corpse whose spirit has not dispersed [but has no power]. Therefore, if you want to personally experience this realm, you must practice with everything you have. It does not depend on meditation or croaking like a bullfrog.

Verse

What is the principle of this "secret words unconcealed"?

> It is called the indestructible hidden body;
> That body is empty and bright.

TIANTONG RUJING

Case

The fiftieth patriarch was Priest Tiantong Rujing. He studied with Xuedou. Xuedou asked him, "Disciple Rujing, how can something that has never been soiled be cleaned?" The master spent more than a year [on this question]. Suddenly, he was awakened, and said, "I have hit upon that which is not soiled."

Circumstances

The master was a native of Mingzhou. His initiatory name was Rujing. After the age of seventeen, he abandoned doctrinal studies and practiced Zen. He joined Xuedou's community and spent a year there. He always excelled in zazen. Once, he asked to be the sanitation officer. Xuedou asked him, "How can something that has never been soiled be cleaned? If you can answer that, then I will appoint you to be the sanitation officer." The master was at a loss. After several months, he still had no answer. Once [Xuedou] invited him to his quarters and asked him, "Do you have an answer for our earlier discussion?" The master was still unable to answer. Again, Xuedou asked, "How can something that has never been soiled be cleaned?" [The master] did not answer for more than a year. Again, Xuedou asked, "Can you answer?" The master still could not answer. Xuedou said, "If you can climb out of your old rut, you will be free. Then you will be able to answer." Hearing this, the master investigated with all his strength and determination. One day, he was suddenly awakened. He went to [Xuedou's] quarters and told him, "I can answer." Xuedou said, "This time, say it." The master said, "I have hit upon that which is not soiled." Even before he finished speaking, Xuedou hit him. The master broke out in sweat and bowed. Then, Xuedou gave him his approval.

Later, at Jingci Monastery, he became the toilet cleaner in order to repay the occasion of his awakening. Once, when he was passing the Hall of Arhats,[269] a strange monk said to the master, "Cleaner of toilets at Jingci, Rujing, you repay the Way, repay the master, and repay all people." So saying, he disappeared. The prime minister of the country heard about it and interpreted it to be an omen that the sages approved of the master becoming the abbot of Jingci [Monastery]. Consequently, he became the abbot of Jingci. People everywhere said that the master's merits of repaying [his debt] were really supreme. Since arousing the determination [to be awakened] at the age of eighteen, he stayed in the monastery and never returned to his native home. Not only that, but he never associated with his countrymen or went to the rooms of others in the monastery. He did not speak with those who sat near him [in the meditation hall]. All he ever did was single-minded zazen. He vowed, "I will [sit so long that I will] crush a diamond seat." As a result of doing zazen like this, sometimes the flesh on his buttocks split open, but he would not stop sitting. From the time he first aroused this determination up to the age of sixty-four, while he was at [Mount] Tiantong, there was not a single day or night when he did not do zazen.

From the time he first became abbot of Jingci and during the time he was at [Mount] Ruiyan and [Mount] Tiantong, his conduct was outstanding. He vowed to be the same [as monks] in the monks' hall. Therefore, even though he had the [symbolic] patch robe transmitted by Furong, he did not wear it. Whether giving formal talks or in his own quarters, he wore only a black surplice and robe. Even though he was offered a purple robe and master's title by the emperor of the Jiading era,[270] he declined them. Furthermore, he kept secret the matter of who made him a successor, only revealing it at the end [when he was about to die] by offering incense [in recognition]. He not only kept far away from mundane desires and fame, but was also concerned for the good reputation of Zen. Truly, no one at the time equaled his virtue. His conduct was exemplary then and now.

He always said to himself, "In the last century or two, the Way of the patriarchal teachers has declined. Therefore, no spiritual teacher like me has appeared." All [other teachers] were in awe of him. The master never praised them. He would say, "Since the age of nineteen when I made a strong resolve and went on pilgrimage [to visit teachers], I have not met anyone who is enlightened. Many masters just greet visiting officials and never concern themselves with the monks' hall. They always say, 'Each person must understand the Buddhadharma himself.' So saying, they do not guide the monks. What is more, the present abbots of the great monasteries do the same. They think that not caring about anything is the Way,[271] and they never emphasize Zen practice. What is the Buddhadharma in this? If it is as they say, then why are there [still] sharp old gimlets seeking the Way? It is ridiculous. They do not see the Way of the Buddha patriarchs even in a dream."

In his diary, in which he recorded the master's many virtues, the attendant Huangbing says that [the official] Zhao Tiju requested a Dharma talk at the provincial government office. Because [the official] could not utter a phrase [of understanding], the master did not accept the ten thousand silver coins he was offered but gave them back. When [the official] could not say anything, not only did the master refuse his offering, but he also turned his back on fame and fortune. Therefore, he remained aloof from rulers and grand officials and did not receive the greetings of traveling monks. Truly, his merits in following the Way were extraordinary. Therefore, a Taoist elder named Daosheng and five of his followers vowed to practice in the master's community and not return to their native place unless they experienced the Way of the patriarchal teachers. The master was pleased with their resolve and permitted them to have private practice with him without converting [to Buddhism]. When they lined up in the Dharma Hall, they stood right behind the nuns. This was quite rare at the time.

Also, [a monk named] Shanru said, "I will remain with the master for all my life and never take a step south [toward home]." There were many like him who resolved never to leave the master's community. Fu, the gardener, did not know a single Chinese character. When he was sixty, he aroused the determination [to seek enlightenment] for the first time. The master guided him carefully and finally he clarified the Way. Though he was a gardener, he would upon occasion utter strange and wonderful things. Therefore, the master said that the abbots of the great monasteries were not Fu's equals.

Subsequently, [Rujing] made him the keeper of scriptures. Truly, in a community where the Way exists, there are many who have the Way and are committed to it.

He always encouraged people to just sit in zazen. Persuading them to do nothing but sit, he would say, "There is no need for burning incense, bowing, invoking the Buddha, making repentance, or reciting the scriptures—just sit." He would also say, "The important thing is being committed to the Way when you practice Zen." Even though you have a little understanding, you cannot hold on to what you know without a commitment to the Way. You end up with false views, become indolent, and become a non-Buddhist within Buddhism. People, do not forget the most important matter, commitment to the Way. Utilize that commitment in everything you do. Make the truth foremost. Do not get caught up in the fashion of the times, but continue to investigate the ancient style.

Teisho

If you are like this, then even if you have not yet understood it yourself, you will be an originally unsoiled person. Since you are unsoiled, how can you not be an originally clean, pure person? [Xuedou] said, "It is originally unsoiled, so how can it be cleaned? If you climb out of your rut, you will be free." The former enlightened masters originally did not bring about partial understanding. Committed to the single truth, they got people to practice with one objective without self-concern. If for the entire twenty-four hours of the day there is no view of purity and defilement, you are naturally undefiled.

However, [Rujing] still had not escaped the view of defilement. He held on to the idea of using a broom [to sweep it away]. After a year of not getting it clarified, once there was no more skin to shed, or mind and body that needed to shed, he said, "I hit upon that which is unsoiled." Even though it was so, a spot [of dirt] suddenly appeared. Therefore, it says that [Xuedou] hit him even before he finished speaking. Then, sweat broke out all over his body. He abandoned his body at once, and he found the power. Truly, he realized that he was intrinsically clean and had never been subject to impurity. This is why he always said, "The practice of Zen is the dropping off of mind and body."

Verse

Now, tell me, what is "that which is unsoiled"?

The wind of the Way, circulating everywhere, is harder than diamond;
The whole earth is supported by it.

EIHEI DOGEN

Case

The fifty-first patriarch was Priest Eihei Dogen. He studied with Priest Tiantong Rujing. Once, during late-night zazen, Rujing told the monks, "Studying Zen is the dropping off of body and mind." Hearing this, the master was suddenly greatly awakened. He went at once to the abbot's room and burned incense. Rujing asked him, "Why are you burning incense?" The master answered, "Body and mind have dropped off." Rujing said, "Body and mind have dropped off, the dropped-off body and mind." The master said, "This is a temporary ability; you must not approve me without reason." Rujing replied, "I am not approving you without reason." The master asked, "Why are you not approving me without reason?" Rujing said, "You dropped off body and mind." The master bowed. Rujing said, "You have dropped off dropping off." Then, [Rujing's] attendant, Huangping of Fuzhou, said, "It is no small thing for a foreigner to experience this realm." Rujing said, "How many here have gotten it? Liberated, he is mild and peaceful, and the thunder roars."

Circumstances

The master's initiatory name was Dogen. His secular name was Minamoto. He was a ninth-generation descendent of Emperor Murakami, through [the Emperor's son] Prince Gochusho. He was born in 1200. At that time, a physiognomist saw him and said, "This child is a holy child. He has deep eye pupils and will surely become a great man. An ancient book says, 'When a holy man is born, his mother will die.' When this boy is six, his mother will die." His mother was not surprised or frightened when she heard this but loved and respected him even more. When the master was seven, his mother died. People said, "Despite the discrepancy of a year, the physiognomist was correct."

In the winter of his third year, he read [the Chinese poet] Lijiao's "Hundred Poems" at his grandmother's knee. In the fall of his sixth year, he presented a collection of ancient Chinese poems to his father. At the time, venerable and famous Confucian scholars said, "This lad is not an ordinary person. He must be a child wonder." When he was seven, he lost his mother and his grief was profound. Seeing the incense smoke rising into the air at Takao Temple [at her funeral], he awakened to the impermanence of life and death and subsequently aroused the thought [of enlightenment]. In the spring of his eighth year, he read Vasubandhu's Abhidharma-kosha. Venerable old priests said, "He is as wise as Manjushri and has a real capacity for the Mahayana." Hearing this as a youth, the master treasured those words and studied very hard.

At that time, Fujiwara Moroie was the regent and chief advisor [to the emperor], an unrivaled example for court officials. He took in the master and made him his adopted son. He passed on secrets known only to the family and taught him important things about the country. In the spring of his twelfth year, [his adoptive father] gave the ceremony on his attaining adulthood and tried to make him an important official of the court. However, the master secretly left the villa at Kobatayama and went alone to the foot of Mount Hiei [the great Tendai monastic complex].

At that time, [a priest] named Ryokan Hogen was the director of the monastery and a teacher of both the exoteric [Tendai] and esoteric [Shingon] doctrines. He was the master's uncle on his mother's side. [Dogen] went to him and asked to make his home departure. Hogen was very much surprised. He asked, "Your entering-adulthood ceremony is approaching, and your father and foster father will be upset. What about that?" The master replied, "When my loving mother was dying, she told me, 'Make your home departure and learn the Way,' and I think the same. I do not want to futilely mix with the secular world. I just want to make my home departure so I can repay the debt I owe to my loving mother, grandmother, maternal aunt, and others." Hogen wept in admiration and allowed him to become a student, allowing him to study at the Senko House of Shuryogon-in in Han-nya Valley in Yokawa.

On the ninth day of the fourth month in 1213, when he was thirteen, he made his bows to the chief priest, Koin, and had his head shaved. The next day, he received the Bodhisattva precepts[272] on the precept platform at Enryaku Temple and became a monk. Later, he studied the Tendai system of insight and contemplation meditation. He also studied the esoteric teachings of South India. By the age of seventeen, he had read the entire Buddhist canon once.

Koin was the director of monks at Mii Monastery and was also [Dogen's] maternal uncle. He was unrivaled at the time in both esoteric and exoteric teachings, so Dogen questioned him about the great matter of the tradition. Director of Monks Koin told him, "What you now doubt is the ultimate matter of our religion. It is something that has been passed down orally through the generations since Dengyo [Daishi] and Shikaku [Ennin].[273] I cannot remove your doubt. I heard long ago that the Indian, Great Master Bodhidharma, came to China and transmitted the Buddha seal. His teaching has spread everywhere and is called the Zen tradition. If you want to resolve this problem, you should ask Eisai, the director of monks at Kennin Monastery, investigate the ancient reality, and go far away to China and look into the truth."

So, in the fall of his seventeenth year on the twenty-fifth day of the eighth month in 1217, he joined Priest Myozen's community at Kennin Monastery[274] and took on the life of a [Rinzai] monk. When the director of monks at that time [Eisai] was alive, he had all who came to Kennin Monastery to practice Zen wait for three years before they were permitted to wear robes. However, when the master came, he was allowed to wear them in September. In December he was given the major *kesa* or *sanghati* robe and thus was considered fit to practice. Priest Myozen, Eisai's legitimate [Dharma] heir, transmitted the three traditions of exoteric [Tendai], esoteric [Shingon], and [the Zen school of] Mind. In the records of Kennin Monastery's Priest Eisai, it says, "Only Myozen is entrusted with the Dharma Treasury. Those who want to ask about Eisai's Dharma must ask Myozen."

The master entered Myozen's quarters and received the Bodhisattva Precepts a second time. He was given a robe and bowl, and so on,[275] the one hundred thirty-four practices, instructions in the *goma* ritual,[276] and so on, of the Taniryu sect,[277] and he studied the precepts canon and the cessation and contemplation [types of meditation]. He heard about the Rinzai style for the first time, and received the correct lineage of the three traditions of exoteric, esoteric, and Mind. He was Myozen's sole legitimate heir.

Seven years passed. In the spring of his twenty-third year, on the twenty-second day of the second month in the year 1223, he paid his respects at the memorial monument of Kennin Monastery's patriarch [Eisai], and [accompanying Myozen,] proceeded to China. They arrived at [Mount] Tiantong in the year 1223.

While in China, the first of various teachers he saw was Priest Ruyan of Mount Jing.[278] Ruyan asked him, "When did you arrive here?" The master answered, "In April of last year." Ruyan asked, "Did you come just mimicking others?" The master asked, "What about when I do not come just mimicking others?" Ruyan said, "That is still coming mimicking others." The master asked, "Since I came mimicking others, why is this not correct?" Ruyan struck him and said, "What a talkative fellow." The master replied, "It's not that I'm not a talkative fellow but why am I not correct?" Ruyan said, "Sit a while and have some tea."

He also went to Xiaocuiyan in Taizhou. He visited Master Sizhuo[279] and asked him, "What is Buddha?" Sizhuo replied, "The one in the temple." The master asked, "If he's in the temple, how can he be everywhere in the world?" Sizhuo said, "He fills the world." The master said, "Blunder."

Going around and engaging various masters in dialogue like this, he became very conceited, thinking, "No one in China or Japan is my equal." As he was about to return to Japan, a man named Laoxin encouraged him [to stay]. He said, "The only one in China who has a knowledge of the Way is old Master Rujing. If you meet him, you will have a chance to get it." Thus instructed, it was still more than three years before he visited Rujing.

At the time, Wuji Liaopai had died and Master Rujing of Jingci had become the abbot at [Mount] Tiantong. Thinking that conditions were right, [Dogen] went to see him to inquire about his doubt. At their first meeting, he was humbled, and, consequently, they became master and disciple. Intending to practice fully, [Dogen] wrote a letter that said, "Since youth, I have aroused the thought of enlightenment. Though I sought the Way from various masters in my own country and knew a little about the principle of cause and effect, I still did not know the real goal of the Buddhadharma. I was occupied with its names and forms. Finally, I was instructed by Zen Master Senko [Eisai] and learned about Rinzai teachings for the first time. Now, I have followed Dharma Master Myozen to China and have been able to come here where you teach. It is good fortune resulting from conditions in past lives. I, an insignificant person from a distant land, ask you in your great compassion to allow me to come often to your quarters to respectfully ask about the essentials of the Dharma, regardless of whether it is day or night or how I am dressed. In your great compassion, please hear [my request] and grant it." Then Master Rujing said, "Disciple Dogen, from now on, regardless of whether you are wearing your *kesa* robe, or whether it is day or night, you may question me. I will overlook the absence of ceremony as if we were father and son."

After that, he studied the inner truth day and night and received the truth directly from Rujing. Once, the master was asked to be his attendant. The master declined, saying, "Being a foreigner, if I were to become your attendant in this great monastery in this great land, it might cause trouble in the monastery. I only wish to visit you day and night." Rujing replied, "Truly, what you say is modest and reasonable." Consequently, [Dogen] just had dialogues [with Rujing] and received instruction.

Then once, during late-night zazen, Master Rujing entered the meditation hall and admonished the monks for sleeping, saying, "The practice of Zen is the dropping off of body and mind. It does not require burning incense, bowing, invoking the Buddha, making repentance, or reciting the scriptures. If you just sit single-mindedly, you will get it." When the master heard this, he was suddenly greatly awakened. This is the main case [at the beginning of the chapter].

From about the time that he met Priest Rujing, he practiced the Way day and night, never ceasing for a moment. He never lay down to sleep. Priest Rujing would tell him, "You conduct yourself like former enlightened men. You will doubtlessly spread the Way of the patriarchs. My finding you is like the Venerable Shakyamuni finding Kashyapa." So, in 1225, he became a patriarch in the fifty-first generation. Rujing instructed him, "Return to your own country at once and spread the Patriarchal Way. Seclude yourself deep in the mountains and mature what you have attained."

While in China, he reverently examined the succession documents of the five houses of Zen.[280] First, he met Weiyi Xitang, former abbot of Guangfu Monastery.[281] Xitang said, "It is a great pleasure to see these ancient documents. How many have you seen?" The master replied, "I have never seen them." Then, Xitang said, "I have an old document that I will show you." When the master saw it, it turned out to be the succession document of the Fayan line. Xitang said, "I found it among the possessions of a certain old monk." It was not Xitang's. Though it had its own writing style, Xitang did not have the chance to explain it in detail.

Also, when the Elder Zongyue was the head monk at Tiantong, he reverently showed [Dogen] a succession document of the Yunmen line. [Dogen] asked him, "When I compare the present factions of the five houses, there are several differences, but how can that be? If [the Dharma] came from India to China in intimate contact [between master and disciple], how can there be differences?" Zongyue said, "Even if there are big differences, you should understand that the Buddhadharma of Yunmen is like this. The reason old Master Shakyamuni is respected is that he was enlightened. The reason Yunmen is respected is that he was enlightened." When the master heard this, he got some idea of the situation.

Also, the librarian Chuan, a distant descendent of Priest Qingyuan, otherwise known as Zen Master Foyan of Longmen,[282] had a succession document. In the early 1200s, a Japanese monk, Head Monk Ryuzen, took care of Chuan while he was sick, and, in gratitude, Chuan brought out the document so he could see it. He said, "It is not easy to see this, but I will show it to you so you can see it." A half year later in the fall of 1223, while the master was staying overnight at Mount Tiantong, Head Monk Ryusan asked librarian Chuan to show it to the master. It was the lineage document of the Yangqi faction [of Linji Zen].

On the twenty-first day of the first month in 1224, he reverently inspected the lineage document of Liaopai, who was Zen Master Wuji of Tiantong. Wuji said, "Being able to see this is quite rare. Now you see it. It is the true goal of studying the Way." The master was overjoyed.

After traveling around to Mount Tiantai, Mount Yandang, and other places in the years from 1225 to 1228, he went to Wan'nian Monastery in Pingtian. The abbot there was Priest Yuanji of Fuzhou.[283] Following preliminary remarks, while they were discussing the teaching styles of Buddha patriarchs from ancient times, a story about the succession between Dagui and Yangshan came up. Yuanji asked, "Have you ever seen the succession document I have?" The master replied, "How could I?" Yuanji got up and handed him the succession document, saying, "I would not show this to a close friend or someone who has been my attendant for years. That is the Dharma instruction of the Buddha patriarchs. However, one day [recently], when I was in the city visiting the governor, I had a dream. I dreamed that an eminent monk, whom I thought was Zen Master Fachang of Mount Damei, handed me a plum flower. He told me, 'If you meet a true man who has arrived by boat, do not begrudge him this flower,' and he handed me the flower. In my dream, unaware, I recited, 'Even before he got onto the boat, he deserved thirty blows.' Before five days passed, I met you. You arrived [in China] by boat. This succession document is written on silk with plum blossoms [woven into it]. This must be what Damei instructed. I brought it out because it is connected with my dream. If you want to succeed me, I cannot withhold it from you." The master trusted him and could not help being overjoyed. But even though he was told that he could ask for the succession document, he just burned incense and bowed before it, making offerings and paying homage. The incense-burning attendant, Faming, said that it was the first time he had seen the document. The master reflected, "It would truly be difficult to have this experience without the unseen aid of the Buddha patriarchs. What good fortune an ignorant person from a peripheral land has had to see these." Tears of emotion wet his sleeves.

After the master traveled to these monasteries, while he was staying overnight at Husheng Monastery on [Mount] Damei, he dreamed that the patriarchal master Damei came and gave him a plum blossom in bloom. The master truly opened his Dharma eye like the sages of old. Therefore, he was able to reverently inspect a number of lineage documents and receive unseen aid [from former patriarchs].

Having received recognition by various masters, having received the approval of Rujing, having resolved the great matter of his life, and having received the Dharma instruction of successive patriarchs, he returned to Japan in 1227. First, he settled at Kennin Monastery, where the remains of his original teacher [Eisai] were, and trained for a while. He was twenty-seven at the time.

Later, while seeking a scenic place that would be secluded, he inspected thirteen places offered by patrons in the Osaka-Kyoto region. None met his expectations. For a while, he stayed near Gokuraku Temple in Fukakusa, in the Uji district of Kyoto. He was thirty-four. Monks seeking the teaching gathered gradually, and eventually there were more than fifty.

[Ten] years later, he moved to Echizen Prefecture. He opened a monastery in a Shibi family villa, getting rid of brambles, rethatching it, repairing it with wood and clay, and teaching the Patriarchal Way. This is the present Eihei Monastery. When he was at Kosho [Horin] Monastery, a spirit would come to hear the precepts and participate in the twice-monthly renewal of vows.[284] At Eihei-ji, a dragon-spirit would come asking for the eight precepts and to be included in the daily dedications.[285] Consequently, every day, [Dogen] wrote out the eight precepts and dedicated them [to the spirit]. This has not been forgotten up to the present.

Teisho

In the more than seven hundred years since Buddhism spread to Japan, the master was the first to spread the True Dharma. In 552, fifteen hundred years after the Buddha's nirvana, Buddha images and other articles were brought from Korea, and in 553, two more were brought over.[286] After that, miracles of the Buddhadharma occurred. It is said that eleven years later, Prince Shotoku was born holding a relic of the Buddha in his hand. That was in 587. After [the Prince] lectured on the *Saddharma-pundarika* [*i.e., the Lotus Sutra*], *Shrimala-devi*, [and *Vimalakirti-Nirdesha*] scriptures, the names and forms, teachings, and texts [of Buddhism] were everywhere.

At the request of Princess Tachibana, [Zen Master Yikong,] a follower of National Teacher Jian of Tang [Dynasty China][287] arrived in the southern capitol [Nara], but only his stone epitaph remains. Having no successors, his teaching was not passed on. Later, Saint Kakua[288] became a true disciple of Zen Master Huaitong Fohai Huiyuan [in China].[289] Although he returned to Japan, that teaching style did not prosper. Also, Monk Supervisor Eisai was a successor to Priest Donglin Huaichong [in China] in the eighth generation of the Huanglong line [of Linji Zen].[290] He tried to spread that style, writing such treatises as "Promoting Zen and Protecting the Nation," and writing petitions to the throne. He was supported by authorities in Nara and Kyoto but his Zen was not pure. He established [a hybrid of] Tendai, Shingon, and Zen.

Although the master [Dogen] thoroughly grasped the Rinzai style and was a true descendent [of Eisai], he still called on Priest Rujing, settled the great matter of his life, and returned to Japan to spread the True Dharma. This was truly good fortune for the nation and a blessing for the people. It was like Great Master Bodhidharma, the twenty-eighth Indian patriarch, entering China for the first time. He became the First Patriarch in China, and the master was similar [in introducing Zen to Japan]. Although he was the fifty-first patriarch [of Zen], he is now Japan's first patriarch. Therefore, the master is called the first patriarch of our [Soto] tradition.

Even though China was filled with proper teachers, and the teaching existed far and wide, if the master had not encountered a true teacher and studied with him, how would the Treasury of the Eye of the True Dharma of the patriarchal teachers have been opened and revealed? That time [in China] had become decadent and was in the grip of the last days of the Dharma. Even in China the Buddhadharma had declined, and the spiritual teachers who were enlightened were rare. Therefore, even though Wuji Liaopai, Xiwen Rutan, and others were abbots of great monasteries, their attainment was incomplete. In the belief that there was no one even in China [who was a true teacher], he was on the verge of returning to Japan. Priest Rujing, the twelfth generation [descendent] of Dongshan, alone transmitted the true bloodline of the patriarchs. Although he kept secret his succession, he did not hide it from the master, transmitting the patriarchal teaching to him by not withholding his oral instruction. Truly, this was exceptional.

Moreover, I [Keizan] have been fortunate to gratefully seek out the patriarchal style as a follower of this [Soto] approach. It is like the Chinese Third Patriarch meeting the Fourth Patriarch. The teaching style has not collapsed. Although there are [different] traces in India, China, and Japan, what they transmit has not changed a bit. How could the essential point that utterly pervades [the Dharma] be anything else? You must first clarify Mind. In the situation where the master first acquired the Way, it was said that practicing Zen is dropping off body and mind. Truly, the practice of Zen consists of abandoning [attachment to] the body and leaving [ordinary] mind behind. If body and mind have not been dropped off, it is not the Way. You may think that the body is skin, flesh, bones, and marrow, but when you see thoroughly, not a hair's tip of them can be found.

People think that there are two kinds of "mind." One is mind as thought and discrimination, and this consciousness that discriminates [external events]. The second is mind that is still and unmoving, and does not know or understand a thing, the mind of purity and stillness. People do not understand that such a mind is still not exempt from being the root of [discriminating] consciousness. The ancients referred to it as the place of deep inner brightness that is unmoved. Do not mistake this for Mind and abide there.

Looking more carefully, "mind" is of three kinds: mind, thought, and consciousness.[291] "Consciousness" is mind that likes and dislikes, affirms, and denies. "Thought" cognizes warm and cold and is aware of pain or tickle. "Mind" does not discern right and wrong, nor is it aware of pain or tickle. It is like a wall, or like wood or stone. It can be thought of as truly still, as if it had no ears or eyes. Therefore, speaking from the vantage point of mind, it is like a manikin made of wood, or a human figure made of iron. Though you have eyes, you do not see; though you have ears, you do not hear. At this point, words do not do it justice. Although such a thing is mind, it is the seed of cognition of warmth, coldness, and awareness of pain and tickle. Thought and consciousness arise from it. Do not make the mistake of thinking that it is fundamental Mind.

Learning the Way is said to be apart from mind, thought, and consciousness. These must not be thought of as body and mind. There is still a wonderful brightness that is eternally unmoving. If you look carefully, you will certainly reach it. If you are able to clarify this Mind, no body and mind can be found; no self and others can be involved. Therefore, it is said, "Drop off body and mind." At this point, if you look intensely, even with a thousand eyes, there is not an atom of anything called skin, flesh, bones, and marrow; nothing to be discriminated as mind, thought, or consciousness. How can you [then] be aware of warmth and cold or discern pain or tickle? What is there to affirm or deny? What is there to like or dislike? Therefore, it is said, "When you look, nothing is there." When [Dogen] personally experienced this place, he said, "Body and mind are dropped off." [Rujing] confirmed this, saying, "Body and mind have dropped off, the dropped-off body and mind." Finally, he said, "The dropping off has dropped off."

Once you reach this realm, you become like a bottomless bucket, like a lacquer bowl with a hole punched in it. No matter how much leaks out, it is never empty; no matter how much is put into it, it is never full. Arriving at this occasion is called "the bottom falling out of the bucket." If you think that there is a hair of enlightenment or acquisition [here], it is not the Way. It is nothing but toying with the spirit.

Monks, experience it thoroughly with yourselves. Investigate it fully, and you will find that there is a body unbound by skin, flesh, bones, and marrow. Though you ultimately try to liberate this body, liberation is not possible. Though you try to abandon it, you cannot. Therefore, in speaking of this place [patriarchal teachers] say, "When everything is utterly emptied out, there is something that cannot be emptied." If you can clarify this thoroughly, you will never doubt all the venerable priests in the world or all the Buddhas of the past, present, and future.

Verse

What is this principle? Would you like to hear it?

> *That bright and shiny realm has neither inside nor outside;*
> *How can there be any body and mind to drop off?*

KOUN EJO

Case

The fifty-second patriarch was Priest Eihei Ejo. He studied with Priest Dogen. Once, while asking for instruction, he heard the expression, "a single hair pierces many holes," and was awakened. That evening, he made his bows [to Dogen] and asked, "Irrespective of the single hair, what are the many holes?" Dogen smiled and said, "Completely pierced." The master bowed.

Circumstances

The master's initiatory name was Ejo. His family name was Fujiwara. He was the grandson of Hidemichi, a fourth-generation descendant of the Imperial Minister of State, Fujiwara Tamemichi. He joined Enno Hoin's community on Mount Hiei and had his head shaved when he was seventeen. Subsequently, he studied the Abhidharma and *Satyasiddhi* [treatises].[292] Later he studied the *Mohe Zhiguan* [of Zhiyi].[293] Realizing that there was no value in studying for the sake of fame and profit, he privately aroused the thought of awakening. However, for a while he obeyed the will of his master and continued on through study [of the written teachings].

Once he was at his mother's house and she commanded him, "My intention in having you make your home departure was not that you would be appointed to high rank and associate with important people. Do not work just for fame and fortune. Become a recluse with your rain hat hung over your back, just going about on foot." When the master heard this, he consented, changed his robes, and did not return to Mount Hiei. He studied Pure Land teachings and heard the profound teaching of [the founder of the

Seizan branch of Pure Land Buddhism, Saint Shoku] Kosaka. Later, he went
to see Saint Butchi [Kakuan] of Tonomine,[294] who had received the patriarchal style from Zen Master Fozhao [Deguang] in China[295] and taught the
meaning of "seeing essential nature." The master surpassed the others in
studying vigorously.

One time, in a discussion of the *Shuramgama Sutra,* they came to the sim-
ile of the pitcher that is [shaped like] a *kalavinka* bird.[296] It said that when
emptiness is added to the emptiness [of the pitcher], the emptiness does not
increase, and when emptiness is taken out, the emptiness does not decrease.
[Ejo] was deeply awakened. Saint Butchi said, "How can the roots of evil
and the obstacles of passion that have existed for countless eons just melt
away and all suffering come to an end?" The more than thirty students there
at the time thought that this was wonderful and respected [Ejo] completely.

Priest Eihei Dogen returned to [Japan and] Kennin Monastery in 1227 to
refine his practice. There was a rumor that he transmitted the True Dharma
from China and privately wanted to spread it. The master got wind of this
and thought, "I understand the [Tendai] teaching of the three cessations and
three contemplations and have grasped the essential practices of the one
approach of Pure Land Buddhism. Moreover, I studied at Tonomine and
grasped the essence of seeing essential nature, becoming a Buddha at once.
What could [Dogen] have brought [from China]?" He visited Dogen in order
to find out. During the several days when they first talked, they thought that
they saw things the same way and discussed the inconceivable knowledge of
seeing essential nature. The master was overjoyed, thinking that his understanding was the same as Dogen's and genuine, and he praised [Dogen] all
the more.

After several days passed, Priest Dogen revealed an extremely different
understanding. At that time the master was surprised and was about to raise
an argument, but he realized that there was something beyond his own truth
and quite different. Therefore, when he again aroused a determination to
rely [on Dogen] and hear his teachings, Priest Dogen told him, "I transmit
the teaching style of the patriarchs and intend to be the first to spread it in
Japan. Though I could stay in this monastery [of Kennin-ji], I want to find
another place and stay there. If I can find some place and build a hermitage,
you should come there and see me. It is not good for you to be my student

here." The master obeyed [Dogen's] decree and waited for the right time.

Priest Dogen built a hermitage near Gokuraku Monastery in Fukakusa and remained there alone. After two years passed without a single person visiting, the master arrived. This was in 1234. Priest Dogen was delighted and permitted him to have private instruction in his quarters. They discussed the Patriarchal Way day and night. After three years passed, the present case came up while the master was seeking instruction. That is, the case was, "A single thought-instant is the same as ten thousand years;[297] a single hair pierces many holes. Passing this test is up to you. Surpassing the crowd is up to you." Hearing this, the master was awakened.

After [Ejo] received formal approval, he followed [Dogen] without leaving him for a single day. He was like a shadow following the form for twenty years. Although he was given many duties, he remained [Dogen's] attendant, assuming the position when his other tasks were completed. I [Keizan] heard him say often, "Although Butsuju [Myozen] had many followers, Master Dogen alone studied thoroughly. Although Priest Dogen also had many followers, I alone went [as his attendant] to his quarters. Therefore, although I heard what others did not, I did not miss anything they did hear."

After he finally inherited the teaching style [of the patriarchs], the master was always highly regarded by Priest Dogen, who had him carry out all the ceremonies at Eihei [Monastery]. When the master asked him why, Dogen said, "I will not live long, but you will survive me. You must spread my Way without fail. For that reason, I value you highly for the sake of the Dharma." In the proprieties of [Dogen's] quarters, the master was treated as if he were the master. In each of the four annual periods of the monastery,[298] he was presented with congratulations. In this way he was treated with courtesy and honor. Master and disciple became one. The light of their minds' eyes merged, like water combined with water, or sky merged with sky, without the slightest discrepancy. Only the master knew Priest Dogen's mind, no one else.

While [Ejo] was maturing at Fukakusa, the time period allowed for being absent from the monastery was written on the bulletin board: "Twice a month, three days each time." Even when Ejo's mother was terminally ill and he visited her, he did not violate the time limit. Her request to see him for the last time because she was seriously ill had occurred frequently, so the whole community urged him to go [regardless of the time limit]. Although the master had thought deeply about the matter, he wanted to know what the community thought. He got them all together and announced, "I would like to see my mother for the last time, but I wonder if I should violate the rule and go?" Every one of the more than fifty monks agreed that even though this [time limit] was the rule, he would not be able to see his mother again, so he should go. [Dogen] would not reject the hopes of the community, so how could he refuse? It was a very serious matter, compared to the small matter of a rule. The whole community was united in its suggestion [they said].

The discussion was heard by Dogen, who said to himself, "Ejo's mind is made up and he will not leave. He does not agree with the group." Sure enough, after the community had made its deliberations, the master told the community, "The rules of the Buddha patriarchs are more important than the opinions of the community. [That rule] is without question a rule of conduct [fixed] by former enlightened people. If I were to comply with human feelings toward my mother and transgress the regulations of former enlightened people, how could I avoid extremely unfilial wrongs [toward her]? What I mean is that by transgressing the regulations now, I would cause even greater wrong to my mother after she dies. A person who makes his home departure should make his parents enter the Way. By following human feelings just once, won't he cause his parents to receive eternal ruination?" So saying, he did not follow the community's suggestions. The community was surprised but they did not disagree with what he said. They all praised him as truly a person with a determination that is difficult to come by.

In this way, his steady determination not to violate the master's will was well known to the master and father [Dogen]. Teacher and disciple were truly of one mind. Not only that, but for twenty years, when he was being treated for illness in accordance with [Dogen's] command, he would not stay away from the master for more than ten days at a time. Nanyue Huairang attended the Sixth Patriarch for eight years prior to enlightenment and for eight years after, sixteen years in all. Even though there were many [students] who never left their masters for thirty or forty years, no one like the master has been encountered in the past or present.

Not only that, but during the fifteen years when he was continuing the teaching at Eihei-ji, he kept his master's portrait beside him in his quarters.

He greeted it each morning with, "Good morning," and said, "Good night" every evening, never forgetting for a single day. He wanted to be the master's attendant in life after life, as Ananda was to the Venerable Shakyamuni.[299] Moreover, in order that his illusory body would not be separated [from his master], he had his own remains installed next to his master's memorial marker as if he were still his attendant, without a separate marker, fearing that a marker [for himself] would indicate reverence [for himself]. At Eihei-ji, he was concerned that ceremonies for himself [after he died] would be performed especially for him, so he asked that he be given only a day of memorial service [on the side] during the eight days of memorial services [for Dogen]. As a matter of fact, he died on the twenty-fourth of the same month [as Dogen] and, as he always wished, one day was set aside during the memorial for the founder [Dogen]. This shows the importance of determination.

Not only that, but in emphasizing the truth and protecting the Dharma, he never altered in the slightest the founders community. Therefore, Dogen's whole community—wise and foolish, old and young alike—turned to him. All who are called "followers of Eihei" everywhere are the master [Ejo's] descendants. Because the Dharma fire burned high and was visible from afar, a certain person in the Ono district of Echizen [Prefecture] had a dream. A great fire was blazing high on a northern mountain. People asked, "What kind of fire burns like this?" He answered, "It is the Dharma fire of someone called Saint Buppo." He awoke from the dream and told people, "A man known as Saint Buppo lived in the dreary northern mountains. Years have passed since he left this world, but I hear that his disciple lives on that mountain." Thinking that this was beyond imagination, he took the trouble to record the dream in writing and inquired about it.

Because he did not violate the founder [Dogen's] prediction in transmitting the path and spread the Dharma at Eihei-ji, his descendants continue down to today. His teaching style has not come to an end. As a result, old Priest Tettsu Gikai,[300] his direct heir, has erected the Dharma banner personally at this monastery and advanced the style of the tradition here [at Daijo-ji]. Consequently, brotherly monks study that ancient style heedless of hunger and cold, and they practice wholeheartedly day and night heedless of the many difficulties. It is all because the virtuous style of the master [Ejo] still remains and his hallowed bones are still warm.

Teisho

As a result of such conduct as the master's of emphasizing the Dharma and his manner of spreading virtue, there is nowhere in Japan that his teaching style does not reach, or any place not moved by it. If your minds today are like those of the ancients [such as Ejo,] the future propagation [of Zen] will be like it was during the great Song Dynasty [in China].

As for the meaning of "A single hair pierces many holes," the master subsequently asked, "Irrespective of the single hair, what are the many holes?" Not a single fine hair can be established; not a single thing can take root. Therefore, the ancients said, "The realm of reality will not admit a speck of dust; not a hair sprouts in the clear sky." When [Ejo] understood it in this way, old Master Dogen gave his approval with the words, "Completely pierced."

Hundreds of thousands of subtle principles and countless teachings are totally pierced by the single hair. They do not come in the least from outside it. Therefore, it is not confined by the ten directions, nor is it absent from past, present, and future. It is dazzling bright, crystal clear. Although this realm were illumined by a thousand suns, they would not match its brightness. If you were to gaze at it with a thousand eyes, its boundary could not be found. However, everybody without exception is awake and clear. It is, therefore, not something nonexistent, nor is it some distinguishable form. It is not movement, stillness, hearing, or seeing. Have you fully reached it? Have you thoroughly awakened like this? If you have not personally experienced this realm, then even if you practice for merit for a million years and have audiences with Buddhas as numerous as sands in the Ganges River, these practices and merits remain conditioned [mundane] merits and practices, and you have not discerned the mind of the patriarchs in the least. Therefore, you cannot escape the cycle of suffering in the triple world, nor is there any end of transmigration among the four forms of birth.[301]

All of you are blessed to copy the appearance of the Buddha and use [the bowls and robe] he used. If it has not yet been your lot to personally experience the Buddha Mind, you not only cheat yourself all day long but you also injure the Buddha. You do not demolish the realm of ignorance and you transmigrate with karmic consciousness. Even if you enjoy the fruit of humanness or divinity for a while as the result of good roots, and are pleased with your conditioned happiness, you are like a cart wheel that can be forced into wet or dry places. You will be a sentient being who transmigrates without beginning or end because of karmic results.

Even if you are conversant with the twelve-part canon of the three vehicles and expound its many doctrines, ultimately you are like a cat watching for a rat. Outwardly you appear still, but inside, your mind continues to seek. Even if your practice is meticulous, the realm of mind is never calm day or night. The result is that your doubt is not cleared up. You are like a fox who runs off quickly but doesn't get far because he keeps looking back over his shoulder. This is the life of a fox apparition that has not stopped toying with its spirit.

Thus, do not be fond of much learning or become occupied with extensive study. Even for a short time, for a fraction of a second, arouse a determination like a great fire in which not a speck of dust can survive, like the great sky to which not even a needle can be attached. Even if this is imaginable, you will surely reach a place where thought does not reach. Even if it is inconceivable, you will reach a place that cannot be emptied. If you can arouse such a genuine determination, then when that determination becomes strong, everyone will pass completely through. There will not be the slightest difference from what all the Buddhas of past, present, and future realize.

The founder Eihei said, "When people seek the Way, it should be like an ordinary person trying to meet a great beauty, or like trying to overcome a powerful adversary, or like trying to take a strong castle. When the determination is deep and strong, the beauty is met and the strong castle is overcome. When you apply this determination to the Way, a thousand, even ten thousand people will acquire the Way."

Therefore, monks, do not think that the Way, the formless teaching of the Great Vehicle, evaluates potentials, so that beginners or later starters cannot attain it. In this realm, there is neither sharp nor dull, no distinctions. Once you raise up [a strong determination], you will have a deep experience of it. Now tell me, what is this principle? As I have already told you:

Space, from the beginning, has not admitted even a needle;
Vast, nonreliant, it is beyond all discussion.

When you reach this realm, not even something like a hair exists, much less the "many holes."

Even though the myriad things are extinguished, there remains something that is not extinguished. Even though everything is gone, there is something that is not exhausted. It turns out to be as expected, naturally. Utterly empty, it is marvelously bright by nature. Therefore, it is said to be pure and naked, empty and spotless, obvious, bright, and shining. There is not a hair of doubt, not a whisker of false thought. It is brighter than a billion suns and moons. You cannot say it is white, you cannot say it is red. It is like waking from a dream. It is simply vivid alertness within yourself, so we call it "vivid alertness." Calling it "alertness" means just that you are very awake. Calling it "bright" means just that it is very bright. You do not have to say that it has neither inside nor outside, nor is there any need to say that it extends into the past and extends into the present. Therefore, do not say that "a single hair pierces many holes." What complete piercing can there be?

Verse

If you call it a "single hair," this is what Ejo attained completely. What is this "single hair," then? Would you like to hear?

Space, from the beginning, has not admitted even a needle;
Vast, nonreliant, it is beyond all discussion.
Do not say that a hair passes through the many holes;
Empty and spotless, it is unmarked by any scars.

A Generalized Guide to the Pronunciation of Pinyin Transliterations

Vowels

a is pronounced "ah" as in the English word *swat*.

e is pronounced "uh" similar to the English word *fun*, or the familiar Chinese phrase *feng shui* ("fung shuay").

i alone or after a single (non-compound) consonant other than *r* is pronounced "ee" as in the English word *magazine* (although the syllable *ri* is roughly pronounced "er" as in the English word *batter)*

i after *ch, sh,* or *zh* is a neutral vowel like "uh" almost nonexistent, plus -*r,* somewhat akin to the English word *shirk*

o is pronounced "oh" as in the English word *note*

u is pronounced "ü" like the French word *tu* or German word *über*

Dipthongs

ao is pronounced "ow" as in the name Chairman Mao, and similar to the English word *how*

ou is pronounced "oh" as in the English word *soul*

ui is pronounced "uay" similar to the English word *way* or the familiar Chinese phrase *feng shui* ("fung shuay")

Consonants

c is pronounced "ts" similar to the English word *bats*

q is pronounced "ch" similar to the English word *cheese* or the familiar martial art *qi gong*

x is pronounced somewhere between the English letters *s* and *sh*

zh is pronounced similar to the English letter *j*

pronunciations of most other consonants and consonant combinations are similar to English

ALTERNATIVE TRANSLITERATIONS
AND PRONUNCIATIONS

I. Indian Patriarchs

Name used in this book	Japanese pronunciation
Shakyamuni	Shakamuni
Mahakashyapa	Makakasho
Ananda	Ananda
Shanavasa	Shonawashu
Upagupta	Ubakikuta
Dhritaka	Daitaka
Micchaka	Mishaka
Vasumitra	Vashumitsu
Buddhanandi	Butsudanandai
Buddhamitra	Fudamitta
Parshva	Barishiba
Punyayashas	Funayasha
Ashvaghosa	Anabotei
Kapimala	Kabimara
Nagarjuna	Nagyaharajuna
Kanadeva	Kanadaiba
Rahulata	Ragorata
Sanghanandi	Sogyanandai
Gayashata	Kayashata
Kumarata	Kumorata
Jayata	Shayata
Vasubandhu	Vashubanzu
Manorhita	Manura
Haklenayashas	Kakurokuna
Aryasimha	Shishibodai
Basiasita	Bashashita
Punyamitra	Funyomitta
Prajnatara	Hannyatara
Bodhidharma	Bodaidaruma

II. *Chinese Patriarchs*

Name used in this book	Wade-Giles transliteration	Japanese pronunciation
Dazu Huike	T'a-tsu Hui-k'o	Taiso Eka
Jianzhi Sengcan	Chien-Chih Seng-ts'an	Kanchi Sosan
Dayi Daoxin	Ta-i Tao-hsin	Daii Doshin
Daman Hongren	Ta-man Hung-jen	Daiman Konin
Dajian Huineng	Ta-chien Hui-neng	Daikan Eno
Qingyuan Xingsi	Ch'ing-yüan Hsing-ssu	Seigen Gyoshi
Shitou Xiqian	Shih-t'ou Hsi-ch'ien	Sekito Kisen
Yaoshan Weiyan	Yao-shan Wei-yen	Yakusan Igen
Yunyan Tansheng	Yün-yen T'an-sheng	Ungan Donjo
Dongshan Liangjie	Tung-shan Liang-chieh	Tozan Ryokai
Yunju Daoying	Yün-chü Tao-ying	Ungo Doyo
Tongan Daopi	T'ung-an Tao-p'i	Doan Dohi
Tongan Guanzhi	T'ung-an Kuan-chih	Doan Kanshi
Liangshan Yuanguan	Liang-shan Yüan-kuan	Ryozan Enkan
Dayang Jingxuan	Ta-yang Ching-hsüan	Taiyo Kyogen
Touzi Yiqing	T'ou-tzu I-ch'ing	Tosu Gisei
Furong Daokai	Fu-jung Tao-k'ai	Fuyo Dokai
Danxia Zichun	Tan-hsia Tzu-ch'un	Tanka Shijun
Zhenxie Qingliao	Chen-hsieh Ch'ing-liao	Shinketsu Seiryo
Tiantong Zongjue	T'ien-t'ung Tsung-chüeh	Tendo Sokaku
Xuedou Zhijian	Hsüeh-tou Chih-chien	Setcho Chikan
Tiantong Rujing	T'ien-t'ung Ju-ching	Tendo Nyojo

A NOTE ABOUT THE NAMES
OF CHINESE BUDDHIST PRIESTS

By Andy Ferguson

Chinese Buddhist priests, upon ordination, received a "Dharma name." For example, the Sixth Chinese Ancestor of Zen received the name Huineng, meaning (literally) "Wisdom Able." Such names normally comprised two Chinese characters. Using this two syllable name is a common way to refer to a monk or priest. Strictly speaking, this name is preceded by the (surname) character *shi* (pronounced "sure") which is the surname for Shakya, the Buddha's surname. Thus all monks belong to the "family of the Buddha." However, in ancient times, when itinerant monks would seek out and follow famous teachers, an important bit of information was the location where the teacher lived. Thus, Huineng's "mountain name" (derived from his geographic location) was Caoxi, the geographic location of his temple. Huineng could thus be referred to as Caoxi Huineng (Huineng of Caoxi), or, simply Caoxi. The Chinese words *shan* and *feng*, meaning "mountain" and "peak" are commonly found in mountain names (e.g., Guifeng, Yangshan, Dongshan). After their death, great Chinese Zen teachers sometimes received posthumous names that were bestowed by the emperor. In Huineng's case, his posthumous name was Dajian, meaning "Great Mirror." In later times, he might be referred to by any of these names, together or singly. Thus he might be called Huineng, Dajian Huineng, Caoxi, Caoxi Huineng, and so on. Huineng is even sometimes referred to by his lay name, Lu, or even "the traveler Lu," referring to his travels to see the Fifth Chinese Ancestor.

NOTES

Introduction

1. Material used for this biography has been drawn from the following sources: Sahashi Horyu, *Ningen Keizan*, 2nd ed. (Tokyo: Shunjusha, 1979); Azuma Ryushin, *Dogen sho jiten* (Tokyo: Shunjusha, 1972); Tajima Hyakudo, *Nihon no zen goroku*, vol. 5, *Keizan* (Tokyo: Kodansha, 1978); *Koza bukkyo*, vol. 7, *Nihon bukkyo no shuha* (Tokyo: Daizo shuppan, 1958). Some information is common knowledge among specialists in Japanese Buddhism.

2. At the conclusion of his *teisho* on Huineng, the thirty-third patriarch.

3. Kochi claims (vol. 4, p. 349) that research has established that Keizan was born in 1264 (first year of Bun'ei) rather than 1268 (fifth year of Bun'ei), which is the traditional date assigned. Some scholars have said that the date is the third year of Bun'ei, giving three possible dates of birth.

4. Sahashi Horyu, *Ningen Keizan* (Tokyo: Shunjusha, 1979), p. 220.

5. Kochi, vol. 4, p. 359.

6. Kochi, vol. 4, p. 360.

7. Kochi, vol. 4, p. 360.

8. Kochi, vol. 4, pp. 361–362.

9. Sahashi, p. 212.

10. Details of all these problems can be found in Sahashi's *Ningen Keizan,* pp. 212–239. Some of these problems are discussed by Nagahisa Gakusui, in his *Denkoroku monogatari* (Tokyo, Komeisha, 1965), where he attempts to explain their existence. See pp. 53–93.

11. See note 9.

Main Text

1. "Sun Race" or, alternately, "Sun Lineage," is the Sanskrit *suryavamsha*. Tradition has it that Shakyamuni's first ancestors were descended from the sun; other families are said to be descended from the moon. This kind of identity should not be confused with caste or class. The Buddha was originally a member of the Kshatriya class, which was a hereditary warrior and ruling group. His family name was Gotama and he belonged to a tribe called "Shakya."

2. Only a Buddha possesses all thirty-two major marks and eighty minor marks on his body, which indicate his uniqueness as either a great spiritual ruler or great secular ruler. Only highly advanced bodhisattvas are able to see these marks, ordinarily, but when the future Buddha was born, the sage Asita found the marks on the body of the young prince and on that basis predicted a glorious future for him.

3. Buddhist scriptures have the Buddha predicting that his teaching would pass through three periods, during which the authenticity and integrity of both the teaching and the teaching monks would degenerate. The first period, the period of the "True Dharma," is self-explanatory. It would last for five hundred years. This would be followed by a period called the "Counterfeit Dharma." Like counterfeit money, it looks genuine, but there is only outward show. In reality, the teachings are not well taught or understood, and there is a serious decline in monastic life. The third period is the "Collapsed Dharma," known in China as *mo fa* and in Japan as *mappo*. During this period, human morality and ability will have degenerated so far, and the teaching itself become so corrupted, that there would be no hope for liberation, enlightenment, or practicing the True Dharma. Japanese calculated this final period to begin at the end of the eleventh century. This view of history had a strong impact on Chinese and Japanese Buddhists, who saw themselves as living during the third period. The arising of Pure Land Buddhism was for the most part a response to the dilemma created by this view of time, society, and individual salvation. Keizan's response to *mappo* is typical of the way Zen masters starting with Dogen dealt with the problem, a response diametrically opposite that of the new faith-oriented Pure Land Buddhism founded by Honen and Shinran.

4. Gotama was Shakyamuni's family name. Keizan switches here from the latter name to the former.

5. Fayan (J. Hogen) is Fayan Wenyi (869–958), teacher of Fayan line of Chinese Zen.

6. Master Dizang Guichen (not to be confused the bodhisattva Dizang/Jizo) lived from 869–928, and was the teacher of Fayan (previous note) and successor to Xuansha Shibei.

7. Well attested as one of the Buddha's followers during his lifetime. He is prominent in Buddhist history as the convener of the first council following the death of the Buddha, at which time an attempt was made to gather, validate, and codify everything the Buddha had taught during his ministry. The event is recounted in the next case, that of the second patriarch, Ananda.

8. First of the four Hindu social classes. It is followed, in descending order of social power and importance, by the Kshatriya (the Buddha's class), the Vaishya, and finally, at the bottom of the social ladder, the Shudra. Outside the four social classes are the Candala or "outcaste" (J. *sendara*), a group of people forced to participate in undesirable occupations such as fishing, hunting, butchering, and selling meat. Hindus abhorred such groups, and the four Hindu classes recoiled from any contact with them. It was

thought that such matters as occupation and social class were the results of karma in previous lifetimes (see Jayata, the twentieth patriarch in this book), and hence carried a moral stigma.

Such class divisions are found in one form or another in most cultures around the world. In these days, the Japanese word *sendara* (which appears in the chapter on the twentieth patriarch) carries quite serious discriminatory overtones and must be examined with clarity and sensitivity. Keizan uses this situation to point to the ignorance of the speaker who is making a statement about karma and not to endorse discriminatory attitudes toward outcaste groups, nor does he provide any indication that he approves of such distinctions. A thoughtful reading of the *Denkoroku* will show that Keizan felt very deeply that distinctions based on race, class, occupation, and the like only promote suffering and confusion and, as indications of profound ignorance, are to be rejected. In fact, any form of prejudice, whether based on class, race, color, or sex, is antithetical to the most basic teachings of Shakyamuni Buddha.

9. See note 3. The significance here is that Mahakashyapa had all but two of the identifying marks. The text says "thirty-one marks," which is an obvious error. If he lacked two marks, he must have had thirty.

10. "Seven past Buddhas" is a common phrase in Zen lineage materials, and it reflects the tradition that Shakyamuni was not the only Buddha to have ever lived but was preceded by several other Buddhas during this and a former eon *(kalpa)*.

11. Chinese records, similar to the present record, of the masters in the Zen lineage. The *Chuan Deng Lu* is better known under its Japanese pronunciation, *Dentoroku*.

12. "Lord" is *shujinko, shujin* being a master or lord, while *ko* is a title for high-ranking people. It is a synonym for such terms as "Buddha nature," "Mind," "essential nature," and so on in Zen writings. Although the term is used often by Keizan, it was never used by Dogen, to the best of my knowledge. The term is somewhat startling in the present work, but careful attention to Keizan's teaching throughout the Denkoroku makes it clear that nothing like a substance or soul is meant. Ultimately, the "Lord" is "no-self."

13. That is, Tushita Heaven. Indian religion prior to Buddhism conceived of twenty-eight celestial realms arranged vertically on top of each other, the higher realm always surpassing the lower realm in terms of blissful delight. These were not "heavens" in the way conceived of by Christians and Muslims, as a place of eternal life and happiness. Human beings are reborn in the celestial realms as a result of good karma in the human life, but when the good karma is finally exhausted after millions of years, the celestial being is then reborn once more in a lower realm—human, animal, etc. The biographies of the Buddha claim that he was a celestial being prior to being born in the human world.

14. A well-known passage from the *Saddharma-pundarika Sutra*, from the chapter named "The Life Duration of the Tathagata."

15. Ananda is well known in Buddhist history as the most beloved of the Buddha's followers and as one who was always with his master. As the present story shows, it was he who was responsible for recalling all he had heard the Buddha say when the council met to codify the teachings. He could do this because he was at the Buddha's side constantly.

16. The warrior and ruling class among the four Hindu social classes. See note 8.

17. See note 15.

18. The meaning is that only those who had exterminated all moral and intellectual defilements and who had experientially grasped the truth of the Four Noble Truths and who had therefore reached the rank of arhat, could attend the council. I do not recall ever encountering the display that follows (in the text) of supernatural power in any of the Indian sources.

19. The reason all Buddhist sutras begin with the statement "Thus have I heard at one time. Once the Buddha was at..." etc., *(evam maya shrutam ekasmin samaye)* is that at the council, Ananda was asked to recite from memory everything he had ever heard the Buddha say. He started each recital with the above phrase, and thus it is presumably a guarantee that the sutra records a genuine utterance of the Buddha. This is why Ananda was referred to as "one who has heard much *(bahushrutam)."*

20. "Three kinds of spiritual knowledge" are the three *vidya:* recollection of the previous lives of sentient beings, the "celestial eye," which can see future rebirths, and the recognition of the extinction of defilements. The "six paranormal powers" are the *abhijna:* these include the above three kinds of knowledge along with clairvoyance, clairaudience, and knowledge of the thoughts of others. The point is that all those at the council were arhats of great spiritual advancement.

21. See note 13. The Celestials of the Pure Abode *(shuddhavasakayika)* are five classes of celestials who inhabit a celestial realm near the top of the twenty-eight realms.

22. His name is given in several alternate forms, some of which occur in the story following the case. The Japanese *shonawashu* seems to indicate an original Shanavasa, hence my reconstitution. Monier-Williams records both Shanavasa and Shanavasika ("name of an arhat") in his *Sanskrit-English Dictionary.* He also translates *shanaka* as "a hempen cloth or garment."

23. "Intermediate period" is Sanskrit *antarabhava.* It is the period often given as forty-nine days between death and rebirth. Buddhist literature shows this period as a "middle existence" during which an individual, in the form of a bodiless ghost, wanders about seeking a womb—human, animal, etc.—in which to take root and mature as a fetus. These spirits have no bodies, not to mention clothes, hence the delightful idea that Shanavasa wore clothes even during this middle time.

24. "Mind and body and external environment" translates the Japanese *sho e ho.* These are

two forms of karmic result. *Sho* means one's own mind and body, and *e* refers to such things as native place, race, social class, economic circumstances, and so on. Both are understood to result from past karma.

25. The "three realms" *(trailokya)* are (1) realm of desire *(kamaloka)*, (2) realm of form *(rupaloka)*, and (3) formless realm *(arupyaloka)*. These are arranged vertically in that ascending order, cosmologically speaking, and all sentient beings dwell within these three realms. However, for the same reason, all three realms are also realms of suffering and rebirth and consequently are understood to be something to transcend in nirvana, which is not a place to begin with and is not within the three realms. Hence Keizan's remarks.

26. "Dependent on grasses and adhering to trees" is a well-known Zen phrase. The direct reference is to the intermediate existence between death and rebirth when the spirit wanders without support (cf. note 23). Supposedly, the only support or refuge for the poor spirit is grass and trees, a kind of temporary shelter. However, Zen uses this as a metaphor referring to Zen students who have left the ordinary secular life and made some progress but who have not decisively concluded their training yet. Thus, in a manner of speaking, they hover like lost spirits between two worlds or lives. The term was used in slightly different form in the *Linji lu (Rinzairoku)* and the koan collection, *Cong Rong Lu (Shoyoroku)*.

27. See note 3.

28. The length of pure white silk is an image of the flowing water and symbolizes the inner Buddha nature as inherently pure.

29. Upagupta's story is about all that is known about him. His name occurs in Indian Buddhist sources such as the *Divyavadana*, which says that he lived about a hundred years after the death of the Buddha. The Chinese *Da Zhi Du Lun* also mentions him. See Akanuma Chizen, *Indo bukkyo koyu meishi jiten*, p. 707, for the small amount of information extant. He is typical of a number of men in this text who are said to be patriarchal teachers in Zen but whose lives are exceedingly obscure. Others, such as Nagarjuna and Vasubandhu, are quite famous as Buddhist thinkers and authors.

30. I cannot reconstitute the Japanese *Dari* into its original Indic form with any degree of confidence. Every common dictionary and encyclopedia simply gives this name without further identification. I would guess that it is a drastically abbreviated transliteration of "Pataliputra," a prominent city in Buddhist history, but given the problems of figuring out what the Chinese or Japanese transliteration points to, this is only a guess.

31. See note 2.

32. See note 25. It is the lowest of the three realms. It includes a number of "heavens" with their resident beings.

33. See note 25. The Brahma Heavens coincide with the realm of form and are located directly above the heavens mentioned in the preceding note.

34. The "ten powers" *(bala)* overlap with the three *vidya* and six *abhijna* mentioned in note 20, and include as well such gifts as the ability to enter all trances, concentrations, and other meditative states. The ten powers are the possession of only the most spiritually advanced, such as a Buddha.

35. In Indian Buddhist custom, to repeat a formula such as the Triple Refuge three times was to make, in effect, a binding commitment similar to a legally binding document. To repeat something three times was thus a very serious form of promise or commitment.

36. "Psychic powers" is my translation of the Japanese *nyoi soku*, which is a common translation of the Sanskrit *rddhi-pada*. There are four: desire to be *(chanda)*, vigor *(virya)*, thought *(citta)*, and exploration *(mimamsa)*. Actually, these are not psychic powers but rather the foundation or base for the powers.

37. Biographies of the Buddha claim that these were the words uttered by the young prince and Buddha-to-be as soon as he was born. Upon being born, he took seven steps, paused, and made this announcement, which is understood to be his proclamation of his destiny of Buddha.

38. Some reference works give his name as "Dhitika," and say that he was from Mathura. I have reconstituted the name on the authority of Monier-Williams Sanskrit-English Dictionary (p. 519), which lists a Dhritaka as "a Buddhist saint or patriarch."

39. The Japanese has *mugaga*, literally, "no-self-self," where one would expect the common *muga*, or "no-self." All texts have *mugaga*, which I assume is intentional. I have, accordingly, translated it as "self which is no self," but it could just be "no self." The term is directly followed by *mugaga sho*, which is clearly translatable as "without what belongs to a self" or simply "without mine." It is obvious that Keizan is using the very common expression in Buddhist literature that says there is no "me" or "mine," or no "self" or "what belongs to a self."

40. A series of well-known phrases that attempt to characterize the true state of things. "The three realms of mind only" comes from the *Sutra of the Ten Stages (Dashabhumika Sutra)*. In East Asian Buddhism, it is interpreted to mean that the world is Buddha or Buddha nature. The other two phrases are from the writings of Zen Master Dogen, the founder of Keizan's line of Zen in Japan, though the original sources of the phrases are the *Avatamsaka Sutra* and *Nirvana Sutra* respectively. The final phrase, "absolutely empty and quiescent," is probably from some version of the *Prajnaparamitra Sutra*.

41. The analogy is an allusion to a well-known parable in the *Saddharma-pundarika Sutra*, which tells of a young boy running away from his wealthy father and becoming utterly poor and destitute. Thus, running away from the truth within oneself and seeking it in the written word is like running away from one's own wealth and becoming destitute.

42. A quotation from the *Chuan Deng Lu (Dentoroku)*. The words were uttered by Wutai Shan Bimo to a monk.

43. See note 24.

44. An allusion to a story told by the Taoist master Zhuangzi in the chapter "The Way of Heaven" in his collected writings. Lunbian was a wheelwright of great ability who realized that much of his skill was beyond the power of words to communicate.

45. "Wizard" is my translation for the Chinese *xian*. Xian are wizards or sorcerers who live in solitude in the mountains, often living to extraordinary ages through special diet and supernatural powers. The Asita mentioned here is not the wizard who appears in biographies of the Buddha making predictions about the future of the new-born prince. That Asita is said to have died prior to the Buddha's enlightenment, as he himself predicted he would do, so the Asita mentioned here in connection with Micchaka must be another.

46. The arhat is the spiritually perfected individual in the pre-Mahayana or non-Mahayana forms of Buddhism, also referred to as "Hinayana" or "Small Vehicle." The arhat has exterminated all defilements *(klesha)*, gained experiential understanding of the truths of impermanence, substancelessness, and turmoil *(anitya, anatman, dukkha)* in all things, and is liberated from future births. Such a state is very close to Buddhahood, but it is still considered slightly less than full, complete Buddhahood. The Buddha was an arhat, but he was also a *samyaksambuddha*, a fully, completely enlightened one. The distinction between arhat and Buddha was an important one to early Buddhists.

47 "Supernatural powers" is *jintzu* (Ch. *Shentong*, which are the ten special powers of a Buddha, including such things as being able to make earthquakes, shoot rays of light from the pores of the skin, and so on.

48. *Pratyekabuddhas* are those who are enlightened without a teacher and who live in solitude, preferring not to teach others. Mahayana literature often disparages pratyekabuddhas, likening them to "Hinayanists" who are deficient in compassion.

49. "Subtle defilements" are *upakleshas* in Sanskrit. They are considered harder to eliminate than the more obvious *kleshas*. Upakleshas consist of such things as arrogance and pride. The distinction between upaklesha and klesha is a common one in such texts as the *Abhidharmakosha*, though Zen as a rule does not tend to concern itself with scholastic niceties such as these.

50. The text is *fukon*, "not now." The character for *kon*, "now," is an obvious error for the character meaning "to understand," *wakaru*. I have followed other editions in amending the text to read "does not understand."

51. "Fortunate eon" is *bhadra-kalpa*, the name of our present eon. It is called "fortunate" or "good" because, during such an eon, a thousand Buddhas appear in the world. The *Bhadrakalpika Sutra (Taisho* no. 425) exists in both Chinese and Tibetan, and in it can be found the names of the thousand Buddhas of our eon.

52. The text has *mirai gusoku* ("future complete") but the *mirai* must be an error for *honrai* ("original," "primordial") and so I have chosen the reading of the other texts.

53. The Japanese has *kamara*. Akamatsu lists a Kamala in his *Indo Bukkyo Koyu Meishi Jiten* (p. 269). Monier-Williams lists Kamala as a town in India in his Sanskrit-English Dictionary, and I have decided to reconstruct the name on the basis of the latter listing.

54. Manjushri, the bodhisattva exemplar par excellence of enlightened understanding, was one of the bodhisattvas who engaged Vimalakirti in a discussion of the correct "entrance to the truth of nonduality" in the *Vimalakirti Sutra*. Neither Manjushri's insistence that speech cannot capture the truth nor Vimalakirti's "thunderous silence" can express the truth, which is (as Keizan says) utterly beyond any predication.

55. The ten abodes are ten of the fifty-two stages of enlightenment given in the *Avatamsaka Sutra*. The first fifty stages are arranged in five groups of ten, and the ten abodes are the second series of ten stages, immediately following the ten stages of faith. Bodhisattvas on this set of stages have obviously already advanced a long way, but they still have thirty more stages to traverse before the final stages of Buddhahood. It is thus not surprising that they still see as if "through a glass, darkly." A discussion of the bodhisattva stages can be found in Har Dayal's *The Bodhisattva Doctrine in Buddhist Sanskrit Literature* (London: Routledge and Kegan Paul, 1932).

56. An allusion to a passage from the *Large Prajnaparamita Sutra*. This and subsequent references to "same sutra, same chapter" refer to that scripture.

57. Dongshan Liangjie (807–869) is considered the founder of the Chinese Caodong [Soto] line of Zen. Guishan Lingyou (771–853) is the founder of the Guiyang line and was one of Dongshan's teachers. Yunyan Tansheng (782–841) is a prominent figure in the Japanese Soto Zen patriarchal lineage. He is included as the thirty-seventh patriarch in this translation.

58. See previous note.

59. "Abides in its dharma state" is *ju hoi*. Here, *dharma* means some thing or event. When something abides in its dharma state it is experienced as just that particular event or thing as it is at that moment, without reference to prior or subsequent states, thus, nondualisticly. An example of this is the analogy of firewood and ashes in Zen Master Dogen's essay, *"Genjo koan,"* in *Shobogenzo*. There, Dogen says that firewood does not turn into ashes, because something like firewood does not cease being what it is. Its dharma state is that of firewood, and this dharma state does not change. It is an analogy, in the text mentioned, for life and death. This means that life does not turn into death, because life and death are two different dharma states. Each remains just what it is, changelessly. A good discussion of this important term can be found in Hee-jin Kim's *Dogen Kigen: Mystical Realist* (Tucson: University of Arizona Press, 1975), particularly pp. 200–22.

60. Chuangzi Decheng (d. 890) was a successor to Yaoshan Weiyan. His name means

"Boat Monk" because later in his life he spent his time ferrying people across the river and helping others who were seeking the Dharma.

61. The Vaishya class is the third of the four Indian social classes, and they are usually merchants. I have not been able to reconstruct the original of *daigya-koku*. The Chinese pronunciation is *dijia*. However, neither Eitel nor Akanuma, nor any other source I have consulted, identifies this dijia/daigya.

62. It is said in biographies of the Buddha that immediately upon being born, he took seven steps. Buddhamitra's seven steps echo the Buddha's steps and thus indicate his own stature. At the same time, the fact that he walks for the first time in fifty years symbolizes his readiness to walk in the true path as embodied by Buddhanandi.

63. The words are those of Bodhidharma's famous manifesto and signify the uniqueness of patriarchal Zen.

64. The twelve *nidanas* or "conditions" are the twelve interdependent links of the "wheel of becoming," starting with ignorance, and ending in old age, sickness, and death (i.e., *dukkha*).

65. All living things are born in one of four ways: from wombs, from eggs, from moisture, as a result of miracles. Karma in a former life determines the form of birth.

66. "Separation and concealment" are *ri* and *bi* (Ch. *li* and *wei*). *Bi/wei* could also be translated as "secret" or "latent." The terms are from the chapter titled "Li Wei Ti Jing" in the *Bao Zang Lun Shan* and also occur as the subject of case 24 of the *Wumen Guan*. "Separation and concealment" refer to the expression of original Mind, "separation" referring to silence and interiority, "concealment" referring to concealment among the many actualities that make up the world. In other words, "concealment" is union or oneness with things. The verse seems to say that the dynamic expression of original Mind does not depend on either speech or silence but rather transcends them. The verse should be read in the light of Buddhamitra's own silence.

67. *Parshva* is Sanskrit for "rib." He was named "Venerable Rib" because he never lay down to sleep. Dogen tells an expanded version of the story in his *Gyoji* ("Continuous Practice"), which can be found in this translator's *How to Raise an Ox* (Los Angeles: Center Publications, 1978), pp. 175–203.

68. I give the Japanese pronunciations because I cannot reconstruct the originals or find any references to the names elsewhere.

69. That is, the *Tripitaka* or "three baskets." These are the three broad categories of Buddhist canonical literature, *sutra* (discourses, sermons), *vinaya* (monastic discipline, moral precepts), and *abhidharma* (scholastic interpretation of sutra and vinaya).

70. See note 20.

71. He had a vision of twenty-one fragments of the *sharira* (relics) left from the Buddha's cremation. Sharira are said to be small, gem-like objects retrieved from the ashes. Other remains include teeth and bone fragments.

72. "Absolute" and "concrete matters" translates the well-known pair of terms, *ri* and *ji* (Ch. *li* and *shih*). The terms are translated in various ways, such as "absolute and relative" and "principle and facts." The terms usually denote two different forms of reality or truth or two ontological realities, and, therefore, the terms often point to a view of two orders of reality or truth. In Zen, the tendency is to see the two as ultimately identical, as indicated, for instance, by Dogen's teaching, *shoho jisso*, "all things are ultimate reality." Keizan touches on this briefly when he says that Mahayana sutras do not recommend "sweeping away dust." His main point, however, seems to be that the sutras not only teach such things as emptiness and nirvana but also thoroughly discuss such ordinary "facts'" or "concrete matters" as those he lists.

73. The three vehicles *(yana)* are those of the *shravaka* (literally, "hearers"), *pratyekabuddha* (the solitary enlightened), and the *bodhisattva*. The five vehicles are the same three plus the vehicles of celestials and humans.

74. In the "Skillful Means" chapter of the *Lotus Sutra*, five hundred arhats of the small vehicle (i.e., *shravakas*) leave the assembly where the Buddha is expounding the truth because, in their arrogance and pride, they reject the Mahayana teachings. This story is typical of the often extremely harsh polemics leveled at the non-Mahayanists by Mahayanists and illustrates the typical Mahayana claim that it possesses the complete truth. Keizan reflects this bias with his distinction between sutras that contain the "complete truth" and those of "incomplete truth."

75. *Tendoku* and *tenkyo* are highly regarded formalized rituals in which vast numbers of sutras are "read" by flipping the pages rapidly or by symbolically reading a short passage from the beginning, middle, and conclusion of a sutra. This allows very long sutras to be read ceremonially in a very brief time. Here, "turning the sutra" seems to contrast with reading or reciting a sutra in the normal way. See the following note.

76. "'Turning' means, literally, "rotating."' In China and Japan, sutras were copied on long, horizontal strips of paper or cloth and rolled up on a spindle. Each roll constitutes a *kan* (Ch. *zhuan*). One read a sutra as the scroll was unwound from one spindle and rewound onto another spindle. Thus, reading a sutra literally involved turning or rotating the sutra. Keizan uses this sutra-turning as a striking image of the appearance and disappearance, through conditioning, of all things. The whole universe is a sutra that preaches conditioned arising and cessation, and, consequently, life and death are merely chapters and phrases in the great sutra. The effectiveness of Keizan's verse derives from the connotations of the word "turning,"' which applies simultaneously to the unrolling of a sutra and to the cyclic turning over and over in life and death. However, for Keizan, "born here, dying there" is nothing more than "chapters and phrases."

77. This is a technical term in Mahayana Buddhist literature and refers to the bodhisattva's ability to see the world unflinchingly and courageously as a place where, in reality, nothing originates or ceases to be; in short, the world as empty. *Prajnaparamita* literature says that such a vision is terrifying to any but very advanced bodhisattvas, but the latter can face this horrendous truth on the eighth stage with emotional and intellectual patience. The Sanskrit is *anut-pattika-dharma-ksanti*, which is translated "patience with regard to the truth of non-arising things." See Har Daya, *The Bodhisattva Doctrine in Buddhist Sanskrit Literature* (London: Routledge and Kegan Paul, 1932), p. 213.

78. The text is amended in accordance with readings in other versions. The present text has *sho butsu mata hi sonja nari to*. The alternate reading, *sho butsu mata sonja ni arazu*, seems clearer in context, hence my choice.

79. Ashvaghosa (ca. 100 A.D.) is well known to students of Buddhism and Indian literature as the author of the *Buddhacharita (The Acts of the Buddha)*, a long, verse biography of the Buddha, describing his life in ten "acts." He was also credited in China and Japan with the composition of the *Dacheng Qi Xin Lun* or *Awakening Mahayana Faith*, the title often being reconstituted into the Sanskrit *Mahayana-shraddhotpada* on the assumption that it was written by Ashvaghosa in Sanskrit. However, modern scholarship has pretty much discredited the story and believes that it was composed by a Chinese writer and attributed to the Indian writer.

80. A literal translation of the Japanese *ku sho*, "Merit-superior." However, Eitel *(Handbook of Chinese Buddhism)* translates the name as "Absolute Conqueror," reading the first character as the Japanese *setsu*, meaning, among other things, "acute," "the most," and so on. The two characters, *ku* and *setsu*, are very similar in appearance. Eitel says that the name is a posthumous name given to Buddhist monks. I have followed the reading of the text if for no other reason than that the reading remains consistent with Keizan's interpretation.

81. See note 2.

82. He appears as an *asura*, one of the five or six forms all life takes in the Buddhist cosmology. Asuras are frequently depicted with three faces and eight arms. The point here, and in the rest of the passage, is that Buddha nature appears in all the realms of existence, including the celestial realms, hells, etc.

83. When celestial beings are about to end their stay in the celestial realm and be reborn elsewhere, the impending departure is signaled by a number of signs, such as the withering of flower ornaments, casting a shadow, perspiring, and so on. These signs are discussed in biographies of the Buddha that depict him as a celestial being prior to his birth as a prince.

84. Horns and hair refer to the realm of animals. Shackles and chains are a reference to the hells.

85. Lingyun was a Chinese Zen master who became enlightened while wandering in the

mountains and suddenly seeing red peach blossoms. Keizan's predecessor, Dogen, was very fond of telling this story. One recounting can be found in the essay, *"Keisei sanshoku"* ("Sounds of Valley Streams, Forms of Mountains") which is in this translator's *How to Raise an Ox* (Los Angeles: Center Publications, 1978), p. 105. In his enlightenment poem, Lingyun says, "After once seeing the peach blossoms, - There is nothing more to doubt."

86. See note 20.

87. Dogen, the founder of Soto Zen and a predecessor of Keizan, also uses the expression "ocean of nature," in Shobogenzo Bussho ("Buddha Nature"). The lines attributed here to Ashvaghosa are also attributed to him in the "Buddha Nature" chapter. I have frequently interpolated "Buddha" in square brackets in the translation where only "ocean of nature" is given in the text, in order to clarify that it is the ocean of Buddha nature.

88. *Shuramgama* is the name of a samadhi, as well as the name of a sutra in which twenty-five samadhis are discussed. The title translates as something like *Heroic Advance*.

89. See note 20.

90. "Beyond number" is my translation for a well-known Zen expression that literally reads, "three by three in front and three by three in back." The expression seems to have originated in the koan, "Three by three in front and three by three in back," which is case 35 in the *Bi Yan Lu (Hekiganroku)*.

91. The text has simply *kokoro*, or *shin*, which is vague in context. It could refer simply to what we mean ordinarily by "mind," and therefore the passage would be denying the duality of mind and body. However, I have taken the term to be a common Zen synonym for what is elsewhere called "Buddha nature," "Buddha Mind," and so on. I take it that Keizan's point is that all things are nothing other than Buddha nature in these forms. Consequently, Keizan is saying that to see Buddha nature is to see things, and to see things is to see Buddha nature. The same idea pervades Dogen's Shobogenzo.

92. Xuefeng Yicun (822–908) was the sixth patriarch in the line of Qingyuan Xingsi. He was an important master in Chinese Zen and appears to have been a favorite of Dogen and Keizan. Dogen quotes him often, and in his *Three Hundred Cases (Sambyaku soku)* he records several koans in which Xuefeng figures prominently, in contrast to many masters who appear in only a single case.

93. It is called "fantasy-like samadhi" *(nyogen zammai)* because from the perspective of Buddha nature, or ocean of essential nature, the manifestations of the latter are no more than fantasies or dreams. Keizan here uses the term samadhi as a synonym for "ocean of essential nature" and other such terms. His intention appears to be to emphasize that all dualisms, such as subject and object, are obliterated in the light of reality, since samadhi itself is the absence of the subject-object dichotomy. However, *nyogen zammai* is not the name of a particular samadhi.

94. The Sanskrit original is *chinta-mani* and is usually translated as "wish-fulfilling jewel." As the name implies, the possessor of the jewel can have every desire fulfilled. The "cow of desires" is similar in that its inexhaustible udders grant all desires. Keizan's "mind-jewel" is similar, although it does not fulfill ordinary desires.

95. *Nagas* are mythical creatures mentioned often in Indian Buddhist literature, along with *kinnaras*, *gandharvas*, and several other forms of being. They are portrayed in art as creatures with the bodies of cobras and the heads of men. The Chinese translated the word *naga* as *long*, which is the dragon so prominent in Chinese art. However, *nagas* are not dragons, and I have retained the original Sanskrit term rather than perpetuate the error. The two other names given here are listed in Eitel's *Handbook* and Soothill's *Dictionary of Chinese Buddhist Terms*. Much of Soothill's information comes from Eitel's dictionary.

96. Shingon and Tendai are two schools of Mahayana Buddhism that were imported into Japan from China in the early ninth century. These two schools, along with the Pure Land schools and several other Mahayana traditions, claim the great Nagarjuna as a patriarch, which attests to the enormous esteem with which he and his work is held. He is thought to have lived sometime in the first or second century. His treatment of the teaching of emptiness is considered definitive and, consequently, he had an immense influence on the development of subsequent Indian Buddhist thought and on the later Chinese schools such as Huayan, Tiantai, and Chan. In a very real way, he is a patriarch of all the later Mahayana schools.

97. These are all stories of precious jewels being hidden or guarded by various people, black dragons, and so forth. In the case of the drunk, he does not know that he possesses the jewel that is hidden in his clothes. The fierce black dragon keeps the jewel tucked under his chin so that it is almost impossible for someone to acquire it.

98. Xuansha Shibei (J. Gensha Shibi) lived from 835 to 908. He was a master in the line descended from Qingyuan Xingsi and was one of the most noteworthy Zen teachers. He is an important patriarch in the Japanese Soto Zen line. Both Dogen and Keizan esteemed him highly.

99. The "wheel-turning monarch" is the *chakravartin raja*, so called because he is so great and powerful that wherever his chariot wheels touch, the earth belongs to him.

100. See note 71.

101. Damei (J. Daibai) and Guishan (J. Isan) are both famous Chinese Zen masters, their dates being, respectively, 752–839 and 771–853. Damei meditated with a miniature pagoda on top of his head so that if he fell asleep, the pagoda would fall and wake him up. Dogen cites this practice with great approval in his essay *Shobogenzo Gyoji* ("Continuous Practice"). See my translation of the essay in *How to Raise an Ox* (Los Angeles: Center Publications, 1978).

102. Yinshan was a successor to Fayan. Luoshan was a successor to Yantou.

103. A *shravaka* is literally a "hearer," and refers to the Buddha's immediate followers who heard him while he lived. A *pratyekabuddha* is someone who is enlightened without a teacher and who chooses not to teach others. Both are mentioned often in Mahayana literature and have become archetypes of a kind of person who is either inadequately enlightened or who does not follow the bodhisattva path of altruism and compassion. They represent people who, from Keizan's perspective, have lost their way on the religious path.

104. Koun Ejo (1198–1280) was Dogen's successor as patriarch. His successor was Tettsu Gikai, whose own successor was Keizan, author of the present work.

105. The reference is to the Chinese Zen Master, Yuanwu Keqin (J. Engo Kokugon) who lived from 1063 to 1135. He was not only a noteworthy Zen teacher but is also remembered for the important contribution he made to the final form of the koan collection, *Bi Yan Lu* (J. *Hekiganroku*).

106. Huanglong Huinan (1002–1069) is best known as founder of the Huanglong line of Chinese Zen.

107. His name means "One-eyed Deva," for apparently obvious reasons. He is better known in Buddhist history as Aryadeva. He was a follower of Nagarjuna's Madhyamika school and wrote several treatises expounding that teaching. He is considered one of the founding patriarchs of the Chinese Sanlun school, which specialized in this area of doctrine.

108. The reference seems to be to a samadhi in which mundane things are seen as formless, markless, or signless, the latter being Edward Conze's translation. There are three samadhis, or a samadhi in which things are contemplated in three ways: empty, formless (or signless), and wishless. The term is not the name of a particular samadhi so much as a description of content (or lack thereof).

109. The quotation is from the *Baojing Sanmei* (J. *Hokyo zammai*) or "Jewel Mirror Samadhi," a short text recited frequently in Zen ceremonies. The point here is that snow and a silver bowl are very similar in color, as are cranes and the moonlight they stand in. However, despite the similarity, they are different and can be distinguished. The point of the passage becomes quite clear in the context of the whole text, which concerns identity and difference, and it is this relationship between the two that Keizan is concerned with here.

110. These are references to incidents that triggered the awakening of the Chinese masters Lingyun and Xiangyan. To Dogen and Keizan, such incidents became archetypes of the kind of event that can trigger *satori* once the mind is prepared.

111. Indian thought saw the cosmos as passing through these phases in a cyclical manner. The cosmos comes into being, lasts for a very long time (often given as 4,320,000,000

years), is destroyed, and then passes through an "empty eon," during which time there is nothing. Then the cycle starts up again. Keizan is making the point that the individual who has actualized the True Self remains totally imperturbable in the midst of all this change, a center of eternal stillness in the midst of change and destruction.

112. See note 3.

113. The triple world *(trailokya)* is the ancient Indian cosmology consisting of three planes or realms arranged vertically, like a three-story building. The lower realm is the realm of desire *(kama),* containing humans, the hells, animals, and several of the lower celestial realms. The second realm, the realm of form *(rupa)* is inhabited by celestial beings. The third and highest realm is that of formlessness *(arupya)* and is inhabited by celestial beings without form. All these are still included within the conditioned world of birth and death, so to "leave the triple world" means that one becomes enlightened and, therefore, liberated from rebirth and suffering.

114. Yama is the judge of the dead, who studies the record of the life of the deceased and metes out the appropriate torment in one of the hells (or, more accurately, purgatories).

115. Yunfeng Wenyue (998–1062) was a Chinese Zen master in the Linji line.

116. "Field of monkhood" is literally a "field of black," referring to the black robes worn by monks.

117. The iron mountains are one of the torments in the Buddhist hells. Bodies of the wicked are crushed as the iron mountains crash together. The bodies are then reproduced to be smashed again, and so the long process continues.

118. The udumbara tree blooms only once in a hundred years. Hence, it has become a favorite Buddhist figure of speech denoting rarity.

119. The term translated here as "Self" is *ga-ga,* literally, "self-self." I have not found the term in any standard Buddhist dictionaries, so this may be Keizan's own unique usage. I have translated the terms simply as "Self," capitalized, to indicate that the discussion concerns what Zen sometimes calls the "True Self." Although Yasutani Roshi interprets *ga-ga* to refer to the well-known Buddhist "self and what belongs to self," or "me and mine," (Sanskrit *atma-atmıya)* in his *Denkoroku dokugo,* I believe that this is inaccurate. My own reading is based on several factors, one of which is the use of the term in the concluding verse, where *ga-ga* is said to appear many times *(ikubakuka)* with different faces, or many forms, a teaching found frequently in Keizan's text. It is the True Self, or formless Self, that does this, not the false self and its possessions. Also, Keizan's own use of the term "True Self" *(shinjitsu ga)* following this verse leads me to believe that the term is a synonym for the "True Self," while the *ga* of the same verse simply denotes the false self or is a reflexive pronoun. Finally, the *Shusho Bokun Keizan Denkoroku* (ed. Yoshida Gizen, Kyoto, 1887) glosses *ga-ga* with *muga no shinga* or "selfless True Self" (vol. 1, p. 53).

120. Again, I have been frustrated in my attempt to find the original form of this individual's name, so I have no choice but to retain the Japanese pronunciation of the Chinese transliteration of the Indian original.

121. A *li* is a Chinese linear measurement, one *li* being roughly the equivalent of one-third of a Western mile, or about 1,890 feet.

122. The four great elements are earth, water, fire, and wind. Everything is made up of these elements. The five aggregates *(skandha)* are matter, feeling, thought, karmic impulses, and consciousness.

123. "True Self" is *shinjitsu ga*. Following as it does the verse that uses the term *ga-ga* (see note 119), and apparently continuing the point made in the verse, the obvious conclusion is that *ga-ga* and *shinjitsu ga* are the same thing.

124. The third fruit refers to the third of the four result stages of development in early Buddhist texts. The first fruit is that of *stream-winner*, the second is *once-returner*, the third is *non-returner*, and the fourth is *arhat*. The third fruit means that a monk who reaches this stage but does not become liberated will not be reborn in human form but will nevertheless arrive at the stage of arhat in a nonhuman form after death.

125. The "ten good actions" probably refers to the abstention from the ten evil things: killing, stealing, sexual misconduct, lying, "double tongue," coarse language, lewd language, covetousness, anger, and perverted views.

126. In ancient Indian cosmology, there were several circles or spheres underlying the world. The diamond circle was the bottom circle.

127. See note 12.

128. See note 12.

129. Keizan is referring to the establishment of Soto Zen in Japan by Dogen in the early thirteenth century. Keizan was the third patriarch after Dogen in this tradition. However, other forms of Buddhism had existed in Japan since the sixth century, but Keizan, like Dogen, did not think that they were the True Dharma.

130. The Udraramaputra, or Udrakaramaputra, family were descendants of a Brahmin priest of the same name who is said to have been one of Shakyamuni's teachers.

131. I have failed to restore the Japanese to its original Indian form, so here, I have translated the name to English.

132. A kingdom in Central Asia, north of India.

133. In Buddhist cosmology, the realm of desire *(kama loka)* is the lowest of the three realms (see note 113). Along with humans, it contains celestial beings who live in six realms arranged in vertical order. The highest of the six celestial realms is that of the

Paranirmitavasha-vartin (gods). Kumarata fell, through rebirth, to the next-to-lowest celestial realm, that of the *Trayastrimshas* (or "thirty-three" celestials). He subsequently "rose" through rebirth to the second of the realms of the triple world, the realm of form, which is inhabited by the so-called Brahma celestials.

134. See note 133.

135. See note 133. The words in parentheses are Keizan's.

136. The reference is to the six stages of the bodhisattva according to Tendai Buddhism, and the "way of names and words" is one of the six. When the bodhisattva hears the names and words of the scriptures and treatises, he realizes that he or she is of the same essence as all the Buddhas. Keizan is speaking of the mere intellectual grasp of this teaching.

137. This is a traditional Buddhist list of offenses. These five—making a Buddha bleed, killing one's father, killing one's mother, killing an arhat, and creating a schism in the Buddhist order—are unpardonable because they are so horrendous. The offender thus falls immediately into hell, as did Devadatta, the Buddha's cousin, when he wounded the Buddha. The seven offenses are the above five plus killing one's teacher and killing a sage. The traditional list of five can be found in the *Brahmajala Sutra*.

138. See note 25 for the three realms. See note 65 for the four forms of birth. The six destinies are celestial, ashuras, humans, animal, hungry ghosts, and hells. The nine forms of existence are these six plus the realms of arhats and bodhisattvas. The tenth realm, that of Buddhas, is excluded because it is exempt from karmic consequences.

139. Vasubandhu is one of the most famous and influential Buddhist thinkers and writers. He was the brother of Asangha, also a famous and influential figure in Indian Buddhism. Vasubandhu was converted from the Hinayana to the Mahayana by his brother and went on to compose several very important Buddhist texts, among which are the *Mahayana-samgraha*, *Karmasiddhi-prakarana*, *Vimshatika-karika*, and *Dashabhumika-sutra shastra*. He is credited with the composition of more than thirty-five treatises.

140. My translation of the Japanese. Sanskrit unknown.

141. My translation of the Japanese. Sanskrit unknown.

142. The name translates as "magpie," but I cannot find a Sanskrit original. *Suni* is the Japanese pronunciation of the two characters.

143. *Kido* is the Japanese pronunciation of the two characters.

144. I am guessing here what the Sanskrit might be.

145. The teaching of the sudden realization or awakening.

146. "Flowers in the eyes" is an expression found often in Buddhist literature. It refers to a defect or disease of the eyes in which the individual thinks that he sees flowers in the

air in front of him, whereas there are no real flowers. The flowers are illusions generated by faulty vision.

147. Jiashan (d. 881) was a successor to Panzi, in the line started by Qingyuan Xingsi. He was a prominent Zen teacher, and his life and sayings are recorded in the *Chuan Deng Lu* and elsewhere.

148. The text does not specify that it is Zen masters who do this, but I have presumed from the context that this is what is meant.

149. The twenty-second patriarch's name is somewhat problematical, being given in several forms in different sources. He is sometimes called Manora, Manura (Eitel), as well as Manorhita. I have decided to use the last name, which is Eitel's primary listing, and which Monier-Williams lists in his Sanskrit-English Dictionary and translates as "Benefit to Man."

150. These are the eighteen *dhatu.* Comprising as they do both the subjective and objective realms in their totality, they embrace all of existence. Consequently, to say that they are all empty is tantamount to saying that everything is empty *(sarvam shunyam).*

151. A translation of the Japanese name of the king.

152. I am guessing at the Indian original. It could also be Makala or something similar.

153. A paraphrase and interpretation of the original, which says, literally, "Do not think of seeing as the route (or track) of the eye's light."

154. It is difficult to capture the original in English. The Chinese word for "crane" is *he,* and *lena* is a transliteration of the Sanskrit; so the whole name is part semantically meaningful Chinese, part transliteration. The name is given usually as Haklena but he is also known as Haklenayashas. I assume that the latter is the correct name on the basis of the explanation of the name in the story. That is, he became famous *(yashas)* because of a flock of cranes. The original might therefore have been Hakulenayashas, "famous *(yashas)* because of a flock *(kulena)* of cranes *(ha)*."

155. According to Hindu and Buddhist cosmology, the world passes through four eons *(kalpa):* origination, subsistence, destruction, and nothingness. The last is the empty eon, during which time nothing exists.

156. If one does not have to sit in any prescribed seat in the meditation hall during zazen, one does not have to distinguish between the left side or right side. In context, the statement means that one does not have to distinguish between Buddhas and ordinary beings.

157. Kubha is present-day Kabul in Afghanistan.

158. These are the Japanese pronunciations. I cannot reconstitute them into their originals.

159. The four perverted views *(viparyasa)* are: the world is permanent, the world is substantial (or has a self), the world is pleasant, and the world is pure. The three poisons are craving, hatred, and delusion.

160. These are the three bodies of a Buddha *(trikaya)*. The *dharma-kaya* is the eternal, formless body; the *sambhoga-kaya* is the glorified body adorned with the major and minor marks of a Buddha, seen only by the spiritually advanced; the *nirmana-kaya* or transformed body is the historical form taken by the *dharma-kaya*. Shakyamuni was the transformed body of the *dharma-kaya*.

161. Another problematic name. Just about all reference works list this individual as "Basiasita," but whether that is the correct Sanskrit name is unclear. The story shows that the name can be divided into *basia* and *sita*. *Sita* means "light," and may be a synonym for enlightenment, but I find no *basia* in any Sanskrit dictionary. The original could be *vashya* or *vashi*. The correct form of the last part of the name could be *asita*, meaning "non-light" or "darkness."

162. A quotation from the *Zhaozhou Chanshi Yulu*, the saying of Zen Master Zhaozhou (Joshu).

163. See note 138.

164. See note 155.

165. Mahasthamaprapta is "He who has achieved great power," one of the more prominent bodhisattvas of the Mahayana pantheon.

166. I translate his name, Prajnatara, as "he who brought across prajna," on the assumption that *tara* means "to carry across," which is what the Sanskrit means. The Tibetan Buddhist female savioress, Tara, is "she who carries us across," or "she who delivers us." My interpretation is based on the story in which this individual brought his *prajna* from a former life.

167. The editor of the text, Kochi Egaku, attributes this to Zen master Sanping Yizhun. See *Keizan Zen*, vol. 2, *Denkoroku kokai*, Tokyo: Sankibo, 1985.

168. "Seal of approval" is *inka*, given to the disciple by the master in recognition of superior achievement and fitness to become a teacher. To receive *inka* means that one becomes the master's successor.

169. "Heaping snow in a silver bowl and hiding a heron in bright moonlight" is a line from the *Baojing Sanmei* (J. *Hokyo zammai*), chanted often in Zen liturgy. Though snow is similar to a silver bowl in color, they are not the same, nor are a heron and bright moonlight. They are similar but different.

170. "Formless" is *muso*, or Sanskrit *animitta*. The Sanskrit is usually translated as "markless" or "signless," meaning that things are not perceived by the wise as having marks

or characteristics such as male, female, tall, short, and the like. "Formless" thus stretches the meaning somewhat, but is probably acceptable in context.

171. "Nature of things" is *hossu*, literally, "Dharma nature." The original Sanskrit is probably *dharmata*.

172. I cannot identify the Sanskrit original of Koshi, so I give the Japanese pronunciation.

173. The passage can be found in the *Bi Yan Lu* (J. *Hekiganroku*) in the commentary to case 73.

174. The original has *iken-o*, meaning either "a king with a heterodox view," or "King Heterodox View." The term is not explained, but at any rate, it is a minor problem, and I have simply called him "the king."

175. Bodhiruci was a prominent missionary and translator in China at the time, and Guandong was also prominent. Why they are picked out as a rather rascally pair is not very clear, but both have bad reputations in Zen writings. Dogen also speaks of them with great contempt and vehemence.

176. "They remain just what they are, changeless," is my rather loose translation of *ju hoi*, which is often translated literally as "abiding in a dharma state." Dogen made the term famous in such essays as *Genjo koan*, *Uji*, and similar texts. It means that anything remains just what it is and does not decay and change. Consequently, something appears, is what it is for its duration, and then disappears to be replaced by another thing. Dogen says, for instance, that spring does not become summer. Spring is just spring, then it is replaced by something different, summer. Life does not turn into death but remains life and is ultimately replaced by death. Each thing, thus, is never other than what it is, although it has predecessors and others that follow it.

177. Hairs become very fine in winter, so that an autumn hair is very fine.

178. Attributed to the Chinese master, Yunmen.

179. My interpolation is based on the comments of several scholars and Zen writers who doubt that Daoxin was enlightened at such an early age. This may be simply a condensation of a sequence of events, whereby he met the Third Patriarch at age fourteen and then, later, was awakened. However, given the nature of biographies such as this, which tend to be more laudatory than historical, the text may really mean that he achieved awakening at such an early age.

180. This should not be confused with Mount Putou (Mount Niutou). Niutou, or "Ox-head" is famous for being the center of an important branch of Zen. The Ox-head tradition was founded by Farong.

181. This is the concluding statement in the koan "Dongshan's No Heat or Cold," case 43 in the *Bi Yan Lu (Hekiganroku)*. Dogen's essay, *"Shunju"* ("Spring and Fall") in *Shobogenzo*, is an extended talk on this case. The entire chapter is in this translator's *How to*

Raise an Ox. Becoming totally hot means to encounter heat without the presence of the reactive self, so that when it is hot, there is only hot.

182. "Relative and absolute" are allusions to Dongshan's "Five positions." "Relative" is *pian*, which literally means "bent," and "absolute" is *zheng*, which means "straight."

183. The original is *hossho zammai*, the samadhi of Dharma nature or samadhi of Dharmata. It is not the name of a specific samadhi but probably means, in context, that beings are eternally part of the always so (or ultimately real).

184. This is a well-known koan and story from Huineng's life. Here, "Mind" does not mean ordinary mental activity but, as is clear from so many of Keizan's writings in *Denkoroku*, rather denotes what he sometimes calls "Mind essence" and "original nature." See *Wumen Guan (Mumonkan)*, case 23.

185. Gunabhadra was an Indian Buddhist monk-scholar who was active in China in the fifth century. He translated many Indian Buddhist texts into Chinese.

186. Paramartha was an Indian Buddhist scholar-monk who translated a large number of texts into Chinese in the sixth century. Among works attributed to him is the *Dacheng Qi Xin Lun (Daijo kishinron)*, a text that has had a great impact on the development of East Asian Buddhism. He either edited or actually composed the text. All in all, he translated about fifty texts.

187. The chapters of *Denkoroku* were composed as talks to the monks. The reference is to the traditional intensive training period, lasting ninety days, called *ango*. This particular *ango* took place in the summer of 1300.

188. This is case 11 in the koan collection, *Cong Rong Lu (Shoyoroku)*. Not passing completely through one's attainment leads to a Zen sickness of attachment to the Dharma.

189. The *hossu (fuzi)* is a kind of whisk made of white horse hair and attached to a handle. It is a symbol of authority carried only by Zen masters.

190. The Zhaolun is a well-known treatise by the Chinese monk Sengzhao (374–414), a student of the Indian scholar-monk, Kumarajiva. It is a very early Chinese Buddhist text which attempts to explain the meaning of emptiness *(shunyata)* as found in Indian Buddhist texts.

191. See notes 25 and 138 for the triple world and six destinies.

192. Qingyuan and Nanyue were two of Huineng's successors, each establishing his own teaching tradition. Keizan's line is descended from Qingyuan. Baizhang, mentioned in chapter 37, was a successor in Nanyue's line.

193. These are some of the many students who studied with Yaoshan. Yunyan is the subject of the next chapter. Daowu was Yunyan's Dharma brother. Chuanzi ("The Boat-

man") also succeeded Yaoshan. The others were laymen, Li'ao being a Confucian scholar and author.

194. Baizhang Huaihai was a successor in Nanyue's line (see note 42) in the late eighth and early ninth centuries. His most important successor was Huangbo Xiyun. He is best remembered for inventing the Zen monastic system.

195. See note 92.

196. I cannot find the characters translated as "bullfrog" in either Chinese or Japanese dictionaries, but my text gives a *kana* pronunciation of *gama* for the characters, and bullfrog *(gama)* makes sense in context.

197. Yaoshan is the thirty-sixth patriarch. See note 194 for Baizhang. Daowu was Yunyan's Dharma brother, and a dialogue between the two can be found in *Bi Yan Lu* (*Hekiganroku*) case 89.

198. Wuxie Limo (747–818) was one of Mazu Daoyi's successors. After he studied first with Mazu, he studied with Shitou, with whom he had his awakening.

199. "Realm of the Satisfied Celestials" is Sanskrit *Tusita deva-loka*, one of the many celestial realms or worlds inhabited by beings who enjoy the results of very good karma in former lives. The Buddha is said to have been a celestial in this world prior to being reborn as a human in his last life.

200. Nanquan Puyuan (748–834) was a successor to Mazu Daoyi and an important Chinese Zen master. He is the subject of the koan "Nanquan's Cat."

201. Guishan Lingyou (771–853) was a successor to Baizhang Huaihai (note 194). He and Yangshan Huiji founded the important Guiyang line of Chinese Zen.

202. Nanyang Huizhong (d. 776) studied with Huineng and was eminent enough in his time to be given the posthumous title of Guo shi, "National Teacher." He is the subject of the koan "National Teacher Chung's Seamless Tower" in *Bi Yan Lu* (*Hekiganroku*) case 18.

203. See note 189.

204. The *Amida Sutra* is a short scripture that describes the paradise of Amitabha (Amida) Buddha in great detail. Kumarajıva translated the text into Chinese, and, along with two other similar scriptures, it became the basis for the Pure Land form of Mahayana Buddhism.

205. Hongzhi Zhengjue (Wanshi Shogaku, 1091–1157) was a Caodong master in the line of Yunju. He studied with Kumu Facheng and later with Danxia Zichun, from whom he received Dharma transmission.

206. "Beyond" is *kojo*. As an ordinary term, it denotes advancement, progress, improve-

ment, and upward movement in general. Its opposite is *koge*. However, as a more or less technical term in Zen, it denotes transcendence. In this sense, it is often used, by Dogen for instance, to denote a continuing upward movement beyond any temporary state of awakening or understanding. Thus, in Dogen's essay *Bukkojo-ji*, the term means "going beyond Buddha," and it refers to the Zen insistence that the student not get stuck in any stage of development but transcend it to the next stage, and so on and on endlessly. To constantly "go beyond" thus precludes attachment to some stage of understanding. In the present chapter, Yunju seems to use the term to mean something like "absolute," or "transcendent," so that his question is, "Tell me who you are from the standpoint of absolute truth." From this point of view, Daoying cannot say that his name is Daoying.

207. See note 46. Chinese temples sometimes had images of several arhats, and, as is shown in the present chapter, certain ritual acts such as offering food were sometimes performed for the arhats.

208. Si Da Heshang is Nanyue Huisi (514–577), or Great Master Si. He was also the second patriarch of the new Tientai school of Chinese Buddhism.

209. See note 200.

210. The scripture is the *Miluo Xiasheng Cheng Fo Jing*, an account of the career of Maitreya, the future Buddha of this cosmic eon.

211. "Someone without Buddha nature" translates the Sanskrit *icchantika*. One form of Buddhism classified certain individuals as beings who were so depraved and lost that they would never attain Buddhahood. They were thought to be lacking in Buddha nature, the innate seed in beings that is the cause for enlightenment. Most of the Buddhist schools rejected this idea as incompatible with other teachings. Later, however, the term came to be applied to bodhisattvas. The reasoning was that all other beings would eventually meet the proper teacher and repent their wicked lives. They would someday become perfectly enlightened Buddhas. The bodhisattva, however, deliberately postpones or rejects perfect enlightenment in order to be reborn endlessly among the various suffering beings of the world. Since, realistically, there will always be beings to guide and help, the bodhisattva is, oddly, the one kind of person who will never become a Buddha. He or she is referred to as the "great icchantika."

212. Caoshan Benji (840–901) was successor to Dongshan Liangjie. The two of them together formed what was to known as the Caodong (Soto) tradition. It and the Linji (Rinzai) tradition eventually emerged as the two dominant forms of Chinese Zen. The name of the school came from combining the first part of the names Caoshan and Dongshan.

213. The six senses are eye, ear, nose, tongue, skin (body), and mind, mind being classified as a sense because it has objects like the other senses. The seven consciousnesses are visual, auditory, olfactory, gustatory, tactile, and two forms of mental perception.

214. The ellipses are Keizan's own, showing that he omitted certain parts of what was originally a longer talk by Tongan.

215. The text actually has "twelve-part sutras and treatises," referring to a traditional division of Buddhist texts into twelve parts.

216. The "two vehicles" are non-Mahayana forms of Buddhism. They are the *shravakas* or "hearers," meaning those disciples of the Buddha who heard him speak, and *pratyekabuddhas*, those individuals who are enlightened without a teacher and who choose not to teach others. They are often singled out in Mahayana texts as having an imperfect or incomplete understanding of the truth, as is evident from Keizan's own remarks.

217 See the life of Mahakashyapa, the second biography in this translation.

218. Buddhists believe that there are several hells, the worst being the Avici hell, in which suffering is incessant or uninterrupted. These are not hells in the way hells are imagined in popular Christianity. They correspond more with the Roman Catholic idea of purgatory, a place where one can purge oneself of sin in order to leave purgatory and ascend to a happier realm. Buddhists believe that after one has served one's term in a place like Avici, one is reborn in another realm, such as animal or human.

219. See notes 25 and 113.

220. See note 3.

221. See note 3.

222. The second line has no stated subject. I have given "pearl" as the unstated subject because the line says that it is lustrous and requires no cutting and polishing. This, along with the reference to clear water in the first line, seems to be an oblique reference to a pearl, which, of course, is the True Self, the subject of most of these appreciatory verses. Yasutani Roshi says (*Denkoroku dokugo*, p. 404) that the Self is likened to a pearl in clear water. Yoshida says, in his edition of the text (vol. 2, p. 127), that the clear water is the natural liberated state of mind and body (*jinen datsuraku*).

223. "Site of enlightenment" is the Sanskrit *bodhimanda*. It originally referred to the place where Shakyamuni was enlightened. Keizan extends the term to refer to Mind as the true *bodhidmanda*.

224. The *Transmission of the Lamp* is the *Chuan Deng Lu* (*Dentoroku*), a collection of stories of enlightenment and Dharma transmission of Indian and Chinese patriarchs, and consequently it is somewhat similar to Keizan's collection. However, the format and focus of the biographies of the two collections differ considerably. Also, Keizan's collection traces a single line of transmission from the Buddha down to Ejo in Japan, while the *Dentoroku* has biographies of all the successors of a master. Hence, it is more diffuse and extensive than the present collection, not to mention longer.

225. There was a taboo on using the same name as the reigning monarch, and the custom was to change one's own name accordingly.

226. The *Scripture on Perfect Enlightenment (Yuan Wu Jing)* is not of Indian origin but is a work composed in China. However, it seems to have been widely read and respected in China and Japan, where it is cited frequently in other texts.

227. The "mirror of Qin" is explained further on in the text. "Qin" means the emperor of the Qin dynasty.

228. The *Treatise on the Hundred Dharmas* is Vasubandhu's *Shata-dharma shastra*, translated into Chinese by Xuanzang. It is devoted to the analysis of the hundred dharmas that make up the world of larger objects. It is similar to the *Abhidharma-kosha*, which analyzes and categorizes seventy-five dharmas.

229. *Zhulin pusa* refers to various bodhisattvas with the name "Lin," such as Huilin, Rulai Lin, etc. In chapter 16 of the *Avatamsaka Sutra* (T. 278, p. 463ff.), several bodhisattvas, each having the word *lin* (forest) as part of his name, utter verses. Touzi was reading these verses from the *Avatamsaka Sutra*.

230. "Self-essence of Mind" *(soku shin jisho)* does not mean that Mind has a self-essence or that self-essence belongs to Mind. Rather, Mind *(soku shin)* is self-essence or True Self.

231. This is the first line of the *Can Tong Qi (Sandokai)*, which is recited often as part of Zen liturgy.

232. Zen Master Shexian Guixing was descended from the Nanyue line through Linji and his own master, Shoushan Xingnian. As the text shows, his own successor was Fushan Yuanjian. Even though he was a Dharma successor in the Linji line, Yuanjian temporarily "held the Dharma" as a kind of surrogate for Dayang until a successor to Dayang could be found, even though that successor would never have had the face-to-face transmission with Dayang.

233. This is a text named *Wu Deng Hui Yuan (Compendium of the Five Lamps)*. It was one of Keizan's main sources for the stories in the *Denkoroku*, along with the *Chuan Deng Lu*. It is a compendium of five different biographical sources, hence the name of the work.

234. This is a continuation of *Essential Sayings of the Ancient Elders* by Sengding Shouze. The author of the cited work was Huishi Shiming and contains records of eighty-two Zen masters omitted from the earlier work by Seng-t'ing.

235. The text has *i-on-o* (Ch. *weiyin wang*), which translates the Sanskrit *Bhishma-garjita-ghosha-svara-raja*, "Buddha who reigned prior to the present eon," which is to say, a very long time ago. I have simplified by paraphrasing it as "prior to the first Buddha," meaning the first Buddha of this eon, Dipamkara.

236. The reference is to Shakyamuni and his six predecessors, all of whom lived during the present eon. Dipamkara was the first. There were, of course, other Buddhas in previous eons.

237. See note 232.

238. Master Sanjiao Zhisong. The text has San Song Jiao. He was a successor to Shoushan Xingnian and student of Shexian Guixing (note 232).

239. The reference is to the well-known koan, "Zhaozhou's Oak Tree,"' which is case 37 in the *Wumen Guan (Mumonkan)*.

240. Both masters were successors to Huineng, each starting his own line of transmission but, despite this, Keizan is attempting to emphasize their essential agreement. Qingyuan's line later led to Dongshan and the Caodong tradition, while Nanyue's line led eventually to Linji and the establishment of the Linji tradition. As the text following this passage shows, Keizan is trying to eliminate any sense of superiority or inferiority in either Rinzai or Soto Zen.

241. This is not Danxia, the forty-sixth patriarch, but a much earlier student of Mazu and a successor to Shitou (Sekito).

242. The five houses are the schools or lines of Guiyang, Linji, Caodong, Yunmen, and Fayan. The seven traditions are the above five plus the Huanglong and Yangqi factions, which broke off from the main Linji line.

243. The *Records of Shimen and Linjian* is by Jiaofan (1071–1127), a follower of the Huanglong faction of Linji Zen. The title derives from the fact that the contents are from the records of two men, Shimen and Linjian.

244. Chenggu, "The Keeper of the Old Tower," is further explained several paragraphs later on in the text. See also the following note.

245. Zen master Qianfu Cheng'gu is listed as a successor to Yunmen Fayan, founder of the Yunmen line, who died in 949. Cheng'gu seems to have lived about a hundred years later.

246. Yongjia Xuanjue (d. 840) is famous for having received Huineng's seal of approval after spending just one night at Huineng's monastery. He is well known in Zen history as the author of the verse known as *"Zheng Dao Ge" (Shodoka)*. Huangbo Xiyun (d. 850) was Baizhang's most important Dharma heir.

247. Xiangyan Zhixian (d. 840) is famous for having been awakened when he heard a pebble strike a bamboo. He was a successor to Guishan Lingyou (see following note).

248. Guishan Lingyou (771–853) was wandering in the mountains and was awakened when he suddenly saw some peach blossoms.

249. See note 189.

250. The ellipses are in the text. Keizan is abridging his source.

251. Standing, walking about, sitting, and lying down.

252. *Mathews' Chinese-English Dictionary* (p. 1149) defines "jade bones" as "a man of lofty and pure aims." Here, it is apparently a figure of speech for either the diligent Zen student or, more likely, one's essential nature and inner spiritual beauty. It is contrasted with artificial adornments such as powder and lipstick, which may mean any kind of artifice or cultivation. Keizan means that one's True Self does not need embellishment.

253. "Non-empty emptiness" translated *fuku no ku*. Kochi's note in the text [vol. 4, p. 106] defines the term as "the absolute [*zettai*] that runs through different individuals." There is a long history in Buddhism of debate concerning whether there is something that is non-empty *(agunya)*. Some said that emptiness itself is not empty, a violation of the Madhyamika position that even emptiness is empty. Keizan may simply mean that emptiness must not be construed negatively as a blank or void, an interpretation supported by the context of the term. This emptiness is none other than the realm of the True Self that Keizan speaks of over and over in these biographies. Consequently, it is something positive and grand, not a nihilistic void. It may also be called "true emptiness," meaning that though it empties the world of categories, concepts, and structures that the world does not actually possess, the world remains in its empty actuality as an area of action.

254. The Chinese original for this last phrase in quotation marks is *miao xie jian dai*, which I take to mean something like "subtle union." I have not translated the final *tai*. It means "belt" or "sash," (J. *obi*), and this whole phrase is the seventh of nine *tai* in a group of statements known as "Fushan's Nine Tai." The phrase at hand refers, of course, to the blending of relative and absolute. The complete list of Fushan's nine *tai* can be found in Yamada Kodo, *Zenshu jiten* (Tokyo, 1965), p. 944.

255. The universe passes through four successive phases: the phase of formation, the phase of persistence or continuity, the phase of destruction, and the phase of emptiness or nothingness. Then the whole process is repeated, and this process is eternal. The "empty eon" is the fourth phase. "Prior to the empty eon" for people in the present time would be equivalent to "eternity," or "before the beginning of time."

256. See note 255.

257. My text does not have the negative "not showing signs" *(kizasezu)* but all other versions do, and the sentence is problematical if not read as a negative statement. I suspect that the text's *kizasu* is a misprint.

258. Panshan Baoji (no dates) was a successor to Mazu Daoyi. Of his own successors, little is known with the exception of Puhua, who was later closely connected to Linji.

259. Kumu Facheng was a successor to Furong Daokai, the forty-fifth patriarch in this present collection of biographies. His dates of birth and death are unknown.

260. The seventh of the eight forms of consciousness *(vijnana)* cataloged and studied by Buddhist psychologists is the *manas*. Its primary function is to create the illusion of self-

hood by interpreting the existence of memories as the existence of a permanent self. It is, therefore, that function of the mind that is self-aware and consequently self-attached.

261. Zhenxie Qingliao was a Caodong master who was active in the middle of the twelfth century. He had twelve successors, but not much else is known about him.

262. Yanshou is not well known. He should not be confused with Yongming Yanshou, who died earlier in 975.

263. He is the thirty-fifth patriarch in this present collection of translations.

264. He is the thirty-sixth patriarch.

265. Changqing Huileng (864–932) was a successor to Xuefeng. He appears in several koans in *Bi Yan Lu (Hekiganroku)*.

266. When the world arrives at its phase of destruction (see note 255), three disasters occur. First, a great fire consumes the world. Then, a wind blows away the ashes. Finally, a torrential downpour washes away any remnants. Then, during the empty eon, there is absolutely nothing for a very long time, after which the world is recreated.

267. For "triple world," see note 25. The six paths are the six forms taken by sentient beings in the round of rebirth. They include the human, celestial, animal, hells, and so on.

268. The "eight winds" are gain and loss, praise and ridicule, defamation and eulogy, and sorrow and joy.

269. The Hall of Arhats was a building sometimes found on temple or monastery grounds that contained the images of a number of arhats, those perfected individuals of earlier Buddhism, such as Ananda. There were special ceremonies in honor of the arhats.

270. The Jiading era lasted from 1208 to 1225. The emperor was Ningzong.

271. "Not caring about anything" translates *buji* (Ch. *wushi*). *Buji* Zen is a false Zen characterized by an "I-don't-care" attitude. Nothing matters, everything is false and empty, and there are no concerns, even for practice. It is a nihilistic attitude condemned by Keizan and other Zen masters.

272. Bodhisattva precepts are Mahayana precepts, as distinguished from so-called Hinayana precepts. Their source is the *Brahmajala Sutra*.

273. Dengyo Daishi, otherwise known as Saicho, traveled to China early in the ninth century to study Buddhism and collect Buddhist literature. While there, he studied Tiantai, Zhenyan, and Zen traditions, all of which he took back to Japan. He set up a new monastery on Mount Hiei, which became the headquarters of Japanese Tendai Buddhism. Shikaku Daishi, or Ennin, went to China in 835. His travels were recorded, and his account has become an important source of information about the state of Buddhism during the

great persecution of Chinese Buddhism in 845. The record was translated by Edwin O. Reischauer, and it is discussed in his *Ennin's Travels in Tang China* (New York, 1955).

274. Myozen was the successor of Eisai (or Yosai), who established Kennin-ji in Kyoto. As the text goes on to say, Dogen returned here shortly after his return from China. Eisai seems to have died at about the time Dogen first met Myozen. The text says several times that Dogen studied with Eisai, but there is some question in scholarly circles as to whether this actually happened.

275. This apparently does not mean that he was given another set of robes and bowls after having received them earlier. It must refer to the earlier occasion.

276. The *goma* ritual was taken over from Indian Brahminism, where the *homa* sacrifice was carried out as a way of making offerings to the gods. This rite was adopted and adapted by esoteric Buddhism, such as Japanese Shingon and some branches of Tendai, where it symbolized the burning up of intellectual and emotional faults *(klesha)* through an offering to all the Buddhas.

277. This refers to the Taniryu faction of Tendai Buddhism, so named because of the location of its headquarters.

278. Ruyan of Mount Jing was a Linji master who received confirmation *(inka)* from Fozhao Deguang (1144–1203), a spiritual descendent of Dahui Zonggao.

279. No information can be found for Fanshan Sizhuo. He should not be confused with others known as Fanshan. Mount Fan had many abbots over a long time and many were known, as was the custom, by where they taught.

280. See note 242.

281. Weiyi Xitang of Guangfu Monastery (1202–1281) was a Linji Zen master in the Yangqi line.

282. Qingyuan, or Longmen Foyan (d. 1120) was a Linji master who succeeded Wuzu Fayan (Goso Hogen).

283. I can find no additional information on this person.

284. The twice-monthly renewal of vows is the *fusatsu* ceremony, during which the bodhisattva precepts are recited, and all involved have a chance to renew their awareness of the vows as well as to renew their commitment to their observance. It is a survival of one of the oldest practices in Buddhism, dating from the early years of Indian Buddhism.

285. This daily dedication is known as *eko*, literally, a "transference." Any virtue one has accumulated is transferred to others, both the living and the dead, in order to aid them in their progress toward enlightenment. It is a good reminder that one should not hold

on to anything, even personal merit.

286. The text has "Buddha images," but the numerical counter is "two scrolls" *(ni-jiku)*, so there is a problem with the passage. It could be that the passage should say something like "Buddha scriptures," but I am assuming from the context that it was two more images that were brought from Korea, so that the error is with the counter. All texts have the same line. Keizan's dates are incorrect. Shotoku was born in 574, not 587.

287. I have found no information on this teacher and disciple.

288. Kakua was a Tendai monk who traveled to China in 1171, where he practiced and studied and had an awakening. He returned to Japan and Mount Hiei, where he attempted to spread the Yangqi form of Linji Zen, but he was unsuccessful. The dates of his birth and death are unknown.

289. He is unknown except for what Keizan says about him.

290. Donglin Huichang is not well known except that he was a Linji master with whom Eisai studied and by whom he was confirmed while in China. He was the abbot of monasteries on Mount Tiantai and Mount Tiantong.

291. "Mind, thought, and consciousness" are, respectively, Sanskrit *citta*, *manas*, and *vijnana*. They are all aspects or functions of what might generally be designated as "mind." *Citta* usually refers to the mental function of storing up impressions, memories, and so on. *Manas* is the thinking capacity of mind and is responsible for discrimination and the illusion of selfhood. *Vijnana*, translated as "consciousness," might be better translated as "awareness," or "perception." Its function is to allow an individual to be aware of an external world. Keizan's point is that none of these is what he means by "mind," or "Mind."

292. These are two well-known Buddhist scholastic traditions. Each treatise became the focal point of study, teaching, and writing for a school or tradition. In Japan, the two traditions were, respectively, the *Kusha* and *Rojitsu*. Their headquarters were in the old capitol of Nara.

293. Zhiyi was an important patriarch of the Chinese Tiantai school in China. His most important writing is the *Mohe Zhiguan*, a lengthy treatise dealing with the cessation or tranquillity *(zhi)* and insight or contemplation *(guan)* types of meditation. The text was taught on Mount Hiei, in Japan, which was the center of Tendai Buddhism.

294. Saint Butchi, otherwise known as Kakuan, was a follower of Dainichi Nonin, a Rinzai Zen teacher who apparently had a self-awakening without benefit of a teacher and sent two monks to China to seek verification and approval for him. The monks found Fojiao Deguang (see following note) and returned to Japan with documents approving Nonin. He taught a short-lived tradition known as the Daruma tradition, named after Bodhidharma who was the first patriarch of China. The tradition eventu-

ally failed in Japan, but a number of Dogen's own students were men who originally practiced in the Daruma group, including Ejo himself.

295. Fojiao Deguang was a successor to Dahui, one of the great Chinese Zen masters and a leading exponent of koan practice.

296. A mythical bird from Indian zoological lore, known for its enchanting song. Here, a pitcher is shaped like a *kalavinka.*

297. A thought instant is *nen* (Ch. *nian*), the very brief period of time it takes for a thought to occur. It is the same as a *ksana,* the briefest measurable length of time. Various texts estimate that it takes from four hundred to seven hundred *ksana* to make one second.

298. These four monastic periods are the beginning of the summer *ango* intensive training period, the end of *ango,* the winter solstice, and New Year's Day.

299. See the biography of Ananda in this collection of translations, where he is said to have been Shakyamuni's personal attendant in many lives.

300. Gikai is Ejo's successor and Keizan's predecessor. He is not given a chapter in the *Denkoroku*, probably because he was still living when Keizan was writing these biographies, and Keizan would not have thought it proper to include him.

301. See note 65.

BIBLIOGRAPHY

Akanuma, Chizen. *Indo bukkyo koyu meishi jiten*. Tokyo: Hozokan, 1967.

Azuma, Ryushin. *Dogen sho jiten*. Tokyo: Shunjusha, 1972.

Dayal, Har. *The Bodhisattva Doctrine in Buddhist Sanskrit Literature*. London: Routledge and Kegan Paul, 1932.

Eitel, Ernest J. *Handbook of Chinese Buddhism*. Amsterdam: Philo Press, 1904.

Kachi, Egaku, ed. *Keizan zen: Denkoroku kikai*. 4 vols. Tokyo: Sankiba, 1987.

Kim, Hee-jin. *Dogen Kigen, Mystical Realist*. Tucson: University of Arizona Press, 1975.

Koza bukkyo, vol. 7, *Nihon bukkyo no shuha* (Tokyo: Daizo shuppan, 1958).

Nagahisa, Gakusui. *Denkoroku monogatari*. Tokyo: Komeisha, 1965.

Ogata, Sohaku, trans. "The Transmission of the Lamp" *(Dentoroku)*. Unpublished typescript, n.d.

Powell, William, trans. *The Record of Dongshan*. Honolulu: University of Hawaii Press, 1986.

Sahashi, Horyu, *Ningen Keizan*. Rev. ed. 1979. Tokyo: Shunjusha.

Soto shu zensho, vol. 8 (Shligen, vol. 2). Tokyo: Soto shu zensho kanko-kai, 1930; rev. ed., Sotoshu Shumucho, 1971.

Tajima, Hyakudo. *Nihon no zen goroku* Vol. 5: *Keizan*. Tokyo: Kodansha, 1978.

Yamada, Kodo, ed. *Zen shu jiten*. Tokyo, 1965.

Yasutani, Hakuun. *Denkoroku dokugo*. Tokyo: Sambo koryukai, 1964.

Yoshida, Gizan, ed. *Shusho bokun Keizan denkoroku*. 2 vols. Kyoto, 1886.

ALSO AVAILABLE FROM WISDOM PUBLICATIONS

The Art of Just Sitting:
Essential Writings on the Zen Practice of Shikantaza

Edited by John Daido Loori
Introduction by Taigen Dan Leighton
224 PAGES, 0-86171-327-3, $16.95

Edited by one of America's preeminent Zen teachers, *The Art of Just Sitting* brings together writings from ancient and modern teachers, and stands as the best available collection on the subject. This is essential reading for any practitioner.

"Daido Loori has given us the single most comprehensive treasury of writings on the subject—it is indispensable to meditators and scholars alike."
— John Daishin Buksbazen, author of *Zen Meditation in Plain English*

The Art of Just Sitting offers essential guidance in meditation from Zen's great ancestors, from Chinese and Japanese Zen's most influential ancient masters, and from some of modern Zen's preeminent teachers.

How to Raise An Ox
Zen Practice as Taught in Master Dogen's Shobogenzo

Francis Dojun Cook
Foreword by Taizan Maezumi Roshi
208 pages, cloth, ISBN 0-86171-317-6, $14.95

Francis Dojun Cook, a Dogen scholar for many years, has translated and illuminatingly introduced ten practice-oriented chapters of Dogen's masterwork, the *Shobogenzo*. We see clearly what is involved in the wholehearted, moment-to-moment practice of Zen, through examples from the lives of past masters.

"An authentic record of some of Master Dogen's most important teachings and an important sourcebook for Zen practitioners." —John Daido Loori, abbot, Zen Mountain Monastery

Mud & Water
The Collected Teachings of Zen Master Bassui

Arthur Braverman
256 pages, ISBN 0-86171-320-6, $14.95

Though he lived centuries ago in a culture vastly different from our own, Bassui speaks with a voice that spans time and space to address our own modern challenges — in life, and in our spiritual practice.

Like Dogen before him, Bassui was dissatisfied with what passed for Zen training, and taught a radically reenergized form of Zen. Accessible and eloquent, his teachings point directly to the importance of seeing our own original nature and recognizing it as Buddhahood itself.

"No matter how far we go, Bassui is there, coaxing us deeper." — Zen teachers Chozen and Hogen Bays, co-abbots of Great Vow Zen Monastery

Zen's Chinese Heritage
The Masters and Their Teachings

Andy Ferguson
512 pages, ISBN 0-86171-163-7, $24.95

Zen's Chinese Heritage surveys twenty-five generations of enlightened Buddhist teachers through brief biographies and starkly beautiful prose and poetry from Chinese Zen sources. *Includes a full-color, poster-size lineage chart.*

"An indispensable reference for any student of Buddhism."
—John Daido Loori, Abbot, Zen Mountain Monastery

"A monumental achievement."
—Robert Aitken, author of *The Gateless Barrier*

Browse through Wisdom's many Zen classics at wisdompubs.org.
While you're there, be sure to sign up to receive the Wisdom Reader,
our free e-newsletter, for additional updates and offers.

WISDOM PUBLICATIONS
Publisher of Buddhist Books.
199 Elm Street, Somerville, MA 02144 ✦ ORDERS: 800-272-4050

WISDOM PUBLICATIONS

Wisdom Publications, a not-for-profit publisher, is dedicated to preserving and transmitting important works from all the major Buddhist traditions as well as related East-West themes.

To learn more about Wisdom, or browse our books on-line, visit our website at wisdompubs.org. You may request a copy of our mail-order catalog on-line or by writing to:

WISDOM PUBLICATIONS
199 Elm Street
Somerville, Massachusetts 02144 USA
Telephone: (617) 776-7416
Fax: (617) 776-7841
Email: info@wisdompubs.org
www.wisdompubs.org

THE WISDOM TRUST

As a not-for-profit publisher, Wisdom is dedicated to the publication of fine Dharma books for the benefit of all and dependent upon the kindness and generosity of sponsors in order to do so. If you would like to make a donation to Wisdom, please do so through our Somerville office. If you would like to sponsor the publication of a book, please write or email us at the address above.

Thank you.

Wisdom is a nonprofit 501(c)(3) organization affiliated with the Foundation for the Preservation of the Mahayana Tradition (FPMT).